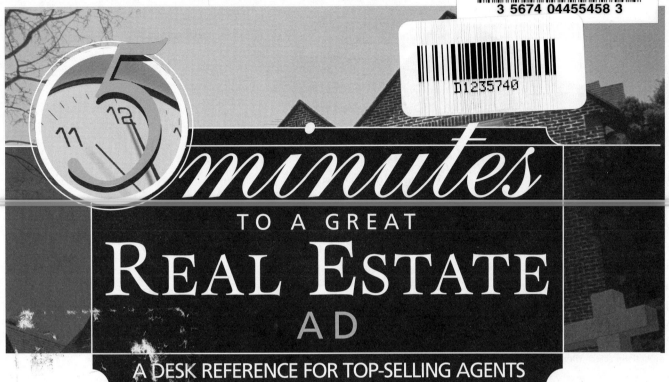

# 5 minutes

## TO A GREAT

# REAL ESTATE

## AD

### A DESK REFERENCE FOR TOP-SELLING AGENTS

# JOHN D. MAYFIELD

*ABR®, ABRM, GRI, e-PRO®, CRB*

THOMSON
★
SOUTH-WESTERN

Australia · Brazil · Canada · Mexico · Singapore · Spain · United Kingdom · United States

## THOMSON

### SOUTH-WESTERN

5 Minutes to a Great Real Estate Ad
John D. Mayfield

**VP/Editorial Director:**
Jack W. Calhoun

**VP/Editor-in-Chief:**
Dave Shaut

**Executive Editor:**
Scott Person

**Associate Acquisitions Editor:**
Sara Glassmeyer

**Developmental Editor:**
Arlin Kauffman

**Marketing Manager:**
Mark Linton

**Production Project Manager:**
Brian Courter

**Manager of Technology, Editorial:**
Vicky True

**Sr. Technology Project Editor:**
Matt McKinney

**Web Coordinator:**
Karen Schaeffer

**Manufacturing Coordinator:**
Charlene Taylor

**Production House:**
International Typesetting and Composition

**Printer:**
West Group
Eagan, MN

**Art Director:**
Linda Helcher

**Internal Designer:**
Chris A. Miller

**Cover Designer:**
Chris A. Miller

**Cover Images:**
© Getty Images
© SuperStock

Library of Congress Control Number:
2005935617

For more information about our products,
contact us at:
Thomson Learning Academic Resource
Center
1-800-423-0563

**Thomson Higher Education**
5191 Natorp Boulevard
Mason, OH 45040
USA

# Dedication

I dedicate this book to Chelsea Faye Briley who left this life at such a young age. Although handicapped and unable to live life like most young boys and young women, Chelsea always had a smile on her face and the ability to warm anyone's heart she met. Her attitude and happiness are like this book in a similar way. We can spend thousands of dollars advertising ourselves and our products, but if we cannot communicate a love and positive attitude to others, it will all be in vain.

"Thank you" Chelsea for touching my life and my family's life in a special way!

# About the Author

John Mayfield received his real estate license at the age of 18 in 1978. John was one of the first sales associates in his board of REALTORS® to reach the Missouri Association of REALTORS® Million Dollar Club. John achieved this award during a time when interest rates were record highs. John has been a practicing broker since 1981 and he owns and manages three offices in southeast Missouri, and manages over 35 real estate agents. John has taught pre- and post-license real estate courses since 1988. John has earned the ABR®, ABRM, CRB, e-PRO®, and GRI designations throughout his real estate tenure.

John is an avid real estate speaker and trainer. John is a GRI instructor for The Missouri Association of REALTORS® and the Arkansas Association of REALTORS®. John was one of the featured speakers at the 2004 National Association of REALTORS® convention in Orlando, Florida. He is the author of two books, *5 Minutes to a Great Real Estate Sales Meeting* and *5 Minutes to a Great Real Estate Letter* by Thomson Learning. John is also one of the contributing editors to the "Sales Coach" section for *REALTOR® Magazine Online,* and is a real estate writer for Hewlett Packard's Web site. John is also active on a local, state, and national level for the REALTORS® Association. John is also an NAR Director for the state of Missouri.

John and his wife, Kerry, have two children, Alyx and Anne. They also own and run a "Pick Your Own" Blueberry and Blackberry Farm (Liberty Farms) in southeast Missouri.

# Contents

# Introduction

Writing ads can be a fun and rewarding experience for the real estate agent. Unfortunately, many real estate professionals fail to recognize how important it is to write good advertising copy.

Questions often arise: *How much information do I give in the ad? Should I include the price, school district, and location? Do I write the ad in such a way leaving out critical information to entice the reader to call us about the listed property?* Over my years of experience I've tried and continued to use both methods in my advertising practices. Sometimes the price is so reasonable on a particular listing that you know by including the price, many potential buyers will pick up the phone and call you about the advertisement. Other times you know by experience that if a price is too high, it will produce no leads. There are two schools of thought on this issue and both have valid arguments. First, why give too much information and not get any leads from your marketing efforts? In reality that's what your advertisement is all about—to produce leads, make the phone ring, build a relationship with the callers, and help them find what they are looking for.

The second rationale about including and not including information is the argument on wasting the buyers' valuable time. Why mislead the buyers by teasing or leading them on if a home is out of their budget? Most buyers would rather we list the key essentials—price, location, school district, etc. According to the National Association of REALTORS® Profile of Home Buyers and Sellers, "price" is the most requested piece of information buyer's want in real estate ads!

So is there a right or wrong method to advertise your listed properties? The answer is no, and the choice is up to you. What you should strive to do is create great real estate advertisement copy, and describe your client's property in a true description.

Finding out what features your clients will miss when they move from this home or what they (the sellers) feel a potential buyer will appreciate most about their home will profit you when you construct your advertising copy. How does your property compare with other competing homes? As a real estate professional, you should analyze these questions and many others while writing your real estate ads.

Writing good ads should be fun and enjoyable, and is a part of our fiduciary duty we owe our client. Make sure you use time and care when preparing advertising copy for newspapers, Web sites, Multiple Listing Service®, postcards and flyers, and any other forms of marketing you plan to do. To help you carry out this task, we have developed the following acronym and provided a worksheet (Appendix A) to prepare your future ad copy.

## GET CALLS!

Try remembering this phrase each time you begin to write your ad copy:

**G** rab the reader's attention! To perform this task, use a headline or phrase that will cause the reader to stop and want to read more. Your local television station is excellent at getting our attention and causing us to tune in to the newscast. *"You won't believe what this six-year-old boy did today at the zoo!"* They've got your curiosity and you want to know more. **Grab the reader's attention!**

**E** ntice the reader with information about the home. Grabbing the reader's attention is your first goal when writing ad copy for your real estate listings; "enticing" them with more information is the next step. It should be more than a 3-bedroom/2-bath bungalow for $159,900. What's appealing about this bungalow? How's the floor plan, the woodwork, and what words can you use to paint a picture about this home? **Entice the reader!**

**T** ruthful in all advertising! You may have heard the saying, *"Don't let the truth interfere with a good story,"* but in advertising to the public it's bad business practice. Always paint an accurate picture in all of your advertising. No one profits to portray information or "overexaggerate" features that are not what they are, especially after the consumer visits the property and discovers the misleading information. For a long and prosperous real estate career, be **truthful in advertising!**

**C** lose the sale! It seems odd that we should ask for the consumer's business in our classified ads; however, it is a smart practice to follow. There are a number of ways to ask for the business: *"For more information, ask for John Smith," "To schedule a private showing, contact Judy Lee at 431-MOVE,"* or *"To see a virtual tour of this home and to arrange an appointment to preview, go to http://www.mayfieldre.com/123Smith.htm."* Whatever method you decide, make sure you **close the sale!**

**A** sk the sellers what they'll miss about their home. This is an overlooked task with many real estate professionals but one most sellers understand when asked. Think about your own home for a moment. If you planned to sell your house today, what features would you miss? I'm sure you can come up with a lengthy list of positive features you will hate to leave behind. The same is true for your clients, so always **ask the sellers what they'll miss about their home.**

**L** ist key features about the home, such as bedrooms, baths, central air-conditioning, location, school, price, and other common features the consumer needs to know. As noted earlier, the debate on providing price, school, or location has pros and cons for both sides whether you should include them or not. However, certain key features about the home are essential to any classified ad. Normally, you would include this information somewhere in the middle of the ad; however, it can go before any features you list the sellers will miss or just after it. **List key features about the home!**

**L** ook at other ads and pay attention to what other successful real estate agents are doing. If you're new to the real estate business or trying to increase your sales normally, one good way to improve your advertising copy is to watch and read what other "successful" real estate professionals are doing. DON'T COPY! Simply read and watch to help create new ideas for you when developing classified ads in the future. It will make a huge difference in the way you market yourself and your clients' properties if you practice the art to **look at other ads and pay attention to what other successful real estate agents are doing.**

**S** pend time preparing and writing your ads, and write several ads for each listing you have! This is an overlooked practice in the real estate industry. We spend thousands of dollars on marketing our listings, hours of time earning new business, and we agree to follow a strict fiduciary obligation with our clients only to write one or two ads in a brief 60-second drill before moving on to our next "to do" item. I hope you don't fall into that category but if you do, remind yourself to **spend time preparing and writing your ads, and write several ads for each listing you have!**

By following this format you will build effective ads to carry out your main objective (GET CALLS!). We've included an ad template worksheet in Appendix A to copy and use while composing and writing classified ads for your clients.

There is also an added space for you to write as you think of new ad headings, buzzwords, or sample ads. The book also comes with a CD-ROM that contains the sample ads in the book so you can merge data from Microsoft® Excel and Microsoft® Word.

*5 Minutes to a Great Real Estate Ad* does not replace your ad writing but, rather, it is a resource you can go to in finding examples and ideas you might use in your daily business.

With this book and the tools on the CD-ROM, you're only five minutes away from a great real estate ad!

Best of luck!

John D. Mayfield

# Acknowledgements

I would like to say thank you to all of my real estate agents at Mayfield Real Estate. I also could not have completed this manuscript without the aid of a "GREAT" assistant. Thank you Amanda for all of your help! I also want to say thank you to Sara Glassmeyer, my editor and original first contact person at Thomson, who has helped and guided my real estate writing career. Thanks to Scott Person, Mark Linton, and Dave Shaut who also do such a good job for Thomson and have become good friends of mine. Thanks to Arlin Kauffman who pitched in at the last minute to help in final editing. Thank you to all of my friends at the Missouri Association of REALTORS® for your positive feedback and support on all of my books. I also want to say thank you to the CRB® (Certified Residential Brokerage Council) for all of their support and promotion of my books. Thanks Ginny Shipe, Katie Dwyer, and Tara Maric!

Of course, I owe a deep gratitude to my family. Thank you Alyx and Anne for being patient and understanding to your dad's busy schedule, my mom for brainstorming a few ad headings with me, and my lovely and wonderful wife, Kerry, for being my "BEST" friend!

# What Buyers Want in a Home Purchase—Recap of NAR 2004 Study

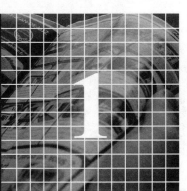

In 2004 the National Association of REALTORS® conducted a study of home-buyers across the U.S. on features and characteristics that they felt were important to recent homebuyers.[1] This section will contain a few of the facts and characteristics as outlined in the study.

- Most homes purchased had a median size of 1,727 square feet. Median home size among first-time buyers was 1,451 square feet and 1,920 square feet for repeat buyers. Custom-built homes were larger, with a median size of 2,186 square feet.
- The most desirable home feature was central air-conditioning, with 73% of recent buyers viewing this as very important. Also considered very important by homebuyers were walk-in closets in the main bedroom (51%), having a main-level bedroom (42%), and a patio or oversized garage (41%).
- Repeat homebuyers wanted a bedroom on the main level more than first-time homebuyers.
- Most buyers who took part in the survey (66%) said they would pay for an extra cost for a walk-in closet in the main bedroom.

Some of the top desired features that buyers reported in the homebuying process were:

- Central air-conditioning
- Walk-in closet in main bedroom
- Bedroom on the main level
- Patio
- Oversized garage
- Cable and satellite TV-ready
- Fencing

[1] P. Bishop, T. M. Beers III, and S. D. Hightower from The National Association of REALTORS® Research Division, "2004 National Association of REALTORS® Profiles of Buyers' Home Feature Preferences," http://www.realtor.org/Research.nsf/files/HFShilite2004.pdf/$FILE/HFShilite2004.pdf.

- Second shower in master bath
- Porch
- Eat-in kitchen

The above items, if present in your listing, would be good to somehow incorporate into your ad copy. Repeat buyers especially might find this information helpful.

Some other interesting characteristics for buyers that they viewed very important were:

*Structural features:*
- A home that is less than ten years old
- A single-story home
- One or more fireplaces
- Nine-foot or greater ceilings

*Interior features:*
- A separate shower in master or main bedroom

*Exterior features:*
- Fencing
- Deck

*Natural features:*
- Professional landscaping
- A flat lot
- Wooded lots and many trees
- Water view
- Waterfront property

*Neighborhood features:*
- Sidewalks
- Close to schools
- Near shopping

Buyers who recently bought homes and took part in this survey said they would be willing to pay more for some of these desired features:

- One or more fireplaces
- A home that is fewer than ten years old
- Full or partially finished basement
- Separate shower in master/main bath
- Whirlpool bath
- Hardwood floors
- Granite or similar countertops

The same study also shows that home searchers thought finding homes with particular rooms was very important. Most buyers felt that a garage was very

What Buyers Want in a Home Purchase

important followed by the living room, two or more full bathrooms, laundry room, family room, dining room, and den/study. The three most popular items in the study for home improvements since buyers purchased a home were:

- Repaint wallpaper interior
- Landscaping
- New window treatments

The complete "2004 National Association of REALTORS® Profile of Buyers' Home Feature Preferences" can be ordered from the National Association of REALTORS® at 1-800-874-6500. Highlights of the study can be viewed at the National Association of REALTORS® Web site at http://www.realtor.org. Understanding and knowing what buyers are looking for in their home purchase can be a huge benefit in writing ad copy to attract possible buyers for your properties and for their needs.

# Budgeting for Ads  2

One of the hardest tasks for new real estate agents to understand is the need to spend money on advertising. Like it or not, advertising is an investment that we cannot afford to do without. How much money should you spend on your advertising as a real estate agent? In a May 2004 article from *Texas REALTOR®* magazine, Greg Herder, CEO of Hobbs/Herder Advertising in Newport Beach, California, points out, "Anywhere from 10%–30% of your gross commissions should be spent on marketing. If you are just starting out, you will need to be closer to 30%. If you are a seasoned veteran, you will be closer to 10%."[1] Cyndi Cook, director of marketing and promotions for RE/MAX DFW Associates, adds, "An agent's advertising budget can range from 25%–30% of their total commissions earned depending on their media selection."[2] Those are big numbers compared to what many real estate agents spend on their advertising. But if you want to do better than average, you have to invest money in yourself and in advertising! When starting out you may need to invest some of your savings or take out a loan to get your career moving. However, if your advertising campaign takes a little while to get started don't become discouraged. Most experts will tell you that advertising will take some time. The following table illustrates how an agent who makes $50,000 needs to spend $12,500 dollars on advertising. That may seem mind-boggling; however, think of the impact $12,500 dollars would have on creating new business.

| Gross Commission Earned | Multiplied by Advertising Factor | Advertising Budget |
|---|---|---|
| $50,000 | × 25% (.25) | $12,500 |

It won't take long until that $50,000 could multiply two-, three-, or even four-fold. And don't forget, you can't stop there! Keep increasing your advertising until your referral base reaches the level where you are working with a steady flow of clients. At that point, experts have suggested to back off your advertising to a more comfortable level. However, you will still need to spend a minimum of 20% on all your gross commissions for marketing to be an effective real estate professional in today's competitive market.

---

[1] M. Woolard, "Does Your Advertising Work?" *Texas REALTOR®*, May 2004, http://www.texasrealtors.com/web/7/54/magazine/issues/04/0504/advertising.cfm.

[2] Ibid.

# Condominiums 3

Have a new listing in a condominium complex? Before you write that ad, let's consider why most people move into a condominium and what some of the most common objections might be from these consumers.

Normally, condominium buyers are looking for a change in lifestyle. Doing away with yard work, snow shoveling, and the need for upkeep in other exterior home maintenance items can be a big blessing to the condominium owner.

Fearful objections that many condominium buyers worry about are the lack of space and the storing of cherished items. *Will I feel trapped and enclosed? Will there be a noise level? Can I adjust to this new way of living?* All of those questions are good ones and areas we should try to address in our advertising so the potential buyer may consider condominium living. One point to keep in mind when writing condominium ads is your target audience and why it would be worthwhile for them to consider condominium living.

It's easy to build a condominium Web page on your Web site or to add a link for all your condominiums for sale. If you choose to do this, be sure to incorporate that into your advertising so buyers can simply type in your URL address and be directed immediately to your "Special Condo" page.

Many of the ads included in this section are simply examples for you to try to consider and complete when constructing real estate ads for condos. Naturally, you will need to change specific information to match your listing criteria. You can also use many of the headings found throughout the condominium section in other types of properties for sale.

# Sample Headings

Take the Big Step in Downsize *(Ad #1)*

Who Said Downsizing Can't Be Fun? *(Ad #2)*

Go Ahead and Indulge *(Ad #3)*

Condo Time and the Living Is Easy *(Ad #4)*

Toot Your Horn in This Townhouse *(Ad #5)*

Quit Worrying! *(Ad #6)*

Townhouse for Three *(Ad #7)*

Terrific Townhouse with Terrific Features! *(Ad #8)*

No More Yard Work *(Ad #9)*

Auctioneer, You Can Sell That Rake Too . . . *(Ad #10)*

You'll Pinch Yourself *(Ad #11)*

Do You Miss Cooking? *(Ad #12)*

It's Like a Dream Come True When You View This Condo *(Ad #13)*

Say Goodbye to Shoveling Snow! *(Ad #14)*

Imported Italian Marble *(Ad #15)*

Say Goodbye to Cutting the Grass *(Ad #16)*

A Little Bit of Paradise *(Ad #17)*

Should Have Done This Years Ago! *(Ad #18)*

Custom Condo *(Ad #19)*

Why Worry About *(Ad #20)*

Tiled Verandah with This Condo *(Ad #21)*

No Need to Worry About *(Ad #22)*

Grand Scale Living *(Ad #23)*

Casual and Comfortable *(Ad #24)*

High above the Clouds, "Almost" *(Ad #25)*

Skyline Condo *(Ad #26)*

Views for Miles *(Ad #27)*

Country Oasis Condo *(Ad #28)*

Endless Views *(Ad #29)*

Urban Oasis Condo *(Ad #30)*

A Little Oasis *(Ad #31)*

Condo with a Loft *(Ad #32)*

A Little Bit of Perfection *(Ad #33)*

Condo with a View *(Ad #34)*

Work of Art *(Ad #35)*

Tradition and Taste *(Ad #36)*

Elegant and Private *(Ad #37)*

Unlimited Possibilities *(Ad #38)*

A Condo with Class! *(Ad #39)*

A Condo for Collectibles *(Ad #40)*

Fire the Lawn Keeper! *(Ad #41)*

Watch the Birds *(Ad #42)*

No More Snow Removal *(Ad #43)*

Watch the Boats *(Ad #44)*

Sun-Splashed Sunroom Every Morning *(Ad #45)*

Need Space without the Work? *(Ad #46)*

A Patio with a Condo? *(Ad #47)*

Charming and Quaint *(Ad #48)*

Read a Book, or Two, or Three . . . *(Ad #49)*

Luxurious Condo *(Ad #50)*

Old World Grandeur *(Ad #51)*

Pamper Yourself with Rest *(Ad #52)*

Bold and Beautiful *(Ad #53)*

Serious Rest Desiree's Only! *(Ad #54)*

Every Day's a Day of Sunshine *(Ad #55)*

A Condo with Concierge *(Ad #56)*

A Cut above the Rest! *(Ad #57)*

Savor the Splendor *(Ad #58)*

Miracles Do Come True! *(Ad #59)*

Last Chance *(Ad #60)*

Watch Your Golf Game Improve! *(Ad #61)*

Almost Sold Out! *(Ad #62)*

Get Rid of the Lawnmower *(Ad #63)*

Forget about the Cruise *(Ad #64)*

No Need for Bermuda *(Ad #65)*

Nest Is Too Big? *(Ad #66)*

Kids Are Gone? *(Ad #67)*

Have We Got a Condo for You! *(Ad #68)*

Never Wash the Windows Again! *(Ad #69)*

Who Cleared the Snow? *(Ad #70)*

No Maintenance Required *(Ad #71)*

Enjoy Your Own Pool without the Maintenance *(Ad #72)*

Safe and Secure *(Ad #73)*

Top Ten Reasons to Own This Condo! *(Ad #74)*

This Condo + You = A Great Life *(Ad #75)*

One-of-a-Kind Condo *(Ad #76)*

Condo Tranquility *(Ad #77)*

Perfection Meets This Condo *(Ad #78)*

Townhouse for Two *(Ad #79)*

Finding a Condo That Offers Plenty of Room *(Ad #80)*

# Sample Ads

### Take the Big Step in Downsize

by investing in this exquisite *[#Bedrooms] bedroom/[#Baths] bath* condominium. Many upgrades are found throughout this home including walls framed by wood moldings. A great buy at only *[Price]*. For more information, contact *[Listing Agent]* at *[Phone Number]* or visit us on the Web at *[Web Site Address]*. *[Listing Code Number]*
**(Ad #1)**

### Who Said Downsizing Can't Be Fun?

With a large in-ground swimming pool, tennis courts, and a walking track you'll enjoy living at *[Name of Condo Development]*. This condo offers *[#Bedrooms]* bedroom/*[#Baths]* bath with a two-car attached garage. Call today before it is too late. Ask for *[Listing Agent]* at *[Phone Number]*. *[Listing Code Number]*
**(Ad #2)**

### Go Ahead and Indulge

yourself with all the great amenities this condo has to offer. Features whirlpool tub, walk-in closets, gourmet kitchen, and more! A great buy for the money! Call *[Listing Agent]* today to schedule a showing. Call *[Phone Number]*. *[Listing Code Number]*
**(Ad #3)**

### Condo Time and the Living Is Easy

No grass to mow, no snow to shovel, no windows to wash. With this home located at *[Name of Condo Development]*, you'll have easy access to golf. For a private tour, call *[Listing Agent]* at *[Phone Number]*, or you can e-mail *[Listing Agent]* at *[Listing Agent E-mail]*. *[Listing Code Number]*
**(Ad #4)**

### Toot Your Horn in This Townhouse

with special extras like a formal dining room, master bath and suite, screened-in porch, and more. It's a great place to call home and it is affordably priced. Call *[Listing Agent]* at *[Phone Number]* for all of the details! *[Listing Code Number]*
**(Ad #5)**

### Quit Worrying!

Your new theme to live by for this condo at *[Name of Condo Development]*. Why worry about all the extra upkeep in your present home when you can make more time for golf, fishing, travel, and more. Lots of extras are included with this townhouse. Call *[Listing Agent]* at *[Phone Number]* for more information. *[Listing Code Number]*
**(Ad #6)**

### Townhouse for Three

or four or five, you decide. With all the room in this new listing, you'll wonder what you ever did before. Awesome condo with plenty of amenities! You can view more about this property at *[Web Site Address]*, or call *[Listing Agent]* at *[Phone Number]*. *[Listing Code Number]* *(Ad #7)*

### Terrific Townhouse with Terrific Features!

Spacious living room and kitchen are just two of the many features you will find in this condo. Lovely long row of sash windows provides lots of morning light! Call *[Listing Agent]* at *[Phone Number]* about all of the extras included with this condo. *[Listing Code Number]* *(Ad #8)*

### No More Yard Work

when you invest in this condo! All of your exterior chores are included in one low maintenance fee. Each owner has available space for his or her favorite outdoor activities, such as gardening. Great price on this condo so call quick! *[Feature 1]* and *[Feature 2]*. Call *[Phone Number]* and ask for *[Listing Agent]*. *[Listing Code Number]* *(Ad #9)*

### Auctioneer, You Can Sell that Rake Too...

because the condo I'm buying includes maintenance of all my outdoor work-related activities. I'll use my extra time reading a few of my favorite books on my enclosed sun porch (that is when I am not playing golf at *[Name of Golf Course]*). Stop dreaming, it could be yours today! *[Feature 1]* and *[Feature 2]*. Call *[Listing Agent]* at *[Phone Number]* for all of the details. *[Listing Code Number]* *(Ad #10)*

### You'll Pinch Yourself

when you walk around this condo and soak up all the beauty it contains. *[#Bedrooms]* bedrooms and *[#Baths]* baths, *[Feature 1]*, and *[Feature 2]*. This condo also includes a two-car attached garage with plenty of storage space. Great association amenities with this unit, so call *[Listing Agent]* at *[Phone Number]* for all of the details! *[Listing Code Number]* *(Ad #11)*

### Do You Miss Cooking?

With all the yard work and indoor cleaning you have to do it is no wonder you have such little time to enjoy your kitchen. With this *[#Bedrooms]* bedroom/*[#Baths]* bath condo you can reignite your cooking skills. You'll appreciate all of the gourmet amenities this spacious kitchen has to offer. *[Feature 1]* and *[Feature 2]*. Call *[Listing Agent]* at *[Phone Number]* for all of the details! *[Listing Code Number]* *(Ad #12)*

### It's Like a Dream Come True When You View This Condo

as you witness the fine craftsmanship and detail this condominium has to offer. A stunning Terracotta-tiled floor in the kitchen makes way to a large breakfast area. Features *[#Bedrooms]* bedrooms and *[#Baths]* baths and *[Feature 1]* and *[Feature 2]*. Call *[Phone Number]* and ask for *[Listing Agent]*. *[Listing Code Number]* *(Ad #13)*

### Say Goodbye to Shoveling Snow!

It's included with your monthly maintenance fees at *[Name of Condo Development]*. Less than ten units remaining! Colors and carpet choices available to choose from, but don't delay because the balance of these condos are sure to go quick. Extra features included are *[Feature 1]*, *[Feature 2]*, and *[Feature 3]*. For more information, call *[Listing Agent]* at *[Phone Number]*. *[Listing Code Number]*
*(Ad #14)*

### Imported Italian Marble

in the main foyer is just the beginning of all the extras you'll find in the *[#Bedrooms]* bedroom/ *[#Baths]* bath home. You can view a virtual tour at *[Web Site Address]*. Call *[Phone Number]* and ask for *[Listing Agent]*. *[Listing Code Number]*
*(Ad #15)*

### Say Goodbye to Cutting the Grass!

With condo living, your exterior work activities are included! You'll appreciate the glass-fronted bookcase doors on each side of the living room fireplace. This condo features a large master bath to enjoy during your downtime. See how enjoyable life can really be! For a private tour, call *[Listing Agent]* at *[Phone Number]* or e-mail *[Listing Agent]* at *[Listing Agent E-mail]*. *[Listing Code Number]*
*(Ad #16)*

### A Little Bit of Paradise

It's just the beginning when you stand on the balcony and overlook the city. This condo offers plenty of amenities for you and your family such as *[Feature 1]* and *[Feature 2]*. Best of all, it is priced to sell at only *[List Price]*. Detailed information is available at *[Web Site Address]*. For a color brochure, call *[Listing Agent]* at *[Phone Number]*. *[Listing Code Number]*
*(Ad #17)*

### Should Have Done This Years Ago!

You will say to your friends after purchasing this *[#Bedrooms]* bedroom/*[#Baths]* bath condo. Lots of extras in the kitchen such as refrigerator and warming drawers. Formal dining room with wide pine flooring. Still spacious for entertaining and family gatherings. Priced at *[List Price]*, with immediate occupancy. To view this condo, stop by Saturday from 1 P.M.–5 P.M. and visit *[Listing Agent]* or call *[Listing Agent]* for a previewing at *[Phone Number]*. *[Listing Code Number]*
*(Ad #18)*

### Custom Condo

is a great way to describe all of the extras in this unit. From the ceramic tile, maple cabinets, gourmet kitchen, to the hardwood floors in the foyer and living rooms, no corners have been cut. A real gem at *[List Price]*. Oh yes, you'll appreciate the views off of the main bedroom balcony. This condo is sure to go quick, so call *[Listing Agent]* at *[Phone Number]* before it is too late. *[Listing Code Number]*
*(Ad #19)*

### Why Worry About

all the upkeep and work your home requires. You can buy this *[#Bedrooms]* bedroom/*[#Baths]* bath condo and let someone else do the lawn work. Oversized great room with fireplace and a stunning arched trellis between kitchen and dining room is just the beginning to the extras in the condo that's waiting for you. Priced at *[List Price]* and available for immediate occupancy. Call *[Phone Number]* and ask for *[Listing Agent]*. *[Listing Code Number]*
**(Ad #20)**

### Tiled Verandah with This Condo

is just the beginning when describing the elegant details you will find in this *[Name of Condo Development]* condo for sale. Offers an oversized kitchen with abundant cabinets, granite counter tops, large walk-in pantry, and more! Yes, it's a condo but the space is unbelievable! Priced at *[List Price]*, and ready for immediate occupancy. Open Saturday from 12 P.M.–4 P.M. for viewing. Refreshments will be served. Call *[Listing Agent]* at *[Phone Number]* for a pre-showing if that time doesn't work for you. *[Directions]*, *[Street Address]*. *[Listing Code Number]*
**(Ad #21)**

### No Need to Worry About

the lawn anymore. All the exterior maintenance and upkeep is included with your low monthly condo fees. There's even a pool and tennis courts to enjoy with your extra time. Features a *[Feature 1]* and *[Feature 2]*. Priced at *[List Price]*. Call *[Listing Agent]* at *[Phone Number]* for all of the details. *[Listing Code Number]*
**(Ad #22)**

### Grand Scale Living

are just a few words to describe the *[Name of Condo Development]*. Indoor and outdoor swimming pools, tennis courts, walking trails, and recreation hall are just a fraction of the amenities you'll enjoy everyday. Several units to choose from. For a full-color package brochure, call *[Listing Agent]* at *[Phone Number]*. *[Listing Code Number]*
**(Ad #23)**

### Casual and Comfortable

is the feeling you receive as you enter this *[#Bedrooms]* bedroom/*[#Baths]* bath condo. Enjoy the hardwood floors from the foyer to the living area. This condo is brand new and never lived in. Still time to choose your own colors. For more information, call *[Listing Agent]* at *[Phone Number]*.
**(Ad #24)**

### High above the Clouds, "Almost"

is the feeling you'll have from the 34th floor of your own spacious condo. Over *[# of Square Feet]* square feet of living area and plenty of windows to enjoy the views from anywhere. All walls are framed by lovely wood moldings. Priced at *[List Price]*! For a private tour, call *[Listing Agent]* at *[Phone Number]* or e-mail *[Listing Agent]* at *[Listing Agent E-mail]*. *[Listing Code Number]*
**(Ad #25)**

### Skyline Condo

Located on 43<sup>rd</sup> floor in the heart of downtown. Over *[# of Square Feet]* square feet to enjoy in this lovely showplace. Great views from the study will allow your creative mind to think at its maximum potential. The *[Name of Condo Development]* building offers many amenities such as workout gym facilities, salon and spa, and several restaurants. For more information, call *[Listing Agent]* at *[Phone Number]*. *[Listing Code Number]*
*(Ad #26)*

### Views for Miles

are three words the owners describe to their friends when they first visit this condo. Over *[# of Square Feet]* square feet of living area to enjoy. You'll discover a fireplace and whirlpool tub in the main bedroom suite with large walk-in closets. A chef's kitchen boasts state-of-the-art appliances with center island. Located on the 38<sup>th</sup> floor! Priced at *[List Price]*. Additional information or a private showing can be obtained by contacting *[Listing Agent]* at *[Phone Number]*. *[Listing Code Number]*
*(Ad #27)*

### Country Oasis Condo

is the feeling you'll have when you drive one hour south of the city to explore *[Name of Condo Development]*. All units feature *[Feature 1]* and *[Feature 2]*. Two or three bedrooms to choose from. Only six left! Call *[Listing Agent]* at *[Phone Number]* for all of the details. *[Listing Code Number]*
*(Ad #28)*

### Endless Views

describe a small part of the amenities this condo has to offer. *[#Bedrooms]* bedroom/*[#Baths]* baths, *[# of Square Feet]* square feet of living area, and on the 28<sup>th</sup> floor. This is truly upscale living at its best! Priced at *[List Price]*. Call *[Listing Agent]* at *[Phone Number]* for all of the details. *[Listing Code Number]*
*(Ad #29)*

### Urban Oasis Condo

Cotswold moulded-stone fireplace is the backdrop for a large and open living room. Features *[#Bedrooms]* bedrooms and *[#Baths]* baths, and a spacious chef's kitchen with all the extras. Two large walk-in closets off the main bedroom area. Also boasts an attached garage with storage area. All this for *[List Price]*! Call *[Phone Number]* and ask for *[Listing Agent]* for a showing or a free color brochure with all the details. *[Listing Code Number]*
*(Ad #30)*

### A Little Oasis

with plenty of room for the entire family. Naturally well-lit *[#Bedrooms]* bedroom/ *[#Baths]* bath condo, and a large family room with fireplace in this one-of-a-kind condo. Contact *[Listing Agent]* to preview this home today at *[Phone Number]*. *[Listing Code Number]*
*(Ad #31)*

### Condo with a Loft

and the views are outstanding! You'll appreciate the woodwork and detail that accompanies this condo. Cherry wood cabinets, oversized kitchen, and two-car garage with extra storage are just a few of the extras included at a low price of only *[List Price]*. Call *[Phone Number]* and ask for *[Listing Agent]*. *[Listing Code Number]*
*(Ad #32)*

### A Little Bit of Perfection

is what the owners had in mind when they constructed this *[#Bedrooms]* bedroom/ *[#Baths]* bath condo at *[Name of Condo Development]*. Vaulted ceilings along with six panel wood doors give off an unprecedented feel. Italian marble in the foyer will welcome your guests to your special showplace. For more information, call *[Listing Agent]* at *[Phone Number]*. *[Listing Code Number]*
*(Ad #33)*

### Condo with a View

describes this new *[#Bedrooms]* bedroom/ *[#Baths]* bath unit in *[Name of Condo Development]*. Patio with privacy fence, garage, and new central air unit. Also features *[Feature 1]* and *[Feature 2]*. Priced at *[List Price]*. Call *[Phone Number]* and ask for *[Listing Agent]*. *[Listing Code Number]*
*(Ad #34)*

### Work of Art

is a great description for this luxury townhouse in *[Name of Condo Development]*. *[#Bedrooms]* oversized bedrooms with *[#Baths]* full baths, and formal dining room. Master suite features whirlpool tub, *[Feature 1]*, and *[Feature 2]*. For a complete listing and brochure of all the extras details, contact *[Listing Agent]* at *[Phone Number]*. *[Listing Code Number]*
*(Ad #35)*

### Tradition and Taste

is throughout this *[#Bedrooms]* bedroom/ *[#Baths]* bath condo in *[Name of Condo Development]*. Marble entry foyer leads to delightful culinary kitchen. You'll appreciate and love every detail found in this home. You can also view additional photos at *[Web Site Address]*, or call *[Listing Agent]* to arrange a private viewing. Call *[Phone Number]*. *[Listing Code Number]*
*(Ad #36)*

### Elegant and Private

depict this *[#Bedrooms]* bedroom/*[#Baths]* bath condo in *[Name of Condo Development]*. Outstanding views of the countryside. Large laundry room with many built-ins and computer work area. A great buy at only *[List Price]*! For more information, contact *[Listing Agent]* at *[Phone Number]* or visit us on the Web at *[Web Site Address]*.
*(Ad #37)*

### Unlimited Possibilities

are in this *[#Bedrooms]* bedroom/*[#Baths]* bath condo located in *[Name of Condo Development]*. Recently acquired from a bank, this home features *[Feature 1]* and *[Feature 2]*, and has lots of potential for the person with a little imagination. Call *[Listing Agent]* at *[Phone Number]* for more information and to schedule an appointment to look at this newly acquired listing before it is too late. *[Listing Code Number]*
**(Ad #38)**

### A Condo with Class!

Lovely *[#Bedrooms]* bedroom/*[#Baths]* bath condo featuring ceramic tile and hardwood floors. Hard coat plastered ceilings, stone fireplace, gorgeous patio area, and so much more. Available for a special viewing at our Web site at *[Web Site Address]* and detailed color brochure by contacting *[Listing Agent]* at *[Phone Number]*. *[Listing Code Number]*
**(Ad #39)**

### A Condo for Collectibles

Showcase those antique collectibles you've been storing in this condo living room with alcoved bookshelves. Lots of space, *[Feature 1]*, and *[Feature 2]*. Large walk-in closet off main bedroom suite with a sunk-in tub along with separate shower stall. Priced in the mid-200s. Call *[Listing Agent]* at *[Phone Number]* for more information or to preview today. *[Listing Code Number]*
**(Ad #40)**

### Fire the Lawn Keeper!

There's no lawn maintenance in *[Name of Condo Development]*. This *[#Bedrooms]* bedroom/*[#Baths]* bath condo has all of the space and everything you need for a comfortable and happy home. Priced at only *[List Price]*! There's only two units left in the complex so call today before it is too late. Call *[Phone Number]* and ask for *[Listing Agent]*. *[Listing Code Number]*
**(Ad #41)**

### Watch the Birds

from your back porch in this *[#Bedrooms]* bedroom/*[#Baths]* bath condo. Lots of trees outside unit provides for a great bird clientele in this park-like setting. Open this Sunday from 2 P.M.–4 P.M. For more information, call *[Listing Agent]* at *[Phone Number]*. *[Directions]*, *[Street Address]*. *[Listing Code Number]*
**(Ad #42)**

### No More Snow Removal

This *[#Bedrooms]* bedroom/*[#Baths]* bath condo provides all of the exterior maintenance with your low monthly condo dues. Priced at *[List Price]* with immediate occupancy. Spacious main bedroom/bath suite provides large windows for lots of natural light. For a private tour, call *[Listing Agent]* at *[Phone Number]* or e-mail *[Listing Agent]* at *[Listing Agent E-mail]*. *[Listing Code Number]*
**(Ad #43)**

### Watch the Boats

from this fourth-floor condo situated at the Lake of the Ozarks. Great balcony area, swimming pool in complex, private boat dock, and more! A great buy at only *[List Price]*! For more information, contact *[Listing Agent]* at *[Phone Number]* or visit us on the Web at *[Web Site Address]*.
**(Ad #44)**

### Sun-Splashed Sunroom Every Morning

in this *[#Bedrooms]* bedroom/*[#Baths]* bath condo. Coffered ceilings in living room, large country-style kitchen with walk-in pantry, and separate laundry area. Much, much, more! A great buy at only *[List Price]*! Call *[Listing Agent]* at *[Phone Number]* for all of the details. *[Listing Code Number]*
**(Ad #45)**

### Need Space without the Work?

This open and airy *[#Bedrooms]* bedroom/*[#Baths]* bath condo features a large great room, *[Feature 1]*, and *[Feature 2]* with a separate den. There's a one-car garage with attached storage, too! All this for only *[List Price]*! For more information, call *[Listing Agent]* at *[Phone Number]*. *[Listing Code Number]*
**(Ad #46)**

### A Patio with a Condo?

That's right! This *[#Bedrooms]* bedroom/*[#Baths]* bath condo features a large spacious patio with a retractable cover awning. Also features a privacy fence and the ability to have your own small garden with this unit. See for yourself! Call *[Listing Agent]* at *[Phone Number]* for a private showing today. *[Listing Code Number]*
**(Ad #47)**

### Charming and Quaint

expresses this Spanish-style condo in *[Name of Condo Development]*. Only one owner has lived in this unit. Features a large main bedroom/bath suite with separate shower and whirlpool tub. Call *[Listing Agent]* at *[Phone Number]* for all of the details!
**(Ad #48)**

### Read a Book, or Two, or Three...

Or just sit back and relax in this English Tudor Style *[#Bedrooms]* bedroom/*[#Baths]* bath condo in *[Name of Condo Development]*. Attention to detail has been noted in every area of this unit. Over *[# of Square Feet]* square feet and priced at *[List Price]*. Call *[Listing Agent]* at *[Phone Number]* for all of the details. *[Listing Code Number]*
**(Ad #49)**

### Luxurious Condo

on the 38th floor in downtown Chicago. Great views of Lake Michigan! Excellent dining and swimming facilities are included in this building. Priced at *[List Price]*. Full-color brochure available by contacting *[Listing Agent]* at *[Phone Number]*. *[Listing Code Number]*
**(Ad #50)**

### Old World Grandeur

is found throughout this 12-story condo building in the heart of downtown. Lots of exposed brick, gorgeous woodwork, and stained glass windows are found in this *[#Bedrooms]* bedroom/*[#Baths]* bath condo. Located on the third floor. Parking facilities are also available. For a private tour, call *[Listing Agent]* at *[Phone Number]* or e-mail *[Listing Agent]* at *[Listing Agent E-mail]*. *[Listing Code Number]*
**(Ad #51)**

### Pamper Yourself with Rest

in this *[#Bedrooms]* bedroom/*[#Baths]* bath condo in *[Name of Condo Development]*. This complex offers a walking trail, swimming pool, tennis courts, and recreation house as part of its monthly dues. No more need for yard work or exterior maintenance—just sit back and relax! Why just read about it when you can see it in person? Call *[Listing Agent]* at *[Phone Number]* to preview this listing today. *[Listing Code Number]*
**(Ad #52)**

### Bold and Beautiful

Four-panel door with side and transom light greet you on the stone front foyer floor. Lots of character found from the hardwood floors to the large, open, and well-lit kitchen with every imaginable appliance available. Priced at only *[List Price]*! For more information, call *[Listing Agent]* at *[Phone Number]*. *[Listing Code Number]*
**(Ad #53)**

### Serious Rest Desiree's Only!

Close to the golf course and country club! This *[#Bedrooms]* bedroom/*[#Baths]* bath condo features a fireplace, built-in bookcases, and a formal dining room for entertaining. Garage workshop area and storage above makes this unit ideal for you and your family. Call *[Listing Agent]* at *[Phone Number]* for more information. *[Listing Code Number]*
**(Ad #54)**

### Every Day's a Day of Sunshine

in this French country *[#Bedrooms]* bedroom/ *[#Baths]* bath condo in *[Name of Condo Development]*. A fantastic stone fireplace accents the living room along with pine wood floors. Great storage facilities, garage, walk-in closets, and more! This is a great buy at *[List Price]* so don't delay! Call *[Listing Agent]* today at *[Phone Number]* for more information. *[Listing Code Number]*
**(Ad #55)**

### A Condo with Concierge

in the *[Name of Condo Development]* building on the Upper West Side of the city. Located on the 34th floor, this unit provides breathtaking views of the entire city. A large foyer greets your guests as they arrive. Formal dining room, living room, study, gourmet chef kitchen, and so much more! You can view this property online at *[Web Site Address]*. Let *[Listing Agent]* show you this lovely listing today. Call *[Phone Number]* to schedule your appointment. *[Listing Code Number]*
**(Ad #56)**

### A Cut above the Rest!

Attractive and affordable *[#Bedrooms]* bedroom/*[#Baths]* bath condo features hardwood floors throughout the unit and ceramic tile in the foyer. Stunning kitchen with granite counter tops lead to French doors opening to an oversized patio with covered trellis. Priced at *[List Price]*. Why just read about it when you can see it in person? Call *[Listing Agent]* at *[Phone Number]* to preview this listing today. *[Listing Code Number]*
**(Ad #57)**

### Savor the Splendor

with this gracious and comfortable condo. Features large formal living room and dining room, brick fireplace with built-in bookcases, and spacious main bedroom and bath. Priced in the low 200s! Owners will provide home warranty for one year. Call *[Listing Agent]* at *[Phone Number]* for all of the details. *[Listing Code Number]*
**(Ad #58)**

### Miracles Do Come True!

This *[#Bedrooms]* bedroom/*[#Baths]* bath condo has recently been renovated with new carpet, paint, and new kitchen cabinets. Priced at *[List Price]*, which is well below market value in *[Name of Condo Development]*. Call *[Listing Agent]* at *[Phone Number]* before it is too late. *[Listing Code Number]*
**(Ad #59)**

### Last Chance

to own a condo in *[Name of Condo Development]*. These *[#Bedrooms]* bedroom/*[#Baths]* bath units are almost gone. There's still time to pick out your own carpet and wall colors. Available for viewing on Saturday and Sunday from 12 P.M.–5 P.M., or call *[Listing Agent]* at *[Phone Number]* for a private showing today. *[Listing Code Number]*
**(Ad #60)**

### Watch Your Golf Game Improve!

*[Name of Condo Development]* features 27 holes of golf included with your condo association dues when you buy this *[#Bedrooms]* bedroom/*[#Baths]* bath unit. Private setting with great shade trees, patio, and more. Oversized garage is ideal to store your golf cart, too! To score a par on this deal, call *[Phone Number]* and ask for *[Listing Agent]*. *[Listing Code Number]*
**(Ad #61)**

### Almost Sold Out!

These *[#Bedrooms]* bedroom/*[#Baths]* bath units in *[Name of Condo Development]* are just about gone. Pick your own colors and carpeting but most of all enjoy the swimming pool and tennis courts as one of the owners in this new development. Come visit us this weekend during our open house before they are all gone, or call *[Listing Agent]* at *[Phone Number]* for a private showing today. *[Directions]*, *[Street Address]*. *[Listing Code Number]*
**(Ad #62)**

### Get Rid of the Lawnmower

*[Name of Condo Development]* takes pride in lawn maintenance for their homeowners. Adorable *[#Bedrooms]* bedroom/*[#Baths]* bath condo with private patio area and privacy fence. Beamed ceilings provide a rustic feel in the living room, along with the stone fireplace. Also boasts a *[Feature 1]* and *[Feature 2]*. For more information, call *[Listing Agent]* at *[Agency Phone Number]*. *[Listing Code Number]*
**(Ad #63)**

### Forget about the Cruise

you'll have plenty of amenities to enjoy with owning a home in *[Name of Condo Development]*. Stunning stone flagged floor in kitchen provides the perfect backdrop to the enormous amount of kitchen cabinets. Large walk-in pantry, center island, and top-of-the-line appliances. Large formal dining room, along with *[#Bedrooms]* bedrooms and *[#Baths]* baths. You won't believe you're living in a condo! Let *[Listing Agent]* show you this lovely listing today. Call *[Phone Number]* to schedule your appointment. *[Listing Code Number]*
**(Ad #64)**

### No Need for Bermuda

you'll have all the necessities for a perfect day at *[Name of Condo Development]*. Eye-catching stone and brick condo features many upgrades and extras for you to enjoy! *[Feature 1]*, *[Feature 2]*, and *[Feature 3]* give you all the comforts inside your condo. Golf, swimming pool, and walking trail are also included. Why just read about it when you can see it in person? Call *[Listing Agent]* at *[Phone Number]* to preview this listing today. *[Listing Code Number]*
**(Ad #65)**

### Nest Is Too Big?

Here's the perfect cure with this *[#Bedrooms]* bedroom/*[#Baths]* bath condo in *[Name of Condo Development]*. Exquisite style and taste can be found throughout this home. *[Feature 1]* and *[Feature 2]*, along with many more extras. A great buy at only *[List Price]*! For more information, contact *[Listing Agent]* at *[Phone Number]* or visit us on the Web at *[Web Site Address]*. *[Listing Code Number]*
**(Ad #66)**

### Kids Are Gone?

This plush and plaices condo offers you a gorgeous view of the 17th fairway at *[Name of Condo Development]*. Features *[Feature 1]*, *[Feature 2]*, and *[Feature 3]*, along with many more details too numerous to mention. *[List Price]*! Call quick on this one; it's sure to go quick at this price! Call *[Phone Number]* and ask for *[Listing Agent]*. *[Listing Code Number]*
**(Ad #67)**

### Have We Got a Condo for You!

Grace and beauty abound throughout this brick condo building situated in *[Name of Condo Development]*. Offers you a two-car garage with additional storage in attic. Large eat-in kitchen with small breakfast nook. *[Feature 1]* and *[Feature 2]*. You'll thank yourself everyday for making such a smart move! See for yourself! Call *[Listing Agent]* at *[Phone Number]* for a private showing today. *[Listing Code Number]*
**(Ad #68)**

### Never Wash the Windows Again!

*[Name of Condo Development]* provides all of the exterior chores you're tired of worrying with day-in and day-out, including washing the windows! You'll appreciate the lovely oak wood trim throughout this home. Large main bedroom/suite offers a whirlpool tub and separate shower stall. His and her walk-in closets, fireplace, and more. Call *[Listing Agent]* at *[Phone Number]* for all of the details. *[Listing Code Number]*
**(Ad #69)**

### Who Cleared the Snow?

*[Name of Condo Development]* of course! Extra exterior amenities such as snow removal, window washing, lawn mowing, and more are included in your low monthly maintenance fees. Best of all you can enjoy *[Feature 1]*, *[Feature 2]*, and a wealth of other features with this *[#Bedrooms]* bedroom/*[#Baths]* bath condo. Let *[Listing Agent]* show you this lovely listing today. Call *[Phone Number]* to schedule your appointment. *[Listing Code Number]*
**(Ad #70)**

### No Maintenance Required

with this *[#Bedrooms]* bedroom/*[#Baths]* bath condo in *[Name of Condo Development]*. Beautiful boxed hedges line the sidewalk as you approach the gorgeous wooden door with lead glass. A spacious and delightful kitchen will warm any cook's heart. All this for a low price of *[List Price]*. *[Listing Code Number]*
**(Ad #71)**

### Enjoy Your Own Pool without the Maintenance!

*[Name of Condo Development]* offers a wonderful pool and patio area as a portion of your amenities when you invest in this development. You'll also enjoy *[Feature 1]*, *[Feature 2]*, and *[Feature 3]* in this *[#Bedrooms]* bedroom/*[#Baths]* bath condo. For more information, call *[Listing Agent]* at *[Phone Number]*. *[Listing Code Number]*
**(Ad #72)**

### Safe and Secure

Gated *[#Bedrooms]* bedroom/*[#Baths]* bath in *[Name of Condo Development]*. Generous living space is complimented by an open floor plan with vaulted ceilings and large wood moldings. Stone fireplace in living room, *[Feature 1]*, *[Feature 2]*, and a large oversized two-car garage with workbench is included in this home. *[List Price]*. Call *[Listing Agent]* at *[Phone Number]* for all of the details. *[Listing Code Number]*
**(Ad #73)**

### Top Ten Reasons to Own This Condo!

We can't list all ten reasons to purchase this home in our ad but we can tell you about *[Feature 1]*, *[Feature 2]*, *[Feature 3]*, and that you also can enjoy use of the swimming pool with cabana, recreation house, and walking trail at *[Name of Condo Development]*. A great buy at only *[List Price]*! For more information, contact *[Listing Agent]* at *[Phone Number]* or visit us on the Web at *[Web Site Address]*. *[Listing Code Number]*
**(Ad #74)**

### This Condo + You = A Great Life

An open and airy living room greets you as you enter through the front door of this *[#Bedrooms]* bedroom/*[#Baths]* bath condo in *[Name of Condo Development]*. Center island in kitchen is accompanied by ceramic tile and small breakfast bar. Large pantry provides plenty of storage for all of your needs. *[List Price]*! Call quick on this one; it's sure to go quick at this price! Call *[Phone Number]* and ask for *[Listing Agent]*. *[Listing Code Number]*
**(Ad #75)**

### One-of-a-Kind Condo!

Neat and clean *[#Bedrooms]* bedroom/*[#Baths]* bath home located in quiet and private area of development. Quaint patio offers a sensational large tree nearby providing lots of shade. Two car garage, *[Feature 1]*, *[Feature 2]*, and *[Feature 3]*. Call *[Phone Number]* and ask for *[Listing Agent]*. *[Listing Code Number]*
**(Ad #76)**

### Condo Tranquility

You've never dreamed a sunroom could offer such peace and relaxation until you spend a few minutes sitting in this room in this *[#Bedrooms]* bedroom/*[#Baths]* bath home we recently listed for sale. Also boasts *[Feature 1]*, *[Feature 2]*, *[Feature 3]*, and so much more. See for yourself! Contact *[Phone Number]* and ask for *[Listing Agent]*. *[Listing Code Number]*
**(Ad #77)**

### Perfection Meets This Condo

A large brick fireplace in the living room is flanked by floor-to-ceiling bookcases that provide a stunning entrance from the airy foyer. Imported marble floors are an integral part of several rooms, along with coved molding and many other fine details. *[Feature 1]*, *[Feature 2]*, and *[Feature 3]* are only the beginning of describing this one-of-a-kind listing. A great buy at only *[List Price]*! For more information, contact *[Listing Agent]* at *[Phone Number]* or visit us on the Web at *[Web Site Address]*. *[Listing Code Number]*
**(Ad #78)**

### Townhouse for Two

is a fitting description of this *[#Bedrooms]* bedroom/*[#Baths]* bath home in *[Name of Condo Development]*. Large walk-in closets, fireplace in living room, and pantry off kitchen. One-car garage with small storage area is ideal for keepsakes and other rarely used items. *[List Price]*! Call quick on this one; it's sure to go quick at this price! Call *[Phone Number]* and ask for *[Listing Agent]*. *[Listing Code Number]*
**(Ad #79)**

### Finding a Condo That Offers Plenty of Room

is no longer a problem when you look at this *[# of Square Feet]* square feet condo. *[#Bedrooms]* bedrooms and *[#Baths]* baths, *[Feature 1]*, *[Feature 2]*, *[Feature 3]*, and so much more to offer. Call *[Listing Agent]* at *[Phone Number]* for all of the details. *[Listing Code Number]*
**(Ad #80)**

# Small Homes 4

Writing ads for small homes may be one of the most difficult areas to attract potential buyers. If you are not careful you could describe the home in such a way that many buyers would just feel it's not practical for them to consider looking at. So it almost does not do justice to include a small home category. However, many of the properties that real estate agents market throughout the United States are homes geared to this particular audience.

What are some hot buttons that might entice readers in a small home? Again, go back and look at the clientele. Perhaps some people looking for small homes are downsizing from a larger home where they have had a change in family size because of a death of a spouse, or some may be just starting over. Many times potential buyers in this segment are first-time homebuyers. Offerings of assistance by the seller and paying closing costs or other incentives is one way to reach this market segment. (PLEASE NOTE: Conforming to all Real Estate Settlement Procedures Act (RESPA) and Truth-in-Lending guidelines is important for the real estate professional if you are going to include financing terms in your advertisements. Be sure to follow all Truth in Lending laws when writing such ads. For more information consult your broker and all state and federal laws. You can read more information by visiting www.HUD.gov.)

Incorporate a heading that will get the reader's attention and create an interest by enticing the consumer to read more about what this home has to offer. Don't forget to inquire with your sellers about what they've enjoyed about their home and what they'll miss. Remember to ask for the sale and the appointment in all of your advertisements! By following a few simple steps, writing small home ads will be a winner for you!

# Sample Headings

Ivy Cottage *(Ad #1)*

Storybook Setting *(Ad #2)*

Pretty in Pink *(Ad #3)*

A Small Home with a Big Heart *(Ad #4)*

If Walls Could Talk *(Ad #5)*

A Little Bit of House and a Whole Lot of Home *(Ad #6)*

A Cottage with Character *(Ad #7)*

You Can Still Smell the Apple Pies! *(Ad #8)*

A Great Family Was Raised Here *(Ad #9)*

The Perfect Size! *(Ad #10)*

Not Too Big *(Ad #11)*

Affordable and Adorable *(Ad #12)*

The Littlest House on the Block *(Ad #13)*

Cuddle Up *(Ad #14)*

Big on Charm *(Ad #15)*

Great Things Come in Small Packages *(Ad #16)*

A Little Bit of Sunshine *(Ad #17)*

Energy Saver *(Ad #18)*

Small Size for the Spacious Conscious Eyes *(Ad #19)*

Tiny Treasure *(Ad #20)*

Little and Bright *(Ad #21)*

A Cottage for Two *(Ad #22)*

Small and Adorable Especially Affordable *(Ad #23)*

What an Entrance! *(Ad #24)*

Small but Roomy *(Ad #25)*

Small but Spacious *(Ad #26)*

Bungalow with Character *(Ad #27)*

Cottage Like a Castle *(Ad #28)*

Room to Take Care of *(Ad #29)*

Save on Your Utility Bills *(Ad #30)*

No More High Taxes *(Ad #31)*

Gingerbread Cottage *(Ad #32)*

Quaint and Romantic *(Ad #33)*

There's More to Life Than Square Footage *(Ad #34)*

Neat and Clean and the Perfect Size *(Ad #35)*

Now That the Kids Are Gone *(Ad #36)*

Just the Right Size *(Ad #37)*

You'll Be Glad You Downsized! *(Ad #38)*

Why Worry? *(Ad #39)*

No More Empty Rooms *(Ad #40)*

No More Wasted Space *(Ad #41)*

Call the Auctioneer *(Ad #42)*

Father Knows Best *(Ad #43)*

Now You Can Garden *(Ad #44)*

Spend More Time with the Family *(Ad #45)*

Little Is Good *(Ad #46)*

A Small Home with Large Rooms *(Ad #47)*

It's a Secret *(Ad #48)*

It's Not a Secret *(Ad #49)*

The Best of Both Worlds *(Ad #50)*

The Little House That Could *(Ad #51)*

A Spanish Bungalow *(Ad #52)*

A Cottage with a Contemporary Flare *(Ad #53)*

### Ivy Cottage

This Mediterranean style *[#Bedrooms]* bedroom/*[#Baths]* bath home has a cobbled courtyard with lovely wild flowers as a backdrop. It has all the flare you've been looking for including a large eat-in kitchen with newly installed cabinets, granite counter tops, and fireplace in the living room. A real charmer! For a private tour, call *[Listing Agent]* at *[Phone Number]*. Or you can e-mail *[Listing Agent]* at *[Listing Agent E-mail]*. *[Listing Code Number]*
**(Ad #1)**

### Storybook Setting

It's not often we find a home to sell that's nestled among the tress with a cobblestone brook nearby! You'll appreciate the attention to detail the original builder put into the woodwork and trim. An absolute gorgeous setting! Sure to go quick at this low price! Extra features included are *[Feature 1]*, *[Feature 2]*, and *[Feature 3]*. For more information, call *[Listing Agent]* at *[Phone Number]*. *[Listing Code Number]*
**(Ad #2)**

### Pretty in Pink

This charming *[#Bedrooms]* bedroom/*[#Baths]* bath bungalow is a dollhouse! Fresh herbs await your picking off the rock patio. Large kitchen with nook area, pantry, and more. Just listed! Call quick on this one! Call *[Phone Number]* and ask for *[Listing Agent]*. *[Listing Code Number]*
**(Ad #3)**

### A Small Home with a Big Heart

This *[#Bedrooms]* bedroom/*[#Baths]* bath bungalow has been the home to only one owner and has offered many enjoyable holidays for this family. Large dining room adjoins formal living room with fireplace and floor-to-ceiling built-in bookcases. *[Feature 1]* and *[Feature 2]*. See for yourself! Contact *[Phone Number]* and ask for *[Listing Agent]*. *[Listing Code Number]*
**(Ad #4)**

### If Walls Could Talk

you could hear all of the great stories this family and home has shared during the past forty-five years. Only one proud owner has enjoyed the comfort and warmth now offered to you. *[Feature 1]*, *[Feature 2]*, and *[Feature 3]*. Let *[Listing Agent]* show you this lovely listing today. Call *[Phone Number]* to schedule your appointment. *[Listing Code Number]*
**(Ad #5)**

### A Little Bit of House and a Whole Lot of Home

This *[#Bedrooms]* bedroom/*[#Baths]* bath bungalow features a large kitchen with breakfast nook, overlooking patio, and flower garden in the backyard. There's a small den that could be used as an additional bedroom or computer room. See for yourself how tidy this home is. Contact *[Phone Number]* and ask for *[Listing Agent]*. *[Listing Code Number]*
**(Ad #6)**

### A Cottage with Character

Angled door frames and open beams provide a look and feel that is unmatched with this new listing. This *[#Bedrooms]* bedroom/*[#Baths]* bath also features a lovely stone entry foyer, *[Feature 1]*, *[Feature 2]*, and *[Feature 3]*. A real dollhouse and priced for a quick sale. Call *[Phone Number]* and ask for *[Listing Agent]*. *[Listing Code Number]*
*(Ad #7)*

### You Can Still Smell the Apple Pies!

This was Grandma's home and she loved to bake apple pies for her friends and family. This *[#Bedrooms]* bedroom/*[#Baths]* bath features a screened-in porch to relax and nap during warm weather. Great garden spot with small storage shed for tools and accessories. Plenty of flowers to enjoy as you soak up the spacious backyard. *[List Price]*! Call quick on this one, it's sure to go quick at this price! Call *[Phone Number]* and ask for *[Listing Agent]*. *[Listing Code Number]*
*(Ad #8)*

### A Great Family Was Raised Here

This *[#Bedrooms]* bedroom/*[#Baths]* bath ranch home is proud to boast that only one family lived here! Features a large eat-in kitchen, cedar-lined closets, and walk-in pantry in the kitchen. Call today so your family can be proud to be raised here too! Call *[Listing Agent]* at *[Phone Number]* for all of the details! *[Listing Code Number]*
*(Ad #9)*

### The Perfect Size!

Entry portico adds a warm touch to this *[#Bedrooms]* bedroom/*[#Baths]* bath cottage. Knotty pine walls accent the enclosed porch off the side of the home. Features plenty of closet space and *[Feature 1]* and *[Feature 2]*. See for yourself! Contact *[Phone Number]* and ask for *[Listing Agent]*. *[Listing Code Number]*
*(Ad #10)*

### Not Too Big

This *[#Bedrooms]* bedroom/*[#Baths]* bath ivy covered cottage has all the warmth and comfort you would expect from a home. Large living room and dining room with glass beveled doors to close off for private gatherings. There's also a fireplace, central air, eat-in kitchen, and more. Call *[Phone Number]* and ask for *[Listing Agent]* to receive a full-colored flyer of this home. *[Listing Code Number]*
*(Ad #11)*

### Affordable and Adorable

Combination living and dining room fitted with French doors provides a cozy yet open feel for entertaining. *[#Bedrooms]* bedrooms/*[#Baths]* baths *[Style of Home]* with all the comforts you would expect. *[Feature 1]*, *[Feature 2]*, and *[Feature 3]*. See for yourself! Contact *[Phone Number]* and ask for *[Listing Agent]*. *[Listing Code Number]*
*(Ad #12)*

### The Littlest House on the Block

is always the best buy to invest in, and we've found it with this new listing! *[#Bedrooms]* bedroom/*[#Baths]* bath cottage is nestled among larger homes in a grand neighborhood. Features *[Feature 1]*, *[Feature 2]*, and *[Feature 3]*. Let *[Listing Agent]* show you this lovely listing today. Call *[Phone Number]* to schedule your appointment. *[Listing Code Number]*
**(Ad #13)**

### Cuddle Up

next to the wide stone fireplace in this *[#Bedrooms]* bedroom/*[#Baths]* bath Craftsman home. You'll appreciate the *[Feature 1]*, *[Feature 2]*, and *[Feature 3]* along with the stained-fir woodwork in the living and dining rooms. Call *[Phone Number]* and ask for *[Listing Agent]*. *[Listing Code Number]*
**(Ad #14)**

### Big on Charm

is this *[#Bedrooms]* bedroom/*[#Baths]* bath bungalow with stenciled box-beamed ceilings. Sits on a quiet corner lot with large shade trees. Also boasts *[Feature 1]*, *[Feature 2]*, and a huge country kitchen with pantry. For more information, contact *[Listing Agent]* at *[Phone Number]*, or visit us on the Web at *[Web Site Address]*. A great buy at only *[List Price]*! *[Listing Code Number]*
**(Ad #15)**

### Great Things Come in Small Packages

Clean and sharp are two words to describe this *[#Bedrooms]* bedroom/*[#Baths]* *[Style of Home]*. Features a granite fireplace with oak mantel and tongue-and-groove ceilings for a special touch. For more information, call *[Listing Agent]* at *[Phone Number]*. *[Listing Code Number]*
**(Ad #16)**

### A Little Bit of Sunshine

is the perfect description for the natural light-filled *[#Bedrooms]* bedroom/*[#Baths]* bath *[Style of Home]*. Features *[Feature 1]*, *[Feature 2]*, and *[Feature 3]*, along with a large deck overlooking the enormous backyard. Call *[Phone Number]* and ask for *[Listing Agent]*. *[Listing Code Number]*
**(Ad #17)**

### Energy Saver

This *[#Bedrooms]* bedroom/*[#Baths]* bath *[Style of Home]* has been recently remodeled by the owners. Features *[Feature 1]*, *[Feature 2]*, *[Feature 3]*, and much more! For a private tour, call *[Listing Agent]* at *[Phone Number]*. Or you can e-mail *[Listing Agent]* at *[Listing Agent E-mail]*. *[Listing Code Number]*
**(Ad #18)**

### Small Size for the Spacious Conscious Eyes

Front door with adjacent side window gives a hearty and warm greeting to you and your guests. This *[#Bedrooms]* bedroom/*[#Baths]* bath Craftsman home on an oversized city lot is sure to sell fast at this low price! *[List Price]*! Call *[Phone Number]* and ask for *[Listing Agent]*. *[Listing Code Number]*
**(Ad #19)**

### Tiny Treasure

This *[Style of Home]* features the character and charm you've been looking for in your next home! Fireplace, eat-in kitchen with breakfast nook, formal dining room, and a full unfinished basement. See for yourself! Contact *[Phone Number]* and ask for *[Listing Agent]*. *[Listing Code Number]*
**(Ad #20)**

### Little and Bright

Here's a *[#Bedrooms]* bedroom/*[#Baths]* bath *[Style of Home]* with lots of windows providing an abundance of natural light. You'll appreciate the sunshine and warmth this home offers as you make your way throughout every room. Cozy breakfast nook with window seats accents a large country kitchen, central air, pantry, and more. A charming home that's priced to sell. Call *[Listing Agent]* at *[Phone Number]* for all of the details. *[Listing Code Number]*
**(Ad #21)**

### A Cottage for Two

Stunning terra-cotta tile floor in the kitchen leads to an open living room with a fireplace and built-in window seat. This new listing has all of the updates you would require in a pre-owned home. Perfect home and a great buy for the money. Why just read about it when you can see it in person? Call *[Listing Agent]* at *[Phone Number]* to preview this listing today. *[Listing Code Number]*
**(Ad #22)**

### Small and Adorable Especially Affordable

Cotswold-stone walls give this *[#Bedrooms]* bedroom/*[#Baths]* bath *[Style of Home]* all of the charm and class it deserves. Features a fireplace in the living room, hardwood floors in most of the home, and a fully refurbished bathroom! Call *[Listing Agent]* at *[Phone Number]* for all of the details. *[Listing Code Number]*
**(Ad #23)**

### What an Entrance!

You'll be greeted by a spacious terrace bordered by brick with inset of plain terra-cotta tiles with this *[#Bedrooms]* bedroom/*[#Baths]* bath *[Style of Home]*. Also found in this home are *[Feature 1]*, *[Feature 2]*, and *[Feature 3]*. A great buy at only *[List Price]!* For more information contact *[Listing Agent]* at *[Phone Number]*, or visit us on the Web at *[Web Site Address]*. *[Listing Code Number]*
**(Ad #24)**

### Small but Roomy

Designed for efficiency, this *[#Bedrooms]* bedroom/*[#Baths]* bath *[Style of Home]* provides an array of extra features. *[Feature 1]*, *[Feature 2]*, and *[Feature 3]*. *[List Price]!* Call *[Phone Number]* and ask for *[Listing Agent]*. *[Listing Code Number]*
**(Ad #25)**

### Small but Spacious

This *[#Bedrooms]* bedroom/*[#Baths]* bath *[Style of Home]* provides a welcoming-covered front porch to greet your guests. Box bay-window in dining room views a well-maintained lawn and flowers. *[#Bedrooms]* bedrooms and *[#Baths]* baths and so much more to offer. *[List Price]*! Call quick on this one; it's sure to go quick at this price! Call *[Phone Number]* and ask for *[Listing Agent]*. *[Listing Code Number]*
**(Ad #26)**

### Bungalow with Character

Burma teak paneling takes center stage as you enter this quaint and inviting home. You'll appreciate the nine-over-nine sash windows that flood every room with natural sunlight. There's also *[Feature 1]*, *[Feature 2],* and so much more. Call today on this new listing. At *[List Price]* it probably won't be around for long! For a special preview of this week's home, view our photos online at *[Web Site Address]*, or call *[Listing Agent]* at *[Phone Number]*. *[Listing Code Number]*
**(Ad #27)**

### Cottage Like a Castle

provides an oversized living room that's awash in afternoon light! *[#Bedrooms]* bedroom/*[#Baths]* baths with extra features of *[Feature 1]*, *[Feature 2],* and *[Feature 3]*. A great buy for the money at only *[List Price]*. For a private tour, call *[Listing Agent]* at *[Phone Number]*, or e-mail *[Listing Agent]* at *[Listing Agent E-mail]*. *[Listing Code Number]*
**(Ad #28)**

### Room to Take Care of

in this *[#Bedrooms]* bedroom/*[#Baths]* bath *[Style of Home]*. Extra features included are *[Feature 1]*, *[Feature 2]*, and *[Feature 3]*. You'll appreciate all of the extras in this new listing, so don't delay! Call *[Listing Agent]* at *[Phone Number]* to arrange a showing. *[Listing Code Number]*
**(Ad #29)**

### Save on Your Utility Bills

*[#Bedrooms]* bedroom/*[#Baths]* bath *[Style of Home]* provides a stone wall with alcoved bookshelves in the spacious living room with wood-burning fireplace. *[Feature 1]* and *[Feature 2]* are also included with this special new listing. *[List Price]*! Call quick on this one, it's sure to go quick at this price! Call *[Phone Number]* and ask for *[Listing Agent]*. *[Listing Code Number]*
**(Ad #30)**

### No More High Taxes

with this *[Style of Home]* home featuring *[#Bedrooms]* bedrooms and *[#Baths]* baths. You'll appreciate the arched hallways and all of the integrate built-ins this listing has to offer. *[Feature 1]*, *[Feature 2]*, and so much more! See for yourself! Contact *[Phone Number]* and ask for *[Listing Agent]*. *[Listing Code Number]*
**(Ad #31)**

### Gingerbread Cottage

A breathtaking home nestled at the bottom of a grassy hillside greets every visitor with an array of sunshine. Flanked by trompe l'oeil shutters, this *[#Bedrooms]* bedroom/*[#Baths]* bath home is the perfect recipe for happiness! See for yourself! Contact *[Phone Number]* and ask for *[Listing Agent]*. *[Listing Code Number]*
**(Ad #32)**

### Quaint and Romantic

depicts this warm and inviting *[#Bedrooms]* bedroom/*[#Baths]* bath *[Style of Home]*. Window alcove along with *[Feature 1]*, *[Feature 2]*, and *[Feature 3]* makes this a special find. See for yourself! Contact *[Phone Number]* and ask for *[Listing Agent]*. *[Listing Code Number]*
**(Ad #33)**

### There's More to Life Than Square Footage

Enter this charming *[Style of Home]* through a small entry portico flanked by stone and brick. Features *[#Bedrooms]* bedroom/ *[#Baths]* baths along with *[Feature 1]*, *[Feature 2]*, and *[Feature 3]*. To preview this new listing, contact *[Listing Agent]* at *[Phone Number]*. *[Listing Code Number]*
**(Ad #34)**

### Neat and Clean and the Perfect Size

Stenciled box-beamed ceilings make way to a dramatic and stunning living and dining room with fitted French doors. Spacious kitchen with breakfast nook and pantry. *[List Price]*! Call quick on this one; it's sure to go quick at this price! Call *[Phone Number]* and ask for *[Listing Agent]*. *[Listing Code Number]*
**(Ad #35)**

### Now That the Kids Are Gone

why worry and fret with a large home and extra rooms to clean. This *[#Bedrooms]* bedroom/ *[#Baths]* bath *[Style of Home]* will be the perfect answer to helping you travel like you want to. Extra features included are *[Feature 1]*, *[Feature 2]*, and *[Feature 3]*. For more information, call *[Listing Agent]* at *[Phone Number]*. *[Listing Code Number]*
**(Ad #36)**

### Just the Right Size

with this *[#Bedrooms]* bedroom/*[#Baths]* bath *[Style of Home]* with clapboard siding. A stone patio in the rear is visible from the cozy breakfast nook off the kitchen. You'll appreciate the knotty pine walls and hardwood floors in this new listing. It's priced to sell at *[List Price]*. Call *[Listing Agent]* at *[Phone Number]* for all of the details. *[Listing Code Number]*
**(Ad #37)**

### You'll Be Glad You Downsized!

Exquisite kitchen awaits you in this small but powerful *[#Bedrooms]* bedroom/*[#Baths]* bath *[Style of Home]*. Dutch door from mudroom to covered porch adds the perfect touch to a loving home with character! First week on market, so call quickly! Call *[Listing Agent]* at *[Phone Number]* for all of the details. *[Listing Code Number]*
**(Ad #38)**

### Why Worry?

This home is the perfect size. You won't need to agonize about all of the extra housework you currently face. Superb *[#Bedrooms]* bedroom/*[#Baths]* bath home features *[Feature 1]* and *[Feature 2]*. A true one-of-a-kind home that's just right for you and your family! A great buy at only *[List Price]*! For more information, contact *[Listing Agent]* at *[Phone Number]* or visit us on the Web at *[Web Site Address]*. *[Listing Code Number]*
**(Ad #39)**

### No More Empty Rooms

to concern yourself with when you downsize into this *[#Bedrooms]* bedroom/*[#Baths]* bath home. A long row of sash windows brings in morning light from the dining room and living room. Large eat-in kitchen with pantry too! There's so much more to tell you about with this listing but we think it's best if you see for yourself. Contact *[Listing Agent]* at *[Phone Number]*. *[Listing Code Number]*
**(Ad #40)**

### No More Wasted Space

in this *[#Bedrooms]* bedroom/*[#Baths]* bath *[Style of Home]*. Vertical wallboard is the perfect touch in the living and dining rooms along with the wood plank flooring. *[#Bedrooms]* bedroom/*[#Baths]* bath home with many more details too numerous to mention. Call *[Listing Agent]* at *[Phone Number]* for more information. *[Listing Code Number]*
**(Ad #41)**

### Call the Auctioneer

you won't need all of the excess furniture in this *[#Bedrooms]* bedroom/*[#Baths]* bath *[Style of Home]*. Extra features included are *[Feature 1]*, *[Feature 2]*, and *[Feature 3]*. Let *[Listing Agent]* show you this lovely listing today. Call *[Phone Number]* to schedule your appointment. *[Listing Code Number]*
**(Ad #42)**

### Father Knows Best

and that's why he insists on getting rid of that big home and being more practical with your living space. Still, there's *[# of Square Feet]* square feet to enjoy in this *[#Bedrooms]* bedroom/*[#Baths]* bath *[Style of Home]*. *[List Price]*! Call quick on this one, it's sure to go quick at this price! Call *[Phone Number]* and ask for *[Listing Agent]*. *[Listing Code Number]*
**(Ad #43)**

### Now You Can Garden

with the extra time you'll have in this *[#Bedrooms]* bedroom/*[#Baths]* bath *[# of Square Feet]* square feet home we just listed. Features *[Feature 1]* and *[Feature 2]*. It's this week's Special of the Week on our Web site. Visit *[Web Site Address]* for more details, or call *[Listing Agent]* at *[Phone Number]*. *[Listing Code Number]*
**(Ad #44)**

### Spend More Time with the Family

by investing in this *[#Bedrooms]* bedroom/ *[#Baths]* bath *[Style of Home]*. Exposed wooden ceiling beams provide a warm and exciting feel in the oversized living room. You'll appreciate the wainscot found throughout this home. A real beauty! Call quick; it's sure to move fast at only *[List Price]*. Call *[Phone Number]* and ask for *[Listing Agent]*. *[Listing Code Number]*
*(Ad #45)*

### Little Is Good

Four-panel door with side and transom light greets you from the wooden front porch with gingerbread railing. The porch swing stays too! A real charmer at only *[List Price]*. Why just read about it when you can see it in person? Call *[Listing Agent]* at *[Phone Number]* to preview this listing today. *[Listing Code Number]*
*(Ad #46)*

### A Small Home with Large Rooms

Provides the perfect combination for your next home, and here it is! *[#Bedrooms]* bedroom/ *[#Baths]* bath *[Style of Home]*. Also features nine-over-nine sash windows and *[Feature 1]* and *[Feature 2]*. See for yourself! Contact *[Phone Number]* and ask for *[Listing Agent]*. *[Listing Code Number]*
*(Ad #47)*

### It's a Secret

That this *[#Bedrooms]* bedroom/*[#Baths]* bath *[Style of Home]* is priced below market value. At least it was until we ran this ad. The owners have said "sell," and recently dropped the price. *[List Price]*! Call quick on this one; it's sure to go quick at this price! Call *[Phone Number]* and ask for *[Listing Agent]*. *[Listing Code Number]*
*(Ad #48)*

*Note: Make sure you obtain the owner's permission in writing prior to running any motivational ads such as the one above.*

### It's Not a Secret!

that you can purchase this *[#Bedrooms]* bedroom/*[#Baths]* bath home for only *[List Price]*. Cast-iron radiators give off an excellent touch to the character and age of this home. Many recent upgrades by owners. For a full-color flyer or more information, contact *[Listing Agent]* at *[Phone Number]*. *[Listing Code Number]*
*(Ad #49)*

### The Best of Both Worlds

A small home with spacious rooms! Wide pine flooring accents the living room and dining room in this *[#Bedrooms]* bedroom/*[#Baths]* bath *[Style of Home]*. Flower boxes say hello to guests and family as they reach the front porch. A delightful retreat that's priced at only *[List Price]*! Call *[Phone Number]* and ask for *[Listing Agent]*. *[Listing Code Number]*
*(Ad #50)*

### The Little House That Could

Although it's compact in nature, this *[#Bedrooms]* bedroom/*[#Baths]* bath *[Style of Home]* is determined to provide you with all of the satisfaction you desire in your next home. *[Feature 1]*, *[Feature 2]*, and *[Feature 3]* are just a few of the many extras you'll be treated with in this home. A great buy at only *[List Price]*! For more information, contact *[Listing Agent]* at *[Phone Number]*, or visit us on the Web at *[Web Site Address]*. *[Listing Code Number]*
**(Ad #51)**

### A Spanish Bungalow

Stucco siding home with ivy walls and a gorgeous flower garden and rock patio will influence you to spend most of your time outside this *[#Bedrooms]* bedroom/*[#Baths]* bath delight. *[List Price]*! See for yourself! Contact *[Phone Number]* and ask for *[Listing Agent]*. *[Listing Code Number]*
**(Ad #52)**

### A Cottage with a Contemporary Flare

This *[#Bedrooms]* bedroom/*[#Baths]* bath home has lots of character and style! The owners have totally refurbished this home with all of today's modern conveniences. Why just read about it when you can see it in person? Call *[Listing Agent]* at *[Phone Number]* to preview this listing today. *[Listing Code Number]*
**(Ad #53)**

# Large Homes 5

Writing ads for larger homes can be an uncomplicated task. Buyers in this category normally want to know square footage, number of bedrooms and baths, and the extra features your property includes. One important note to remember is that consumers looking for a large home normally want to know price and location. As discussed earlier in the book, some agents may prefer to leave this information out to entice more phone calls. However, as a real estate professional you need to weigh between quantity or quality. Do you want to field an enormous amount of leads to where your productivity level drops? Or, would you rather take fewer but more quality buyer leads knowing the prospects are serious inquiries for this price range? Ultimately, the choice is up to you.

Needing More Room? *(Ad #1)*

It Might Be Hard to Locate Your Spouse *(Ad #2)*

Two-Story Colonial *(Ad #3)*

Reminds You of *Gone with the Wind* *(Ad #4)*

Bigger Than South Fork *(Ad #5)*

Lavish and Lovely *(Ad #6)*

Incredible Size *(Ad #7)*

Double the Pleasure *(Ad #8)*

Contemporary Story-and-a-Half Nestled on a Wooded Lot *(Ad #9)*

Immaculate English Two-Story *(Ad #10)*

Big House and a Big Pool *(Ad #11)*

Gorgeous Estate *(Ad #12)*

Immense Estate *(Ad #13)*

Remarkable and Renown *(Ad #14)*

Larger Than Life *(Ad #15)*

Unbelievable! *(Ad #16)*

Tree-Lined Driveway *(Ad #17)*

Can This Be Real? *(Ad #18)*

Room to Grow *(Ad #19)*

Extraordinary in Detail *(Ad #20)*

Grand and Palatial *(Ad #21)*

There's No Way! *(Ad #22)*

You've Got to Be Kidding *(Ad #23)*

You're Not Dreaming! *(Ad #24)*

Imagine Yourself *(Ad #25)*

### Needing More Room?

If so, we've got the perfect home for your family. Floor-to-ceiling casement windows provide a dramatic backdrop in this open and spacious living room. *[#Bedrooms]* bedroom/*[#Baths]* bath *[Style of Home]*. *[Feature 1]*, *[Feature 2]*, and *[Feature 3]* also adorn this gorgeous home. Priced to sell! Let *[Listing Agent]* show you this lovely listing today. Call *[Phone Number]* to schedule your appointment. *[Listing Code Number]* *(Ad #1)*

### It Might Be Hard to Locate Your Spouse

We don't know if that's a good thing or not but this home is so big you can live in separate areas if you choose! Over *[# of Square Feet]* square feet of living area, complete with full finished basement. Master bath includes his and her walk-in closets, and Mediterranean tile in kitchen with granite counter tops make this a real "one of a kind!" Call *[Listing Agent]* at *[Phone Number]* for all of the details. *[Listing Code Number]* *(Ad #2)*

### Two-Story Colonial

This *[#Bedrooms]* bedroom/*[#Baths]* bath home sits on an oversized lot in town. Large eat-in kitchen leads out to a screened-in porch area that's ideal for summer dining. Arched windows in family room give a dramatic look both inside and outside this home. For more information, call *[Listing Agent]* at *[Phone Number]*. *[Listing Code Number]* *(Ad #3)*

### Reminds You of Gone with the Wind

*[#Bedrooms]* bedroom/*[#Baths]* bath home with all of the extras you would expect in a grand estate. Features open foyer with winding staircase, private study area with fireplace, three-car garage, and full finished basement. A great buy at only *[List Price]*! For more information, contact *[Listing Agent]* at *[Phone Number]*, or visit us on the Web at *[Web Site Address]*. *[Listing Code Number]* *(Ad #4)*

### Bigger Than South Fork

Over *[# of Square Feet]* square feet of lush living space provides all of the upgrades and amenities you would expect from a home of this caliber. Exotic finished basement with private screening room, wet bar, rec. room, sleeping quarters, and in-ground swimming pool with hot tub nearby. One word describes it all, "WOW!" For a private tour, call *[Listing Agent]* at *[Phone Number]* or e-mail *[Listing Agent]* at *[Listing Agent E-mail]*. *[Listing Code Number]* *(Ad #5)*

### Lavish and Lovely

This *[Style of Home]* home features over *[# of Square Feet]* square feet of comfort. One-of-a-kind gourmet kitchen with every upgradeable appliance imaginable! Surround sound speaker system built-into family room area. Huge main bedroom and bath suite with double closets, separate shower, and whirlpool tub. *[List Price]*! Call *[Phone Number]* and ask for *[Listing Agent]*. *[Listing Code Number]* *(Ad #6)*

### Incredible Size

Here's a *[# of Square Feet]* square foot home with dozens of amenities too numerous to mention. Keeping room with cooking hearth provides the perfect backdrop for the large kitchen with center island rectangular field tiles and cherry wood cabinets. Full finished basement too! There's even a separate workshop area off the back of the garage. Call *[Listing Agent]* at *[Phone Number]* for all of the details. *[Listing Code Number]*
**(Ad #7)**

### Double the Pleasure

with this *[Style of Home]* on a double lot. *[#Bedrooms]* bedroom/*[#Baths]* bath home features *[Feature 1]*, *[Feature 2]*, and *[Feature 3]*. *[List Price]*! Call quickly on this one; it's sure to go quick at this price! Call *[Phone Number]* and ask for *[Listing Agent]*. *[Listing Code Number]*
**(Ad #8)**

### Contemporary Story-and-a-Half Nestled on a Wooded Lot

Here is your chance to own the home of your dreams. Outdoor pavilion with fireplace allow you to enjoy trees and spectacular lawn with this *[#Bedrooms]* bedroom/*[#Baths]* bath home. Features cathedral ceilings and upper loft with office area. Polished hardwood floors along with multi-pane windows give way to lots of natural sunlight. *[Feature 1]* and *[Feature 2]*, plus much more! Why just read about it when you can see it in person? Call *[Listing Agent]* at *[Phone Number]* to preview this listing today. *[Listing Code Number]*
**(Ad #9)**

### Immaculate English Two-Story

*[#Bedrooms]* bedroom/*[#Baths]* bath home with flare of yesteryear. Features a galley kitchen with pantry, breakfast area, and bay window overlooking water pond and flower garden. Extra features included are *[Feature 1]*, *[Feature 2]*, and *[Feature 3]*. Let *[Listing Agent]* show you this lovely listing today. Call *[Phone Number]* to schedule your appointment. *[Listing Code Number]*
**(Ad #10)**

### Big House and a Big Pool

Stacked-stone chimney with outdoor fireplace arbor make way to a stunning showplace for entertaining guests and family in this *[#Bedrooms]* bedroom/*[#Baths]* bath *[Style of Home]* home. Features circle drive with water fountain in front entrance. Finished basement with rec. room overlooks pool and patio area. A great buy at only *[List Price]*! For more information, contact *[Listing Agent]* at *[Phone Number]* or visit us on the Web at *[Web Site Address]*. *[Listing Code Number]*
**(Ad #11)**

### Gorgeous Estate

Dormer windows peak out from a steeply tiled roof with this *[#Bedrooms]* bedroom/*[#Baths]* bath *[Style of Home]* home. A romantic and exciting entrance welcomes you as you drive up the lengthy stone-paved roadway. You'll appreciate the detail to every minute part of this home. Spectacular kitchen cabinetry appliqués, mosaic tile, and woodwork throughout home; nothing has been missed! You must see this one for yourself to fully appreciate. Contact *[Phone Number]* and ask for *[Listing Agent]* for more information. *[Listing Code Number]*
**(Ad #12)**

### Immense Estate

18th Century Georgian farmhouse features *[#Bedrooms]* bedroom. and *[#Baths]* baths along with *[# of Square Feet]* sq. ft. of living area. Extra features included are *[Feature 1]*, *[Feature 2]*, and *[Feature 3]*. Don't just settle for any home currently for sale, preview this gorgeous estate today! For a private tour, call *[Listing Agent]* at *[Phone Number]* or e-mail *[Listing Agent]* at *[Listing Agent E-mail]*. *[Listing Code Number]*
*(Ad #13)*

### Remarkable and Renown

help describe this *[# of Square Feet]* *[#Bedrooms]* bedroom/*[#Baths]* bath *[Style of Home]* we recently listed. Each wall in this home is framed by wood moldings. Extra features included are *[Feature 1]*, *[Feature 2]*, and *[Feature 3]*. Let *[Listing Agent]* show you this lovely listing today. Call *[Phone Number]* to schedule your appointment. *[Listing Code Number]*
*(Ad #14)*

### Larger Than Life

This *[# of Square Feet]* sq. ft. *[Style of Home]* home features *[#Bedrooms]* bedroom. and *[#Baths]* baths. Boxed hedges line the front of this grand estate with vast windows that provide lots of afternoon sunlight. There's a covered pavilion with grill and wet bar and an outdoor fireplace to entertain guests and family. A home to be proud of! A great buy at only *[List Price]*! For more information, contact *[Listing Agent]* at *[Agency Phone Number]* or visit us on the Web at *[Web Site Address]*. *[Listing Code Number]*
*(Ad #15)*

### Unbelievable!

The best way for us to describe this enormous *[# of Square Feet]* sq. ft. *[Style of Home]* home! Oversized lot provides the essential backdrop to display all of the trees and shrubs it has to offer. Large stone patio in back leads to garden and gardener's shed. You'll even discover several fountains and small water ponds nestled about on this property. Extra features included are *[Feature 1]*, *[Feature 2]*, and *[Feature 3]*. For more information, call *[Listing Agent]* at *[Phone Number]*. *[Listing Code Number]*
*(Ad #16)*

### Tree-Lined Driveway

Leads you to a *[#Bedrooms]* bedroom/*[#Baths]* bath *[Style of Home]* with over *[# of Square Feet]* sq. ft. of living space. Brick arch for alcove cooking area in kitchen along with an adjoining butler's pantry for entertaining in the spacious dining room. French doors lead to an open and airy screened porch where guests can continue conversations on warm summer evenings. Full finished basement with billiard room and family room. You won't feel cramped in this home, but call us quick! At *[List Price]*, we're sure it won't last long! Call *[Listing Agent]* at *[Phone Number]* for all of the details. *[Listing Code Number]*
*(Ad #17)*

### Can This Be Real?

Stunning *[#Bedrooms]* bedroom/*[#Baths]* bath *[Style of Home]* with over *[# of Square Feet]* sq. ft. of comfortable living area surround you and your family! Exquisite kitchen with center island is accented by beautiful ceramic tile. As you explore this palatial retreat, you'll discover *[Feature 1]*, *[Feature 2]*, and *[Feature 3]*. See for yourself all the extras this home has to offer. Contact *[Phone Number]* and ask for *[Listing Agent]*. *[Listing Code Number]*
*(Ad #18)*

### Room to Grow

and grow, and grow in this *[Style of Home]* home. Over *[# of Square Feet]* sq. ft. of living space to enclose your dreams and desires. There are so many extras with this *[#Bedrooms]* bedroom/*[#Baths]* bath that we've made it our "Home of the Week" on our Web site. Visit *[Web Site Address]* for more information and color photos along with virtual tours, or call *[Listing Agent]* at *[Phone Number]* for a color fact sheet. *[Listing Code Number]* *(Ad #19)*

### Extraordinary in Detail

and charm, this *[# of Square Feet]* sq. ft. *[Style of Home]* home has a little bit of everything! *[Feature 1]*, *[Feature 2]*, *[Feature 3]*, along with many more great amenities. See for yourself! Call *[Listing Agent]* at *[Phone Number]* for a private showing today. *[Listing Code Number]* *(Ad #20)*

### Grand and Palatial

details this one-of-a-kind *[#Bedrooms]* bedroom/*[#Baths]* bath *[Style of Home]* with over *[# of Square Feet]* sq. ft. Extended setting area in main bedroom provides a dramatic view of the backyard and pool area. Oversized garage with storage and workshop area is every dad's delight! Also boasts *[Feature 1]*, *[Feature 2]*, and *[Feature 3]*. *[List Price]*! Call *[Phone Number]* and ask for *[Listing Agent]*. *[Listing Code Number]* *(Ad #21)*

### There's No Way!

*[#Bedrooms]* bedroom/*[#Baths]* bath *[Style of Home]* with over *[# of Square Feet]* sq. ft.? You heard right! Listen to some of these extra amenities included with this home: *[Feature 1]*, *[Feature 2]*, and *[Feature 3]*. You can read and see all about it on our Web site at *[Web Site Address]*. Click on "Home of the Week." You can also call *[Listing Agent]* at *[Phone Number]* for more information. *[Listing Code Number]* *(Ad #22)*

### You've Got to Be Kidding

No, you can buy a *[# of Square Feet]* sq. ft. *[Style of Home]* home with *[#Bedrooms]* bedroom. and *[#Baths]* baths for only *[List Price]*! Kitchen with path through to great room and cathedral ceilings give this home an airy feel. Large family room and rec. room in finished basement for the kids. *[Feature 1]* and *[Feature 2]*. Call *[Phone Number]* and ask for *[Listing Agent]*. *[Listing Code Number]* *(Ad #23)*

### You're Not Dreaming!

This majestic home has everything you've wanted and more. Welcoming foyer with large stone tiles greet guests as they view the winding staircase and open loft area above. There's also a grand room with vaulted ceilings, covered air-cooled veranda adjoining the large patio area, and in-ground pool and hot tub. Extra features included are *[Feature 1]*, *[Feature 2]*, and *[Feature 3]*. Why just read about it when you can see it in person? Call *[Listing Agent]* at *[Phone Number]* to preview this listing today. *[Listing Code Number]* *(Ad #24)*

### *Imagine Yourself*

in this lovely *[# of Square Feet]* sq. ft. *[Style of Home]* home. Features *[#Bedrooms]* bedroom. and *[#Baths]* baths, *[Feature 1], [Feature 2]*, and *[Feature 3]*. Expandable area on second floor gives way to more space if you think you need it. Full finished basement with billiard table and theatre. A must to see, and priced at *[List Price]*. Call *[Phone Number]* and ask for *[Listing Agent]. [Listing Code Number]*
*(Ad #25)*

# Luxury Homes 6

I'm sure most of us at least once has driven through a nice neighborhood admiring the homes and dreaming of owning one day. But did you ever think about what the types of owners are of these fine country estates or mansions? Coldwell Banker Real Estate Corporation recently released a profile of million-dollar-plus homeowners culled from a study it conducted of its top luxury home sales associates who are also considered to be the world's premier marketers of high-end properties. The top findings are as follows:

- 31% are cash buyers
- 68% are considered "new money"
- The number one profession among these homebuyers is classified as "Large Business Executives"
- 67% are from the "baby boom" generation (between the ages of 35 and 55)
- 88% of luxury homebuyers are married[1]

So the question is vague to ask: Are luxury homebuyers really going to be interested by a cute and clever heading? The answer is essentially unknown. The object and idea of having a clever heading is to gain the reader's attention. If all we put was "Two-Story Colonial" as the heading, it may not be as effective as adding "Jet Setter's Paradise." A heading does just what it is intended to do—get the readers' attention and get them to begin reading your ad copy. But, luxury buyers are looking for much more. Most of the time they are more detail-oriented and want to know specifics. They are up on the latest home improvements and terminology for décor and home construction. So including this verbiage into your advertising can be a big hit with the luxury home community. Another note of interest regarding luxury homebuyers is that they are probably more computer savvy than the normal buyer. Most would like to have information on how to get to a Web site for a listing with additional details. In fact, most luxury home agents are building complete Web sites around such properties. Virtual tours, interactive CD-ROMs, and other technology advances with color gloss brochures and DVDs are a must to market high-end properties.

---

[1] Coldwell Banker® Press Release, "Who's Buying Luxury Homes in America–Coldwell Banker Study Reveals Answers," July 29, 2003, http://www.coldwellbankerpreviews.com/servlet/ResourceGuide?action=showArticle&articleId=1360.

# Sample Headings

Wooded Estate *(Ad #1)*

Luxurious Living *(Ad #2)*

Magnificent Estate *(Ad #3)*

Pampered with Perfection *(Ad #4)*

Superb Surrounds *(Ad #5)*

Elegance and Detail *(Ad #6)*

Grand Estate *(Ad #7)*

Breathtaking Estate *(Ad #8)*

Breathtaking and Grandeur *(Ad #9)*

Living the Good Life *(Ad #10)*

A Return to Yesterday *(Ad #11)*

Should Have Been on *The Lifestyles of the Rich and Famous* *(Ad #12)*

A Mansion Made Out of Stone *(Ad #13)*

A Garden for Every Season *(Ad #14)*

Spectacular Garden Areas *(Ad #15)*

Your Own Botanical Gardens Awaits You *(Ad #16)*

Olympic Size Swimming Pool *(Ad #17)*

Believe It or Not *(Ad #18)*

Hard to Believe *(Ad #19)*

Outdoor Entertaining at Its Best *(Ad #20)*

Nestled among the Trees *(Ad #21)*

Patio, Pool, and Tennis Courts *(Ad #22)*

Want Your Own Tennis Courts? *(Ad #23)*

Looks Like a Castle *(Ad #24)*

Vanderbilt Similarities *(Ad #25)*

A Master Gardener Lived Here *(Ad #26)*

The Lure of Luxury *(Ad #27)*

Excel in Excellence *(Ad #28)*

Presidential Penthouse *(Ad #29)*

Paradise on the Fifteenth Floor *(Ad #30)*

This Home Has the Three L's (Luxurious, Lovable, and Livable) *(Ad #31)*

First Class Living *(Ad #32)*

This Home Has the Cure (For the Space You Have Been Looking For) *(Ad #33)*

You Won't Believe the Square Footage *(Ad #34)*

Like a Five-Course Gourmet Meal *(Ad #35)*

Five-Star Rating *(Ad #36)*

Does Martha Stewart Live Here? *(Ad #37)*

A Palatial Retreat *(Ad #38)*

Has All the Bells and Whistles *(Ad #39)*

### Wooded Estate

You'll ooh and aah as you approach this stately home from its lengthy paved tree-lined driveway. Every attention to detail has been included in this *[# of Square Feet]* sq. ft. showplace. The circular drive in front of the home greets you with fountains, flowers, and scrubs. The rear of the home features several patios, more flowers, and an Olympic size in-ground swimming pool. Full finished basement, culinary kitchen to die for, and so much more! CD-ROM is available with photos, floor plan, and virtual tours. For more information, call *[Listing Agent]* at *[Phone Number]*. *[Listing Code Number]*
**(Ad #1)**

### Luxurious Living

This *[# of Square Feet]* sq. ft. two-story French provincial home includes everything you would demand for upscale living. Wall-length bookshelves provide a dramatic backdrop to the family room. Gorgeous enclosed sunroom off back overlooks wooded backyard and pool and patio area. Also features *[Feature 1]*, *[Feature 2]*, and *[Feature 3]*. Let *[Listing Agent]* show you this lovely listing today. Call *[Phone Number]* to schedule your appointment. *[Listing Code Number]*
**(Ad #2)**

### Magnificent Estate

English tudor is nestled on a three-acre parcel of land in *[Subdivision Name]*. Features large kitchen with nook, sitting room, and stone fireplace in master suite. Powder room, walk-in closets, and a full finished basement with home theater. For more information, call *[Listing Agent]* at *[Phone Number]*. *[Listing Code Number]*
**(Ad #3)**

### Pampered with Perfection

This two-story home is only three years old and features many upgrades and extras you won't find available in other homes on the market. Large open great room views, upstairs loft, beamed ceilings, and culinary kitchen with soap stone countertops and oak cabinets. You'll be sorry if you let this opportunity pass you by! For a private tour, call *[Listing Agent]* at *[Phone Number]* or e-mail *[Listing Agent]* at *[Listing Agent E-mail]*. *[Listing Code Number]*
**(Ad #4)**

### Superb Surrounds

This two-story home is situated on the 17th hole of *[Name of Golf Course]*. Large outdoor swimming pool with patio, waterfall, and trellis with outdoor cabana to enjoy the views of the golf course. Stunning entry foyer with circular staircase will greet your guests, along with the important Italian marble floors. Wow! A great buy at only *[List Price]*! For more information, contact *[Listing Agent]* at *[Phone Number]* or visit us on the Web at *[Web Site Address]*. *[Listing Code Number]*
**(Ad #5)**

### Elegance and Detail

This *[# of Square Feet]* sq. ft. *[Style of Home]* home features all of the fine qualities you demand for upscale living. Kitchen designed exclusively by Clive Christian interiors. Top-of-the-line appliances along with large walk-in pantry. Keeping room nearby with river stone fireplace for cozy winter evenings. You'll also find a large screened-in porch for summer dining and a full finished basement with billiard room. This home is a must see! Interactive CD-ROM available by contacting *[Listing Agent]* at *[Phone Number]*. *[Listing Code Number]*
**(Ad #6)**

### Grand Estate

First time offered for sale! This two-story Georgian farmhouse has been completely renovated with posh and elegance. Features spacious rooms and large eat-in kitchen with nook. For your enjoyment, there's also an in-ground pool with hot tub area flanked by a gorgeous rock patio. Why just read about it when you can see it in person? Call *[Listing Agent]* at *[Phone Number]* to preview this listing today. *[Listing Code Number]*
**(Ad #7)**

### Breathtaking Estate

Enjoy all of the splendor and comfort in this *[# of Square Feet]* sq. ft. *[Style of Home]* home. Lovely entry foyer is accompanied by a gracious sitting room on one side and a private study/den on the opposite side. Family room includes a rock fireplace and floor-to-ceiling bookcases on both sides. Large kitchen with nook and pantry. This is a treasure you shouldn't pass up. A great buy at only *[List Price]*! For more information, contact *[Listing Agent]* at *[Phone Number]* or visit us on the Web at *[Web Site Address]*. *[Listing Code Number]*
**(Ad #8)**

### Breathtaking and Grandeur

Follow the tree-lined street of *[Street Name]* and you'll find our newest listing. Encompassing a full lot-and-a-half, this *[Style of Home]* home always gets a second look from those driving by. From its spectacular lawn, trees, and shrubs to the character and coziness this home and its design have to offer, it's a home everyone will fall in love with! Features *[#Bedrooms]* bedroom and *[#Baths]* baths, and much more. Call *[Listing Agent]* at *[Phone Number]* for all of the details! *[Listing Code Number]*
**(Ad #9)**

### Living the Good Life

This *[# of Square Feet]* sq. ft. home includes a room for everyone! Culinary kitchen for mom, library/study for dad, and a rec. room and home theater in the basement for the kids. When you're tired of all the extras inside this home, enjoy the pool, hot tub, and large patio area out back. A rare find, so don't let this one pass you by! For more information, call *[Listing Agent]* at *[Phone Number]*. *[Listing Code Number]*
**(Ad #10)**

### A Return to Yesterday

This Victorian farmhouse is situated on its own five-acre parcel of land. Gorgeous shade trees abound on the property with lots of flowers and several small water gardens. Spacious rooms and fully restored. You can't go wrong with this new listing! For a private tour, call *[Listing Agent]* at *[Phone Number]* or e-mail *[Listing Agent]* at *[Listing Agent E-mail]*. *[Listing Code Number]*
**(Ad #11)**

### Should Have Been on The Lifestyles of the Rich and Famous

This contemporary *[# of Square Feet]* sq. ft. home is located on its own 60-acre parcel of ground that includes a 30-acre lake for fishing and boating. You'll enjoy great views of the mountains and lake below from the patio and pool area. Also includes tennis courts, barn with horse stalls, and a paved one-mile driveway giving this home and property security and privacy. We have more information on this property available at our Web site or an interactive CD-ROM available by contacting *[Listing Agent]* at *[Phone Number]*. *[Listing Code Number]*
*(Ad #12)*

### A Mansion Made Out of Stone

This two-story ivy-covered estate has all the grace and charm you would expect at first glance. Formal dining room with French doors leads to covered patio area and swimming pool at the back of the home. Features a large eat-in kitchen with breakfast nook and pantry, leisure room, and upper-floor balcony overlooking the backyard and pool area. Why just read about it when you can see it in person? Call *[Listing Agent]* at *[Phone Number]* to preview this listing today. *[Listing Code Number]*
*(Ad #13)*

### A Garden for Every Season

It's not often we have a home for sale of such splendor and charm with an owner who has cared for and loved their flowers and gardens as in this home. You'll appreciate the artistic detail that each garden offers throughout Mother Nature's seasonal changes. Twelve-over-twelve sash windows allow great views from the breakfast room, dining room, kitchen, and master suite. Over *[# of Square Feet]* sq. ft. along with *[#Bedrooms]* bedrooms and *[#Baths]* baths make this the perfect home for your family. For more information, call *[Listing Agent]* at *[Phone Number]*. *[Listing Code Number]*
*(Ad #14)*

### Spectacular Garden Areas

This *[Style of Home]* home features an overabundance of kitchen cabinets for the culinary person looking for a new retreat. Elegance and charm flow throughout the living room, dining room, and main floor sitting room. You'll find an upstairs landing area that's perfect for reading a book or visiting with friends. Everything is picture perfect about this home! Just listed, so we encourage you to call quickly before this one is gone. Call *[Listing Agent]* at *[Phone Number]* for all of the details. *[Listing Code Number]*
*(Ad #15)*

### Your Own Botanical Gardens Awaits You

Gorgeous grounds and gardens are the focal point of this home, but don't let the [# of Square Feet] sq. ft. of living area be discounted. Oak-beamed ceiling great room features a massive fireplace adorned by large bookcases. Center island in kitchen is the prefect place to visit with friends while preparing a meal. Screened-in patio area provides a great place for dining, after-dinner talks, or napping on a Sunday afternoon. To find out more details and for a private e-mail containing a special Web site address with photos, virtual tours, and more, contact [Listing Agent] at [Phone Number]. [Listing Code Number]
**(Ad #16)**

### Olympic Size Swimming Pool

is only one small gem to this [Style of Home] home. Warm and inviting gazebo on brick patio is perfect for summer dining or visiting with friends and family. Wisteria-covered trellis adjoins a long-covered patio area near the in-ground swimming pool. Inside you'll find everything from a wood-paneled library to a sitting room. Newly renovated kitchen is a must see! Two sets of staircases and loft attic makes this home great for teenagers too! [List Price]! Call [Phone Number] and ask for [Listing Agent]. [Listing Code Number]
**(Ad #17)**

### Believe It or Not

this home has everything you could imagine! Two bowling lanes in the basement, large billiard room with other recreational activities, plus a private movie theater! Passionate cooks will love this kitchen with all the extra amenities. A great buy at only [List Price]! For more information, contact [Listing Agent] at [Agency Phone Number] or visit us on the Web at [Web Site Address]. [Listing Code Number]
**(Ad #18)**

### Hard to Believe

the price we have on this two-and-a-half story home. Features nearly [# of Square Feet] sq. ft. of living space on a three-acre track of ground. A real showplace! You'll be amazed at the patio area with spectacular pool patio and covered arbor. Extended sitting area in bedroom is a great place to get away. [#Bedrooms] bedrooms and [#Baths] baths along with [Feature 1] and [Feature 2]. Let [Listing Agent] show you this lovely listing today. Call [Phone Number] to schedule your appointment. [Listing Code Number]
**(Ad #19)**

### Outdoor Entertaining at Its Best

This two-story home in [Subdivision Name] features [# of Square Feet] sq. ft. of living area. What's really amazing is the patio, pool, and hot tub area. You'll also discover a brick charcoal grill along with water fountains and flower gardens accenting the backyard. Looks like something from a magazine! Interactive CD-ROM available by contacting [Listing Agent] at [Phone Number]. [Listing Code Number]
**(Ad #20)**

### Nestled among the Trees

Here's a gorgeous home with all of the splendor and beauty you would expect from a [Style of Home]. Features a large deck overlooking the private and quiet backyard. Also available with this home is a full finished basement with rec. room and home theater. Master suite includes powder room and his and her walk-in closets. You'll appreciate all of the details and craftsmanship in this new listing. Call [Listing Agent] at [Phone Number] for all of the details. [Listing Code Number]
**(Ad #21)**

### Patio, Pool, and Tennis Courts

What more could you ask for? How about a *[# of Square Feet]* sq. ft. *[Style of Home]* home with dazzling woodwork and flooring? A full finished basement with billiard room, wet bar, and movie theater? A study/library with wood walls and ceilings? Great opportunity on this newly listed estate. Ask for *[Listing Agent]* at *[Phone Number]*. *[Listing Code Number]*
*(Ad #22)*

### Want Your Own Tennis Courts?

Here's a *[# of Square Feet]* sq. ft. *[Style of Home]* home situated on three full acres of ground. Features two regulation lighted tennis courts, swimming pool, hot tub, and large screened-in patio area for summer dining. You'll appreciate the extra features found throughout this home such as *[Feature 1]*, *[Feature 2]*, and *[Feature 3]*. Contact *[Listing Agent]* at *[Phone Number]* for more details. *[Listing Code Number]*
*(Ad #23)*

### Looks Like a Castle

Believe it or not, this *[# of Square Feet]* sq. ft. estate was patterned after a castle seen in Europe. Features *[#Bedrooms]* bedrooms and *[#Baths]* baths, and large open veranda with stone walls and arches for breathtaking views of the countryside. Would make ideal bed and breakfast facility. Enormous living room with massive stone fireplace and beamed ceilings. This is truly a one-of-a-kind estate. Interactive CD-ROM available by contacting *[Listing Agent]* at *[Phone Number]*. *[Listing Code Number]*
*(Ad #24)*

### Vanderbilt Similarities

Gabled dormer windows make way to a magnificent *[# of Square Feet]* sq. ft. *[Style of Home]* home that reminds you of a mini-mansion. *[#Bedrooms]* bedrooms and *[#Baths]* baths, and full finished basement with large wet bar and dance area. Also features a gym, sauna, and special library with floor-to-ceiling shelves on three of the four walls. Outstanding patio, pool, and garden areas with large arched windows in rear of home. To find out more details and for a private e-mail containing a special Web site address with photos, virtual tours, and more, contact *[Listing Agent]* at *[Phone Number]*. *[Listing Code Number]*
*(Ad #25)*

### A Master Gardener Lived Here

You'll appreciate and adore all of the flowers and gardens found throughout this two-acre estate we just listed. Custom *[# of Square Feet]* sq. ft. *[Style of Home]* home contains every possible amenity you would require. Dormer windows provide additional light to the foyer and each bedroom on the upper level. Swimming pool and pool house accent a beautiful Teriyaki tile patio overlooking all of the beautiful flowers. This is a special treat for some lucky family. Call today! Contact *[Phone Number]* and ask for *[Listing Agent]*. *[Listing Code Number]*
*(Ad #26)*

### The Lure of Luxury

Gorgeous *[#Bedrooms] bedroom/[#Baths] bath [Style of Home]* home situated on a large wooded lot in *[Subdivision Name]*. Large arched windows line the back great room overlooking a large stone patio surrounding an in-ground pool. Special unique waterfall on the edge of the pool recycles pool water for a striking effect. *[List Price]*! Call *[Phone Number]* and ask for *[Listing Agent]*. *[Listing Code Number]* *(Ad #27)*

### Excel in Excellence

This two-story English tudor home has been completely refurbished and updated to every modern convenience. Clyde Christian kitchen with large walk-in pantry is accented by a large breakfast nook overlooking the back patio and grounds. Full finished basement with big screen television and surround sound stereo provide the perfect backdrop for the kids and their friends. Extra features included are *[Feature 1]*, *[Feature 2]*, and *[Feature 3]*. Why just read about it when you can see it in person? Call *[Listing Agent]* at *[Phone Number]* to preview this listing today. *[Listing Code Number]* *(Ad #28)*

### Presidential Penthouse

High above the clouds on the 57th floor, you'll find *[# of Square Feet]* sq. ft. of luxurious home overlooking the south side of the city. Private parking in secure garage area. Also included with your amenities are a gym, sauna, and swimming facilities. *[List Price]*! Call *[Phone Number]* and ask for *[Listing Agent]*. *[Listing Code Number]* *(Ad #29)*

### Paradise on the Fifteenth Floor

Enter the stunning oversized kitchen and you'll immediately be drawn to the mile-high hood vent over the commercial grade gas range. *[# of Square Feet]* sq. ft., along with *[#Bedrooms]* bedrooms and *[#Baths]* baths provides an array of natural light almost any time of the day. Building includes gym and private parking with security, too. For a private tour, call *[Listing Agent]* at *[Phone Number]* or e-mail *[Listing Agent]* at *[Listing Agent E-mail]*. *[Listing Code Number]* *(Ad #30)*

### This Home Has the Three L's (Luxurious, Lovable, and Livable)

*[# of Square Feet]* sq. ft. of pure elegance surround you as you walk through the double entry beveled glass doors in this *[Style of Home]*. From the Italian marble floors to the winding white staircase with deep dark walnut accents, your eyes will be drawn to every small detail of this property. Includes powder room off master suite with his and her walk-in closets, second floor sitting area at top of stairs, and family room with fireplace. Call *[Phone Number]* and ask for *[Listing Agent]*. *[Listing Code Number]* *(Ad #31)*

### First Class Living

This Mediterranean style *[#Bedrooms]* bedroom/*[#Baths]* bath home is located right off of the fourth fairway at *[Name of Golf Course]*. Large open great room with floor-to-ceiling windows overlooking backyard and fairway. The kitchen would be a delight to anyone that loves to cook with all the added amenities and built-ins. The whole family will enjoy the private screening room on the lower level. Don't pass up this once-in-a-lifetime opportunity! *[List Price]*! Call *[Phone Number]* and ask for *[Listing Agent]*. *[Listing Code Number]*
*(Ad #32)*

### This Home Has the Cure (For the Space You Have Been Looking for)

Immaculate *[# of Square Feet]* sq. ft. *[Style of Home]* home. Features a unique open floor plan with vaulted ceilings and vintage style windows. Gorgeous patio area with swimming pool and hot tub area. Oversized laundry facility with built-in desk and cabinets that doubles for a computer room. Full finished basement, wine cellar, and much more. Call *[Listing Agent]* at *[Phone Number]* for all of the details. *[Listing Code Number]*
*(Ad #33)*

### You Won't Believe the Square Footage

Literally this home has over *[# of Square Feet]* sq. ft. of living area for you to enjoy and utilize throughout the year. From the spectacular entry foyer to the quiet and cozy sitting room, every attention to detail has been addressed by the present owners who also oversaw the building. Includes a large eat-in kitchen with breakfast nook and butler's pantry with many built-ins leading to the formal dining room. The perfect getaway is found in the study with mahogany walls and ceilings or the piano room with additional seating area. Too many items to mention, so call *[Listing Agent]* for a full interactive CD-ROM with virtual tours, photo galleries, and more! Call *[Phone Number]* and ask for *[Listing Agent]*. *[Listing Code Number]*
*(Ad #34)*

### Like a Five-Course Gourmet Meal

Top-of-the-line home includes a little bit of everything. The culinary kitchen with center island and massive skylights provide natural sunshine throughout the afternoon. Screened-in patio is perfect for summer dining or casual visits on a Sunday afternoon. This home also has a large exercise room that would match almost any professional gym in town. Oversized master suite features powder room, his and her walk-in closets, and deck with trellis over hot tub. A spectacular home and priced below the appraised value! For a private tour, call *[Listing Agent]* at *[Phone Number]* or e-mail *[Listing Agent]* at *[Listing Agent E-mail]*. *[Listing Code Number]*
*(Ad #35)*

### Five-Star Rating

This home has so many amenities and wonderful features, it would receive a five-star rating by anyone. Features a vintage Mediterranean-style look with an open spacious floor plan that's perfect for entertaining. Vaulted ceilings in great room provide roomy and airy feel as you visit with friends and family. You'll also appreciate the extra touches in floor coverings, woodwork, and trim the owners have chosen for this property. A stunning masterpiece and priced just under its appraised value. For more information, call *[Listing Agent]* at *[Phone Number]*. *[Listing Code Number]*
**(Ad #36)**

### Does Martha Stewart Live Here?

Perhaps it's the décor and decorating the owners have done that makes this home portray the image of class and professionalism. But the extra amenities and details from woodwork, floors, walls, and ceilings also provide a touch of class that you will admire and appreciate. This home is so unique that our only words to describe it are "see it today!" Let *[Listing Agent]* show you this lovely listing today. Call *[Phone Number]* to schedule your appointment. *[Listing Code Number]*
**(Ad #37)**

### A Palatial Retreat

Here's a *[Style of Home]* home located on five acres at the edge of town. Features *[#Bedrooms]* bedrooms and *[#Baths]* baths with an oversized kitchen and breakfast area. Large pantry and butler's passthrough lead to a formal dining room where you will also find a stone fireplace that can been seen from both the dining and living room areas. Finished basement includes family room and rec. room that's perfect for family activities. Extra features included are *[Feature 1]*, *[Feature 2]*, and *[Feature 3]*. Why just read about it when you can see it in person? Call *[Listing Agent]* at *[Phone Number]* to preview this listing today. *[Listing Code Number]*
**(Ad #38)**

### Has All the Bells and Whistles

This *[Style of Home]* home features approximately *[# of Square Feet]* sq. ft. of living area. Gourmet kitchen includes center island with soapstone counter and sink. The ventilation hood takes centerstage in this dream room! Expansive master suite includes whirlpool tub and his and her walk-in closets. You'll appreciate all the detail to woodwork and many extras this home has to offer. *[List Price]*! Call quickly on this one; it's sure to go quick at this price! Call *[Phone Number]* and ask for *[Listing Agent]*. *[Listing Code Number]*
**(Ad #39)**

# Lake and Resort— Vacation Homes

**7**

Lake and resort homes often appeal to a wide variety of buyers. Many are buying second and third homes that they will just use for the weekends. Bathrooms and bedrooms are important for those people because they may be bringing friends to spend a mini-vacation at their retreat. Some are just looking for a different way of life. In this case, fishing, golf, and recreation may be important to them. Most lake and resort buyers want to know the following: Is it on the lake? Does it have lakefront? Do I have lake privileges? Try to be as specific as possible for the readers. It is always a great idea to include the amenities and extra benefits and features the resort or lake area may provide to a buyer in this community. Decks, patios, and windows all play important roles to the lake and resort buyers. Size of lakes that can be fished on or skied on are also benefits that you should promote.

Since most lake and resort buyers will want to see numerous properties before making a decision on their future resort home, they will most likely want to view extra information about the properties for sale. Some ways this can be accomplished is by building a specific Web page if you do business in the area or having flyers or bulletins ready to go via e-mail or by mail. Whatever method you choose, be sure to include contact information for you and your company.

As with homes with acreage, lake and resort properties tend to be more popular when advertised in a metropolitan city. Therefore, it is always important to try to provide your lake and resort listings with the right exposure and the right publication to gain the maximum benefit and exposure for your advertising dollars.

# Sample Headings

Living on the Lake *(Ad #1)*

A Stone's Throw from the Lake *(Ad #2)*

Your Own Boat Dock *(Ad #3)*

Covered Boat Dock Included *(Ad #4)*

Feed the Catfish from Your Own Boat Dock *(Ad #5)*

Adirondack Chairs *(Ad #6)*

A Beautiful Sunset *(Ad #7)*

Living on the Water's Edge *(Ad #8)*

Fish from Your Own Boat Dock *(Ad #9)*

Breathtaking Views of the Lake *(Ad #10)*

Only Five Minutes to Water Skiing *(Ad #11)*

Barbeque by the Water *(Ad #12)*

Move Up to a Lakefront *(Ad #13)*

Secluded Hideaway on Shared Lake *(Ad #14)*

No More Daydreaming about Living on the Lake *(Ad #15)*

18-Hole Championship Golf Course Nearby *(Ad #16)*

Enjoy 72 Holes of Golf! *(Ad #17)*

Villa by the Lake *(Ad #18)*

Living Lakeside *(Ad #19)*

Luxurious Lakeside Living *(Ad #20)*

Take the Kids Fishing (In Your Own Backyard) *(Ad #21)*

Take the Grandkids Fishing (In Your Own Backyard) *(Ad #22)*

Enjoy a Boat Ride Every Evening after Dinner *(Ad #23)*

Lots of Windows to Enjoy the Lake *(Ad #24)*

Lakefront Living *(Ad #25)*

Lakeview Living *(Ad #26)*

Bungalow by the Water *(Ad #27)*

Chalet by the Lake *(Ad #28)*

The 18th Green! *(Ad #29)*

You're Only a Chip or Putt Away *(Ad #30)*

Drive Your Golf Cart to the Country Club *(Ad #31)*

Fairway Delight *(Ad #32)*

You'll Be a Scratch Golfer *(Ad #33)*

Better Than a Hole-N-One *(Ad #34)*

### Living on the Lake

Handcrafted woodwork is found throughout this *[#Bedrooms]* bedroom/*[#Baths]* bath *[Style of Home]* home. Extra features included are *[Feature 1]*, *[Feature 2]*, and *[Feature 3]*. Call *[Listing Agent]* at *[Phone Number]* for more information. *[Listing Code Number]*
**(Ad #1)**

### A Stone's Throw from the Lake

Outdoor pavilion with fireplace make this *[#Bedrooms]* bedroom/*[#Baths]* bath *[Style of Home]* a gorgeous place to call home. Black and white checkerboard floors provide a breathtaking backdrop to a stunning culinary kitchen. Lots of large windows to soak up all the views of the lake. Call *[Listing Agent]* at *[Phone Number]* for more information. *[Listing Code Number]*
**(Ad #2)**

### Your Own Boat Dock

provides a panoramic view of the lake and surrounding homes. Gorgeous *[# of Square feet]* sq. ft. *[Style of Home]* home on *[Name of Lake]*. Spiral staircase in foyer provides an attractive look from the arched windows across the back. This home also features *[Feature 1]*, *[Feature 2]*, and *[Feature 3]*. See for yourself! Contact *[Phone Number]* and ask for *[Listing Agent]*. *[Listing Code Number]*
**(Ad #3)**

### Covered Boat Dock Included

with this *[#Bedrooms]* bedroom/*[#Baths]* bath *[Style of Home]* home. Embrace all the views from the large wooden deck across the back. Cobblestone fireplace inside serves as a barbeque grill on the outside. *[List Price]*! Call today on this one; it's sure to go quick at this price! Call *[Phone Number]* and ask for *[Listing Agent]*. *[Listing Code Number]*
**(Ad #4)**

### Feed the Catfish from Your Own Boat Dock

Lovely *[Style of home]* home with a large chef's kitchen and center island to entertain friends and family. You'll also discover a walk-in pantry, breakfast bar, and many upgraded appliances. *[#Bedrooms]* bedrooms and *[#Baths]* baths with walk-in closets. For more information, call *[Listing Agent]* at *[Phone Number]*. *[Listing Code Number]*
**(Ad #5)**

### Adirondack Chairs

are included with this *[#Bedrooms]* bedroom/*[#Baths]* bath *[Style of Home]* home. A stone's throw from *[Name of Golf Course]* and just one block from *[Name of Lake]*. A great buy at only *[List Price]*! For more information, contact *[Listing Agent]* at *[Phone Number]* or visit us on the Web at *[Web Site Address]*. *[Listing Code Number]*
**(Ad #6)**

### A Beautiful Sunset

is an added bonus with this listing for every evening you enjoy in the backyard. Cathedral ceilings provide an open and airy feel throughout this *[Style of Home]* home. *[#Bedrooms]* bedrooms and *[#Baths]* baths with over *[# of Square Feet]* sq. ft. of living space for only *[List Price]*. For a private tour, call *[Listing Agent]* at *[Phone Number]* or e-mail *[Listing Agent]* at *[Listing Agent E-mail]*. *[Listing Code Number]* *(Ad #7)*

### Living on the Water's Edge

A covered veranda is just a small part of this *[#Bedrooms]* bedrooms/*[#Baths]* bath *[Style of Home]* home. Features *[Feature 1]*, *[Feature 2]*, and *[Feature 3]* along with a full finished basement. Why just read about it when you can see it in person? Call *[Listing Agent]* at *[Phone Number]* to preview this listing today. *[Listing Code Number]* *(Ad #8)*

### Fish from Your Own Boat Dock

Arched trellis between kitchen and dining room provide lots of character and comfort with this *[#Bedrooms]* bedrooms and *[#Baths]* bath *[Style of Home]* home. This home is our "Special of the Week" and can be viewed at *[Web Site Address]*. Call *[Listing Agent]* at *[Phone Number]* for all of the details. *[Listing Code Number]* *(Ad #9)*

### Breathtaking Views of the Lake

Large arched windows make up the majority of the rear of this home and provide a grand view of the lake and surrounding hill country. You'll find lots of extras in this beautiful *[# of Square Feet]* sq. ft. *[Style of Home]* home. Welcoming foyer provides a perfect introduction to guests and friends. Keeping room off kitchen with small beehive fireplace that makes a great conversation piece. Why just read about it when you can see it in person? Call *[Listing Agent]* at *[Phone Number]* to preview this listing today. *[Listing Code Number]* *(Ad #10)*

### Only Five Minutes to Water Skiing

Here's a *[# of Square Feet]* sq. ft. *[Style of Home]* home with *[#Bedrooms]* bedrooms and *[#Baths]* baths that is located on *[Name of Lake]*. Passionate cooks will love this kitchen, especially the Thermador® appliances. Too many extra features to mention in this home. Let *[Listing Agent]* show you this lovely listing today. Call *[Phone Number]* to schedule your appointment. *[Listing Code Number]* *(Ad #11)*

### Barbeque by the Water

Covered gazebo near the water's edge provides the prefect place to entertain family and friends. Private boat slip allows you to just be minutes from moving the conversation to the middle of the lake on your own private pontoon boat that the owner is willing to leave. This *[# of Square Feet]* sq. ft. *[Style of Home]* home has all of the extras you would demand in your next abode. For more information, call *[Listing Agent]* at *[Phone Number]*. *[Listing Code Number]* *(Ad #12)*

### Move Up to a Lake Front

Gorgeous arched windows overlook a large lake in *[Lake Development]*. This custom *[#Bedrooms]* bedrooms/*[#Baths]* bath *[Style of Home]* home features *[Feature 1]*, *[Feature 2]*, and *[Feature 3]*. *[List Price]*! Call quickly on this one; it's sure to go fast at this price! Call *[Phone Number]* and ask for *[Listing Agent]*. *[Listing Code Number]*
*(Ad #13)*

### Secluded Hideaway on Shared Lake

Enjoy the good life with two other families on a four-acre lake nestled among the woods. *[Style of Home]* home with *[#Bedrooms]* bedrooms and *[#Baths]* baths. Spacious master bedroom and private deck overlooking the lake is a great way to greet every morning. Master bath features whirlpool tub and separate shower unit. Two walk-in closets, plus much more. For a private tour, call *[Listing Agent]* at *[Phone Number]* or e-mail *[Listing Agent]* at *[Listing Agent E-mail]*. *[Listing Code Number]*
*(Ad #14)*

### No More Daydreaming about Living on the Lake

when you purchase this *[#Bedrooms]* bedroom/*[#Baths]* bath *[Style of Home]* home. Over *[# of Square Feet]* sq. ft. to enjoy with lots of natural sunlight. Large wrap-around deck provides great outdoor entertaining. Extra features included are *[Feature 1]*, *[Feature 2]*, and *[Feature 3]*. To preview this home, call *[Listing Agent]* at *[Phone Number]*. You can also reach *[Listing Agent]* by e-mail at *[Listing Agent E-mail]*. *[Listing Code Number]*
*(Ad #15)*

### 18-hole Championship Golf Course Nearby

Yes, there's great golf in *[Lake Development]* but it's also a great home with lots of extra features the owners have added. Spacious master bedroom with skylights, his and her walk-in closets, full finished basement, culinary kitchen, and a large stone fireplace in the family room. It's a great place to call home and could be yours today for only *[List Price]*. Let *[Listing Agent]* show you this lovely listing today. Call *[Phone Number]* to schedule your appointment. *[Listing Code Number]*
*(Ad #16)*

### Enjoy 72 Holes of Golf!

Excellent golfing accommodations for homeowners in the *[Lake Development]*. You'll also appreciate this *[#Bedrooms]* bedrooms/*[#Baths]* bath *[Style of Home]* home with *[Feature 1]* and *[Feature 2]*. Tastefully decorated with an open and spacious floor plan. Call *[Listing Agent]* at *[Phone Number]* or e-mail *[Listing Agent]* at *[Listing Agent E-mail]*. *[Listing Code Number]*
*(Ad #17)*

### Villa by the Lake

Natural wood makes this *[Style Home]* home a real gem! You'll discover *[#Bedroom]* bedrooms and *[#Bath]* baths, full finished basement, artist studio, and a large open fireplace in dining room. Oversized kitchen with breakfast area make this the perfect combination for your home by the lake. For more information, call *[Listing Agent]* at *[Phone Number]*. *[Listing Code Number]*
*(Ad #18)*

### Living Lakeside

Lovely entry terrace bordered by brick with inset of plain terra-cotta tiles. Covered front porch and dormer windows give this home plenty of character and appeal from the front view. From the back, you'll enjoy a large wooden deck, patio, and gazebo area all soaking up plenty of views of the lake. This home also features *[#Bedrooms]* bedrooms and *[#Baths]* baths, along with *[Feature 1]* and *[Feature 2]*. Why just read about it when you can see it in person? Call *[Listing Agent]* at *[Phone Number]* to preview this listing today. *[Listing Code Number]*
**(Ad #19)**

### Luxurious Lakeside Living

The owner has said she'll miss the upper-floor sitting room that views the lake from several angles when she sells this home. A great place to read a book or to take an afternoon nap. This new listing also features *[#Bedrooms]* bedrooms and *[#Baths]* baths and over *[# of Square Feet]* sq. ft. Full basement, great kitchen setup, and much more. Let *[Listing Agent]* show you this lovely listing today. Call *[Phone Number]* to schedule your appointment. *[Listing Code Number]*
**(Ad #20)**

### Take the Kids Fishing (In Your Own Backyard)

*[#Bedrooms]* bedroom/*[#Baths]* bath *[Style of Home]* home located in *[Lake Development]* will provide you with access to your own fishing lake just a few short steps from your backdoor. This home includes a private covered boat dock and large deck to enjoy all the views of the lake. Extra features included are *[Feature 1]*, *[Feature 2]*, and *[Feature 3]*. *[List Price]*! Call *[Phone Number]* and ask for *[Listing Agent]*. *[Listing Code Number]*
**(Ad #21)**

### Take the Grandkids Fishing (In Your Own Backyard)

*[#Bedrooms]* bedroom/*[#Baths]* bath *[Style of Home]* home located in *[Lake Development]* will provide you with access to your own fishing lake just a few short steps from your backdoor. This home includes a private covered boat dock and large deck to enjoy all the views of the lake. Extra features included are *[Feature 1]*, *[Feature 2]*, and *[Feature 3]*. *[List Price]*! Call *[Phone Number]* and ask for *[Listing Agent]*. *[Listing Code Number]*
**(Ad #22)**

*(Please note: Same copy from the previous ad was used with this ad to show how you can change the heading but use the same ad).*

### Enjoy a Boat Ride Every Evening after Dinner

This *[#Bedrooms]* bedroom/*[#Baths]* bath *[Style of Home]* home features *[Feature 1]*, *[Feature 2]*, and *[Feature 3]*. Located on *[Name of Lake]* with your own private covered boat dock. Call *[Listing Agent]* at *[Phone Number]* for all of the details. *[Listing Code Number]*
**(Ad #23)**

### Lots of Windows to Enjoy the Lake

Natural wood and natural light make this home a spacious delight! Large arched windows provide a view of the lake that is unmatched. Beautiful kitchen with light oak cabinets and center island. Lots of pantry space, skylights, and open ceiling from great room to upstairs loft give this home a roomy feel. Stone fireplace provides the accentual ingredient to cap off this room. It's a must see! A great buy at only [List Price]! For more information, contact [Listing Agent] at [Phone Number] or visit us on the Web at [Web Site Address]. [Listing Code Number]
**(Ad #24)**

### Lakefront Living

Very attractive [Style of Home] home that's near [Name of Golf Course] in [Lake Development]. [#Bedrooms] bedrooms and [#Baths] baths along with [Feature 1], [Feature 2], and [Feature 3]. See for yourself! Call [Listing Agent] at [Phone Number] for a private showing today. [Listing Code Number]
**(Ad #25)**

### Lakeview Living

Although it's not on the lake, you still have excellent views and all of the amenities of using the lake without the high price tag of a lakefront lot. This new [Style of Home] home features [#Bedrooms] bedrooms and [#Baths] baths, as well as [Feature 1], [Feature 2], and [Feature 3]. [List Price]! Call quickly on this one; it's sure to go fast at this price! Call [Phone Number] and ask for [Listing Agent]. [Listing Code Number]
**(Ad #26)**

### Bungalow by the Water

Cute and cozy [#Bedrooms] bedroom/[#Baths] bath home located in [Lake Development]. Lots of closet space, large eat-in kitchen, [Feature 1], and [Feature 2]. Why just read about it when you can see it in person? Call [Listing Agent] at [Phone Number] to preview this listing today. [Listing Code Number]
**(Ad #27)**

### Chalet by the Lake

This [#Bedrooms] bedroom/[#Baths] bath home has a contemporary feel and look you will appreciate and love. Loft area combines some great views of the nearby lake. Stone fireplace and knotty pine walls are the perfect combination for a retreat-like setting. A great buy at only [List Price]! For more information, contact [Listing Agent] at [Phone Number] or visit us on the Web at [Web Site Address]. [Listing Code Number]
**(Ad #28)**

### The 18th Green!

Most of the famous golf courses have the 18th hole as their signature mark, so it's only fitting that this [# of Square Feet] sq. ft. [Style of Home] home is also on the 18th fairway. Fitted with stone and brick, you'll fall in love with all of the features it has to offer, including the field stone retaining wall in patio area with raised fireplace pit. There's also an in-ground swimming pool, gazebo, and so much more to offer while entertaining friends and family. Why just read about it when you can see it in person? Call [Listing Agent] at [Phone Number] to preview this listing today. [Listing Code Number]
**(Ad #29)**

### You're Only a Chip or Putt Away

This *[#Bedrooms]* bedrooms/*[#Baths]* bath *[Style of Home]* home is located off the 8th fairway in *[Lake Development]*. Features *[Feature 1]*, *[Feature 2]*, and *[Feature 3]*, along with a full finished basement boasting a billiard and media room. This is a must see! A great buy at only *[List Price]*! For more information, contact *[Listing Agent]* at *[Phone Number]* or visit us on the Web at *[Web Site Address]*. *[Listing Code Number]*
**(Ad #30)**

### Drive Your Golf Cart to the Country Club

Located just a stone's throw from the golf course, you'll be able to park your golf cart in the three-car garage in this *[#Bedrooms]* bedroom/*[#Baths]* bath *[Style of Home]* home. Formal dining room fitted with French doors and private setting room give this home the elegance and charm it deserves. Spacious patio area with outdoor pavilion and fireplace allow for great outdoor entertaining. Call *[Listing Agent]* at *[Phone Number]* for all of the details! *[Listing Code Number]*
**(Ad #31)**

### Fairway Delight

As you approach this beautiful *[#Bedrooms]* bedroom/*[#Baths]* bath *[Style of Home]* home, you'll appreciate all the flowers and landscaping the owners have provided. Located in *[Lake Development]*, you'll enjoy both water and golfing privileges. Located on the 3rd fairway, this property has a little bit to offer everyone in the family. Extra features included are *[Feature 1]*, *[Feature 2]*, and *[Feature 3]*. See for yourself! Call *[Listing Agent]* at *[Phone Number]* for a private showing today. *[Listing Code Number]*
**(Ad #32)**

### You'll Be a Scratch Golfer

when you invest in this *[#Bedrooms]* bedrooms/*[#Baths]* bath *[Style of Home]* home in *[Lake Development]*. Great golfing and country club privileges are associated with this new listing. Newly remodeled kitchen with all professional top-of-the-line appliances included. For a private tour, call *[Listing Agent]* at *[Phone Number]* or e-mail *[Listing Agent]* at *[Listing Agent E-mail]*. *[Listing Code Number]*
**(Ad #33)**

### Better Than a Hole-in-One!

Stenciled box-beamed ceilings provide a quaint and clever touch to this *[#Bedrooms]* bedroom/*[#Baths]* bath *[Style of Home]* home. Magnificent master suite features a whirlpool tub, separate shower stall, powder room, his and her closets, and dramatic views of the nearby lake. *[List Price]*! Call *[Phone Number]* and ask for *[Listing Agent]*. *[Listing Code Number]*
**(Ad #34)**

# Homes with Acreage  8

When you think of a home in the country, what is the first object you think of? Fresh air? Space? Maybe cows or pigs? Or maybe in your area of the country it's just simply no one close by where you can enjoy life to it's fullest. Keep these points in mind as you write your ads for homes with acreage. What is it that the owners love and appreciate about their home and living out of town? What will they miss? Most buyers looking for homes with acreage want to know: How much acreage is included? Are there are any outbuildings? Is there a pond, fencing, and other essential items that might be included to make living on a mini-farm easier?

Also, consider where you place your ads for homes that include acreage or mini-farms. It's a good idea to target your advertising to those types of publications that will reach people interested in living on a mini-farm.

From the sample headings and ads provided in this chapter, you should be able to develop effective ads that will produce phone calls and leads, leading to sales for your homes with acreage clients. Good luck!

# Sample Headings

Give the Kids a Horse *(Ad #1)*
Room for a Garden *(Ad #2)*
Old McDonald Had a Farm *(Ad #3)*
A Big Red Barn *(Ad #4)*
Cows Grazing in the Pasture *(Ad #5)*
Winding Creek *(Ad #6)*
Get Out and Open the Gate *(Ad #7)*
New Fencing *(Ad #8)*
In the Mood to Fish? *(Ad #9)*
Only a Stone's Throw from the Lake *(Ad #10)*
Nestled in the Pines *(Ad #11)*
The Tractor Is Included *(Ad #12)*
Breathe in the Fresh Air *(Ad #13)*
You'll Need a Dog *(Ad #14)*
Country Charm *(Ad #15)*
Two-Story Country Home *(Ad #16)*
Have You Ever Wanted a Horse? *(Ad #17)*
Horses Included *(Ad #18)*
Better Than Green Acres *(Ad #19)*
Green Acres—We've Finally Found It *(Ad #20)*

Just a Little Tender Love and Care *(Ad #21)*
Your Own Private Hiking Trail *(Ad #22)*
Archery Anyone? *(Ad #23)*
Nature, Nature, Nature *(Ad #24)*
Rock Glade with Nature's Beauty *(Ad #25)*
Country Living Resort *(Ad #26)*
Gingerbread Fence *(Ad #27)*
A Place for Your Own Canoe *(Ad #28)*
Walk to Your Deer Stand *(Ad #29)*
It's Hayride Time! *(Ad #30)*
A Barn with a Loft *(Ad #31)*
You've Never Tasted Drinking Water So Good *(Ad #32)*
Rise and Shine! The Rooster Is Calling Your Name *(Ad #33)*
The Chickens Want to Stay! *(Ad #34)*
The Catfish Will Accept New Owners *(Ad #35)*
Weekend Retreat *(Ad #36)*
Why Go Anywhere Else *(Ad #37)*
Mini-Farm with All the Extras *(Ad #38)*

### Give the Kids a Horse

There's plenty of room on this ten acre parcel, complete with a small barn and two stalls. Lovely *[#Bedrooms]* bedroom/*[#Baths]* bath *[Style of Home]* home with family room, finished basement, and more. A great opportunity at *[List Price]*. Call *[Listing Agent]* at *[Phone Number]* for more information. *[Listing Code Number]*
***(Ad #1)***

### Room for a Garden

and then some, with this *[#Bedrooms]* bedroom and *[#Baths]* bath *[Style of Home]* home on six acres. You'll find plenty of large shade trees for rest and relaxation. Don't delay on this one! It's priced to move at *[List Price]*. Call *[Listing Agent]* to arrange a showing at *[Phone Number]*. *[Listing Code Number]*
***(Ad #2)***

### Old McDonald Had a Farm

and you can too! This 15-acre listing includes a *[#Bedrooms]* bedroom and *[#Baths]* bath *[Style of Home]* farmhouse. Constructed at the turn of the century you'll find one-of-a-kind craftsmanship with built-in bookcases, china cabinets, and French doors. A real showplace and priced at *[List Price]*. Call *[Listing Agent]* at *[Phone Number]* to arrange a showing or visit this property online at *[Web Site Address]*. *[Listing Code Number]*
***(Ad #3)***

### A Big Red Barn

accompanies this white *[Style of Home]* farmhouse. There's plenty of room for hay for the horses in the large barn with three stalls and separate tack room. You'll even have plenty of room to park your tractor, lawn mowers, and more. For more information on this new listing, call *[Listing Agent]* at *[Phone Number]*. *[Listing Code Number]*
***(Ad #4)***

### Cows Grazing in the Pasture

is a site to wake up to every morning on this 40-acre parcel of real estate. *[#Bedrooms]* bedroom/*[#Baths]* bath *[Style of Home]* farmhouse with large country kitchen, walk-in pantry, and screened-in porch off the side. It's hard to find anything as nice as this and it's only been on the market for a short time. Call *[Listing Agent]* at *[Phone Number]* for a private showing today. *[Listing Code Number]*
***(Ad #5)***

### Winding Creek

is only a part of all the added features you'll find with this *[#Bedrooms]* bedroom/*[#Baths]* bath home on 20 acres. Private walking trail, workshop, full finished basement, and covered patio make up a small portion of the many additions this mini-farm has to offer. Listed for sale at only *[List Price]*! *[Listing Agent]* is ready to show you this property at your convenience. Call *[Phone Number]*. *[Listing Code Number]*
***(Ad #6)***

### Get Out and Open the Gate

There's 60 wooded acres to explore with this *[#Bedrooms]* bedroom/*[#Baths]* bath *[Style of Home]*. Two fireplaces, finished family room in basement, and screened-in porch in the back for summer dining and visits with friends. An absolute treat and priced at only *[List Price]*. You can view this property online at *[Web Site Address]* or call *[Listing Agent]* at *[Phone Number]* for more information. *[Listing Code Number]*
**(Ad #7)**

### New Fencing

makes up a small portion of the many features you'll appreciate with this *[Style of Home]* farmhouse. *[#Bedrooms]* bedrooms and *[#Baths]* baths, central air-conditioning, walk-in pantry, and much more. The owners have made many recent updates including wiring, roof, plumbing, and siding. Call *[Listing Agent]* at *[Phone Number]* about his upcoming open house and how you can preview this home. *[Directions]*, *[Street Address]*. *[Listing Code Number]*
**(Ad #8)**

### In the Mood to Fish?

Fish all you want in your own two acre stocked pond. Twelve acres of gently rolling pasture surround this *[#Bedrooms]* bedroom/*[#Baths]* bath *[Style of Home]* home. Extra clean and ready to move into! Call *[Listing Agent]* at *[Phone Number]* for all the details or to schedule and appointment to preview. *[Listing Code Number]*
**(Ad #9)**

### Only a Stone's Throw from the Lake

with this *[#Bedrooms]* bedroom/*[#Baths]* bath home. Sitting on nine level acres, this *[Style of Home]* home features a small detached workshop, fencing and cross fencing, gazebo, and summer kitchen area. Everything is like brand new! Call *[Listing Agent]* at *[Phone Number]* to find out more about this new listing. *[Listing Code Number]*
**(Ad #10)**

### Nestled in the Pines

you'll find a *[#Bedrooms]* bedroom/*[#Baths]* bath *[Style of Home]* home with cathedral ceilings, stone fireplace, and full finished basement. Too many extras to list in this ad, so call *[Listing Agent]* at *[Phone Number]* for more information. *[Listing Code Number]*
**(Ad #11)**

### The Tractor Is Included

with this 40-acre, *[#Bedrooms]* bedroom/*[#Baths]* bath home. Mostly cleared property, paved road, and large covered country front porch that is perfect for visiting with friends or taking a quick nap on a weekend afternoon. Priced at *[List Price]* this home should sell fast! Call *[Listing Agent]* at *[Phone Number]* for more information and to arrange a private tour today. *[Listing Code Number]*
**(Ad #12)**

### Breathe in the Fresh Air

Breathe fresh country air everyday on this 20-acre parcel of land complete with a *[#Bedrooms]* bedroom/*[#Baths]* bath *[Style of Home]* home. A stunning kitchen with oak wood beams, wood stove, and new cabinets. Gorgeous views from almost anywhere you look! A rare find and priced to sell at only *[List Price]*! Call *[Listing Agent]* at *[Phone Number]* for more information. *[Listing Code Number]* *(Ad #13)*

### You'll Need a Dog

to experience all the unique features of this 25-acre parcel of land. Gorgeous *[#Bedrooms]* bedroom/*[#Baths]* bath home with a wet weather creek. Oversized three-car garage, full unfinished basement, private study, and more. Priced at *[List Price]* and ready for immediate occupancy. Call *[Listing Agent]* at *[Phone Number]* for more information. *[Listing Code Number]* *(Ad #14)*

### Country Charm

with this *[#Bedrooms]* bedroom/*[#Baths]* bath *[Style of Home]* farmhouse. Spacious rooms complement oversized hallways and foyer. Your guests will be amazed at all of the room you have in this lovely new listing. Priced at *[List Price]*! Call *[Listing Agent]* at *[Phone Number]* for more information. *[Listing Code Number]* *(Ad #15)*

### Two-Story Country Home

situated on 17½ acres is the talk of the local real estate board. At only *[List Price]*, we're sure it will go quick! Don't delay! Call *[Listing Agent]* today at *[Phone Number]*. *[Listing Code Number]* *(Ad #16)*

### Have You Ever Wanted a Horse?

Now you can with this 30-acre mini-farm on the edge of town. Complete with a small horse barn, new fencing, and small stocked pond. This *[Style of Home]* home includes *[#Bedrooms]* bedroom and *[#Baths]* baths and a large family room. Priced to sale at only *[List Price]*! Call *[Listing Agent]* to arrange a private showing of this property today at *[Phone Number]*. *[Listing Code Number]* *(Ad #17)*

### Horses Included

in this *[#Bedrooms]* bedroom/*[#Baths]* bath home on 15 acres. Close to state equestrian trail, this property also includes a four stall horse barn. Lovely country kitchen accents this extra clean home. For more information or to preview, call *[Listing Agent]* at *[Phone Number]*. *[Listing Code Number]* *(Ad #18)*

## Better Than Green Acres

are words to describe this *[#Bedrooms]* bedroom/*[#Baths]* bath cozy home on three acres. Great spot for a garden, horseshoes, or other family outdoor activities. Features a 30 × 40 workshop with workbench and shelves designed for the craftsman. It's a real treat and sure to move fast at only *[List Price]*. Call *[Listing Agent]* at *[Phone Number]* to see this home before it is too late. *[Listing Code Number]*
*(Ad #19)*

## Green Acres—We've Finally Found It

just six miles south of town! *[#Bedrooms]* bedroom/*[#Baths]* bath *[Style of Home]* home with all the extras you would expect from your next home. Finished basement, three-car garage, and large screened-in patio to relax and dine during summer evenings. Sits on six acres for plenty of enjoyment. Priced to sell fast at *[List Price]*. Call *[Listing Agent]* at *[Phone Number]* for more information. *[Listing Code Number]*
*(Ad #20)*

## Just a Little Tender Love and Care

is all this *[Style of Home]* farmhouse needs. Sits on ten acres with older barn and additional outbuildings. Have an open mind when you call *[Listing Agent]* to arrange a showing. It has lots of potential. Call *[Phone Number]* and ask for *[Listing Agent]* to look at this home today. *[Listing Code Number]*
*(Ad #21)*

## Your Own Private Hiking Trail

is included with this 25-acre, *[#Bedrooms]* bedroom/*[#Baths]* bath *[Style of Home]* home. Nestled at the foot of the *[City Name]* hillside, the owners have carved out a two-mile trail through their property. Gorgeous stone fireplace accents the large airy family room. You'll also discover a big workshop, full basement, and more. To find out all the details, call *[Listing Agent]* at *[Phone Number]*. *[Listing Code Number]*
*(Ad #22)*

## Archery Anyone?

You'll have more than enough room for your favorite outdoor activities with this 15-acre parcel land. Includes a good combination of woods and pasture along with a wet weather creek! *[#Bedrooms]* bedroom and *[#Baths]* baths complimented by a large brick fireplace in family room. Priced at *[List Price]*. Call *[Listing Agent]* at *[Phone Number]* to arrange a showing today. *[Listing Code Number]*
*(Ad #23)*

## Nature, Nature, Nature

describes this 40-acre wooded parcel of land, complete with a *[#Bedrooms]* bedroom/*[#Baths]* bath *[Style of Home]* home. Gorgeous limestone fireplace in massive great room with beamed ceilings. Loft bedroom overlooks outdoor water garden with its own private deck. Absolutely breathtaking home with lots of extras. Detailed brochure or DVD available by contacting *[Listing Agent]* at *[Phone Number]*. *[Listing Code Number]*
*(Ad #24)*

### Rock Glade with Nature's Beauty

Adorns this eight acre *[#Bedrooms]* bedroom/*[#Baths]* bath home. You'll appreciate the large country kitchen with screened-in porch for summer dining. Full finished basement, two-car garage with attached workshop, and more. Call *[Listing Agent]* at *[Phone Number]* for more information on this new listing. It's sure to go quick at *[List Price]*. *[Listing Code Number]*

*(Ad #25)*

### A Place for Your Own Canoe

with this 30-acre resort-like setting on the *[River Name]*. Large wooden deck is ideal for family gatherings and quiet evenings. *[#Bedrooms]* bedroom/*[#Baths]* bath *[Style of Home]* home with workshop. Best of all, there's a gazebo down by the river you have to see for yourself. For more information, contact *[Listing Agent]* at *[Phone Number]*. *[Listing Code Number]*

*(Ad #28)*

### Country Living Resort

best describes this 30-acre majestic *[Style of Home]* home. Over *[# of Square Feet]* sq. ft. living area, with every available upgrade imaginable for the expansive kitchen. Granite countertops, hardwood floors, and top-of-the-line appliances. Best of all, there's a hot tub with a patio area just off the master bedroom. Priced at *[List Price]*. Call *[Listing Agent]* at *[Phone Number]* to arrange a private showing today. *[Listing Code Number]*

*(Ad #26)*

### Walk to Your Deer Stand

This 45-acre wooded track of ground is nestled at the foot of *[City Name]*. The owner has his own private deer stand, which has led to great success over the last few seasons. Lovely *[#Bedrooms]* bedroom/*[#Baths]* bath *[Style of Home]* home with over *[# of Square Feet]* sq. ft. of living area. Full basement, three-car garage, and large master bedroom and suite with jacuzzi tub and shower. Best of all, it's priced at only *[List Price]*! Call *[Listing Agent]* at *[Phone Number]* to look at this home today. *[Listing Code Number]*

*(Ad #29)*

### Gingerbread Fence

encompasses this *[#Bedrooms]* bedroom/*[#Baths]* bath *[Style of Home]* on the edge of town. Sits on three acres, large shade trees, flower garden, and gazebo area for entertaining friends and family. An absolute dollhouse and priced at *[List Price]*. Just listed, so call *[Listing Agent]* at *[Phone Number]* to preview this home before it is too late. *[Listing Code Number]*

*(Ad #27)*

### It's Hayride Time!

25 gently rolling acres with a good balance of pasture and woods accompany this *[#Bedrooms]* bedroom/*[#Baths]* bath *[Style of Home]* home. Why just read about it when you can see it in person? Call *[Listing Agent]* at *[Phone Number]* to preview this listing today. *[Listing Code Number]*

*(Ad #30)*

### A Barn with a Loft

is included with this seven-acre *[Style of Home]* home just minutes from town. This *[#Bedrooms]* bedroom/*[#Baths]* bath home has been completely renovated by the present owners. You'll love the patio and barbeque area and adjoining in-ground swimming pool for those hot summer afternoons. Call *[Listing Agent]* at *[Phone Number]* for a full-color flyer or to arrange an appointment today. *[Listing Code Number]*
**(Ad #31)**

### You've Never Tasted Drinking Water So Good

as you will with this *[Style of Home]* home on five acres just minutes from town. *[#Bedrooms]* bedroom and *[#Baths]* baths with exotic patio flower garden and gazebo accompanied by Koi fish pond. Breathtaking kitchen with center island and every appliance imaginable built in. Large stone fireplace adorns the vaulted ceilings in the great room. Loft study is a great place to write that book you've always wanted to pen. Call *[Listing Agent]* at *[Phone Number]* for a showing today. *[Listing Code Number]*
**(Ad #32)**

### Rise and Shine! The Rooster Is Calling Your Name

Ten-acre mini-farm complete with chicken house, barn, workshop, and fruit cellar. Enjoy the days of yesteryear with this *[#Bedrooms]* bedroom/*[#Baths]* bath *[Style of Home]* delight. Call *[Listing Agent]* at *[Phone Number]* for a showing today. *[Listing Code Number]*
**(Ad #33)**

### The Chickens Want to Stay!

That's right! If you purchase this 20-acre mini-farm with chicken house and barn, the birds have asked to be included with the sale and promise to produce fresh eggs every morning. *[#Bedrooms]* bedroom/*[#Baths]* bath home with all the amenities you desire in your next home. Priced at only *[List Price]*. Call *[Listing Agent]* at *[Phone Number]* to preview this new listing today. *[Listing Code Number]*
**(Ad #34)**

### The Catfish Will Accept New Owners

to feed them every evening. Small stocked pond is just a part of this gorgeous five-acre *[#Bedrooms]* bedroom/*[#Baths]* bath retreat just minutes from town. Priced right and ready for immediate occupancy! Call *[Listing Agent]* at *[Phone Number]* for more information. *[Listing Code Number]*
**(Ad #35)**

### Weekend Retreat

or ideal for year-round living in this *[#Bedrooms]* bedroom/*[#Baths]* bath *[Style of Home]* home on *[River Name]*. Features large wooden deck overlooking the hillside. Stone fireplace, country kitchen with walk-in pantry, and full unfinished basement are just a few of the extras you'll find in this home. A rare opportunity and priced to sell at *[List Price]*. Call *[Listing Agent]* for more information at *[Phone Number]*. *[Listing Code Number]*
**(Ad #36)**

### *Why Go Anywhere Else*

when you can enjoy all the amenities with this *[#Bedrooms]* bedroom/*[#Baths]* bath *[Style of Home]* home on 25 wooded acres? Peaceful setting and just minutes from town. Large great room, oversized bedrooms, and so much more to offer you and your family. You'll never want to take a vacation again it's so nice! A true paradise and priced for *[List Price]*. For more information, call *[Listing Agent]* at *[Agency Phone Number]*. *[Listing Code Number]* *(Ad #37)*

### *Mini-Farm with All the Extras*

make up this 25-acre farmer's paradise. *[#Bedrooms]* bedroom/*[#Baths]* bath *[Style of Home]* home with over *[# of Square Feet]* sq. ft. Large detached workshop ideal for the craftsman in your family. For more information, contact *[Listing Agent]* at *[Phone Number]* to arrange a showing today. *[Listing Code Number]* *(Ad #38)*

Homes with Acreage

# Farms—Ranches 9

The ads and ad headings listed in this chapter may also be used with homes with acreage and the vacant and unimproved land listings. Keep in mind that including the number of acres, fencing, and types of outbuildings are all important to the farm consumer. You might also include information about how much land is cleared, the number of acres in woods, and if the farm has creeks or springs. Consider devoting a portion of your. Web site to photos, plats, and maps for your farm properties you market on a daily basis.

# Sample Headings

Why Are the Tree Trunks Painted White? *(Ad #1)*

Careful Not to Name the Animals *(Ad #2)*

You Won't Believe the Size of the Catfish *(Ad #3)*

It's Okay to Feed the Fish *(Ad #4)*

Sometimes the Deer Want to Be Fed *(Ad #5)*

Black Bears Near This Home? *(Ad #6)*

Nestled in the Valley *(Ad #7)*

Walk the Ridge *(Ad #8)*

Horse Trails and Hiking Trails *(Ad #9)*

The Fall Foliage Is Breathtaking *(Ad #10)*

Rock Climbing Not Allowed *(Ad #11)*

Raise Your Own Black Beauty! *(Ad #12)*

Carefully Crafted Farmhouse *(Ad #13)*

Pre-Civil War Farmhouse *(Ad #14)*

Turn-of-the-Century Farmhouse *(Ad #15)*

Grandma's Quilts Will Look Great *(Ad #16)*

Enjoy the Good Life *(Ad #17)*

Step into the Good Life *(Ad #18)*

City Life or Country Life—You Make the Choice *(Ad #19)*

Most People Would Love This Opportunity *(Ad #20)*

Forget the Smog *(Ad #21)*

No More Hustle and Bustle *(Ad #22)*

It's a Different Way of Life *(Ad #23)*

You'll Wonder How You Went Without *(Ad #24)*

Cowboy Boots Not Included *(Ad #25)*

You'll Need Cowboy Boots *(Ad #26)*

Ask Your Feet if It's Okay to Buy Cowboy Boots *(Ad #27)*

Get Rid of the Tie *(Ad #28)*

No More Sport Coat and Tie *(Ad #29)*

Well Water Never Tasted So Good *(Ad #30)*

Requires a Pony *(Ad #31)*

A Real Country Kitchen *(Ad #32)*

The Kids Will Love It *(Ad #33)*

You'll Need a Flannel Shirt to Enjoy the Crisp Fall Mornings *(Ad #34)*

A Stone Home to Call Home! *(Ad #35)*

Mini-Farm in the Woods with High-Speed Internet Access! *(Ad #36)*

Overlooking the River *(Ad #37)*

Plenty of Firewood *(Ad #38)*

Burn a Fire Every Night *(Ad #39)*

Old McDonald Would Have Loved This Farm *(Ad #40)*

Living a Dream! *(Ad #41)*

Close to the City—But Nestled in the Woods *(Ad #42)*

# Sample Ads

### Why Are the Tree Trunks Painted White?

Maybe it's because the owner's grandpa painted his trees white or perhaps it's the size and beauty of the large shade trees found throughout this *[Acres]*-acre farm. You'll adore the country kitchen with its large windows overlooking the garden and flowerbeds in the backyard. *[#Bedrooms]* bedrooms and *[#Baths]* baths, and so much more to offer at an unbelievable low price of *[List Price]*. Call *[Listing Agent]* at *[Phone Number]* for all of the details. *[Listing Code Number]*
***(Ad #1)***

### Careful Not to Name the Animals

With *[acres]* cleared acres to explore and own, this farm will provide ample opportunity to own a wide variety of animals. Lovely home with open and airy floor plan. Extra features included are *[Feature 1]*, *[Feature 2]*, and *[Feature 3]*. A great buy at only *[List Price]*! For more information, contact *[Listing Agent]* at *[Phone Number]* or visit us on the Web at *[Web Site Address]*. *[Listing Code Number]*
***(Ad #2)***

### You Won't Believe the Size of the Catfish

in the three-acre pond that's included with this *[Acres]*-acre *[#Bedrooms]* bedroom/*[#Baths]* bath *[Style of Home]* home. Stenciled box-beamed ceilings highlight the kitchen and nook area with large nine-over-nine sash windows viewing the back patio. See for yourself! Contact *[Phone Number]* and ask for *[Listing Agent]*. *[Listing Code Number]*
***(Ad #3)***

### It's Okay to Feed the Fish

since the owners do every evening. Large four-acre lake in the middle of *[Acres]* acres provides you with your own piece of tranquility. Accordion folding shutters accompany the family room windows for more privacy. *[# of Square Feet]* sq. ft. *[Style of Home]* home will make the perfect place to call your residence. Call *[Listing Agent]* at *[Phone Number]* for all of the details. *[Listing Code Number]*
***(Ad #4)***

### Sometimes the Deer Want to Be Fed

Stacked-stone chimney with outdoor fireplace arbor is the perfect place to watch the deer feed in the evening on this *[Acres]*-acre farm featuring a *[Style of Home]* home with over *[# of Square Feet]* sq. ft. A great buy at only *[List Price]*! Call *[Phone Number]* and ask for *[Listing Agent]*. *[Listing Code Number]*
***(Ad #5)***

### Black Bears Near This Home?

Not really, but with over *[acres]* wooded acres you're sure to see plenty of other wildlife. Gorgeous farmhouse features a bath tucked under the eaves of the attic, and a large spacious master bedroom with two walk-in closets. Cabinets with glass doors accent a large country kitchen viewing a keeping room with fireplace and ceramic floor. Let *[Listing Agent]* show you this lovely listing today. Call *[Phone Number]* to schedule your appointment. *[Listing Code Number]*
***(Ad #6)***

Farms—Ranches

73

### Nestled in the Valley

Simple yet functional, this *[#Bedrooms]* bedroom/*[#Baths]* bath *[Style of Home]* home features *[Feature 1]* and *[Feature 2]*, along with low-voltage halogen lighting in the kitchen. A real charmer that's sure to please everyone in the family! Why just read about it when you can see it in person? Call *[Listing Agent]* at *[Phone Number]* to preview this listing today. *[Listing Code Number]*
*(Ad #7)*

### Walk the Ridge

on your own *[acres]* wooded acres! Great views from almost anywhere you look out in this *[# of Square Feet]* sq. ft. *[Style of Home]* home. Upper-story setting room is ideal to read a book or to enjoy your favorite hobby. *[List Price]*! Call *[Phone Number]* and ask for *[Listing Agent]*. *[Listing Code Number]*
*(Ad #8)*

### Horse Trails and Hiking Trails

make up a small part of this *[acres]*-wooded acre farm. Features a lovely *[#Bedrooms]* bedrooms/*[#Baths]* bath *[Style of Home]* home with a large covered front porch. Large wood plank floors compliment the stone fireplace in the great room. *[Feature 1]*, *[Feature 2]*, and *[Feature 3]*. Call *[Listing Agent]* at *[Phone Number]* for more information. *[Listing Code Number]*
*(Ad #9)*

### The Fall Foliage is Breathtaking

from the front porch of this new listing. Multiple gables with keystone lintels provide a dramatic backdrop as guests make their way up the paved driveway to your home. Light and airy floor plan features *[#Bedrooms]* bedrooms and *[#Baths]* baths, *[# of Square Feet]* sq. ft., and more. See for yourself! Contact *[Phone Number]* and ask for *[Listing Agent]*. *[Listing Code Number]*
*(Ad #10)*

### Rock Climbing Not Allowed

unless you're an experienced rock climber! Over *[Acres]* acres with your own rock bluffs to climb on or to sit back and enjoy their beauty. Exquisite kitchen in this *[#Bedrooms]* bedrooms/*[#Baths]* bath *[Style of Home]* that will please any demanding cook. Family room with limestone fireplace and more. Price to sell at only *[List Price]*. Call *[Listing Agent]* at *[Phone Number]* for all of the details. *[Listing Code Number]*
*(Ad #11)*

### Raise Your Own Black Beauty!

Stunning *[Acres]*-acre horse farm complete with horse barn, stalls, and storage/tack room. The white board fencing goes great with this traditional *[Style of Home]* home. This new listing provides *[# of Square Feet]* sq. ft., along with *[#Bedrooms]* bedrooms and *[#Baths]* baths. For more information, visit our Web site at *[Web Address]* or call *[Listing Agent]* at *[Phone Number]*. *[Listing Code Number]*
*(Ad #12)*

### Carefully Crafted Farmhouse

is an inspiration to anyone who comes to visit you. The owners have been attentive to detail throughout this *[Style of Home]* home. Built-in plank fireplace in family room on main level, and *[#Bedrooms]* bedrooms and *[#Baths]* baths, along with a welcoming covered front porch to friends and guests. *[List Price]*! Call quickly on this one; it's sure to go fast at this price! Call *[Phone Number]* and ask for *[Listing Agent]*. *[Listing Code Number]*
***(Ad #13)***

### Pre-Civil War Farmhouse

This *[Style of Home]* home was built just prior to the Civil War. Large rooms with wide woodwork frame every area with perfection. Open foyer greets your guests with a heavy sigh. Many original details have been preserved to give this new listing a special touch. A great buy at only *[List Price]*! For more information, contact *[Listing Agent]* at *[Phone Number]* or visit us on the Web at *[Web Site Address]*. *[Listing Code Number]*
***(Ad #14)***

### Turn-of-the-Century Farmhouse

Sidelights and overhead transom frame the six-panel entry door as you enter this stately residence we just listed. Open and airy foyer provides a sense of warmth and comfort in this *[#Bedrooms]* bedroom/*[#Baths]* bath home. Fresh herbs in the garden just off the kitchen backdoor. A real charmer and priced to sell at only *[List Price]*! For a private tour, call *[Listing Agent]* at *[Phone Number]* or you can e-mail *[Listing Agent]* at *[Listing Agent E-mail]*. *[Listing Code Number]*
***(Ad #15)***

### Grandma's Quilts Will Look Great

in this farmhouse! Large *[# of Square Feet]* sq. ft. *[Style of Home]* home features a large open living room with boxed windows overlooking the side lot with large shade trees. Country kitchen with large walk-in pantry, *[#Bedrooms]* bedrooms and *[#Baths]* baths, *[Feature 1]*, and *[Feature 2]*. Call *[Listing Agent]* at *[Phone Number]* for all of the details. *[Listing Code Number]*
***(Ad #16)***

### Enjoy the Good Life

with this *[#Bedrooms]* bedroom/*[#Baths]* bath *[Style of Home]* home located minutes from town. Over *[Acres]* cleared acres makes this a place to make your dreams come true! Extra features included are *[Feature 1]*, *[Feature 2]*, and *[Feature 3]*. For more information, call *[Listing Agent]* at *[Phone Number]*. *[Listing Code Number]*
***(Ad #17)***

### Step into the Good Life

with this two-story 18th-century colonial home with a central chimney. Lovely lawn and landscaping provide a picturesque setting. Features *[Feature 1]*, *[Feature 2]*, and *[Feature 3]*, along with much more. A great buy at only *[List Price]*! For more information, contact *[Listing Agent]* at *[Phone Number]* or visit us on the Web at *[Web Site Address]*. *[Listing Code Number]*
***(Ad #18)***

### City Life or Country Life—You Make the Choice

Over *[Acres]* mostly cleared acres that are ideal for horses or cattle. Wet weather creek and spring-fed pond make owning and raising livestock a breeze. All fencing is in excellent condition. A great buy at only *[List Price]*! For a full-color flyer, contact *[Listing Agent]* at *[Phone Number]* or visit us on the Web at *[Web Site Address]*. *[Listing Code Number]*
**(Ad #19)**

### Most People Would Love This Opportunity

to own *[Acres]* acres of prime farmland just minutes from town. Features a large 30 × 50 metal barn, corral, and fencing for cattle. Good road frontage for possible future development, *[#Bedrooms]* bedroom/*[#Baths]* bath *[Style of Home]* home, along with *[Feature 1]* and *[Feature 2]*. See for yourself! Call *[Listing Agent]* at *[Phone Number]* for a private showing today. *[Listing Code Number]*
**(Ad #20)**

### Forget the Smog

this home is in the country on *[Acres]* acres. Features a lovely *[#Bedrooms]* bedroom/*[#Baths]* bath *[Style of Home]* home with tongue and groove wall paneling in the spacious family room. Features a dining room with bay window, large kitchen with breakfast nook, and a full unfinished basement. Let *[Listing Agent]* show you this lovely listing today. Call *[Phone Number]* to schedule your appointment. *[Listing Code Number]*
**(Ad #21)**

### No More Hustle and Bustle

when you invest in this farm and move to the country. *[#Bedrooms]* bedroom/*[#Baths]* bath *[Style of Home]* home on *[Acres]* acres of land. Several good outbuildings for storage, pond, and great garden area! Ladies, you'll appreciate the oversized kitchen and large pantry that's been completely remodeled. *[List Price]*! Call *[Phone Number]* and ask for *[Listing Agent]*. *[Listing Code Number]*
**(Ad #22)**

### It's a Different Way of Life

on this *[Acres]*-acre farm. A grand foyer greets you when you enter this *[#Bedrooms]* bedroom/*[#Baths]* bath *[Style of Home]* home. Extra features included are *[Feature 1]*, *[Feature 2]*, and *[Feature 3]*. For a private tour, call *[Listing Agent]* at *[Phone Number]* or e-mail *[Listing Agent]* at *[Listing Agent E-mail]*. *[Listing Code Number]*
**(Ad #23)**

### You'll Wonder How You Went Without

living in the country on your own farm. Over *[acres]* acres of cleared pasture that's perfect for horse lovers. Large horse barn with stalls and tack room. Excellent fencing, pond, and a stately *[#Bedrooms]* bedroom and *[#Baths]* bath *[Style of Home]* home. For more information, call *[Listing Agent]* at *[Phone Number]*. *[Listing Code Number]*
**(Ad #24)**

### Cowboy Boots Not Included

with this *[Acres]*-acre farm we just listed! There's a good balance of cleared and wooded acreage including some marketable timber with this property. You'll appreciate the *[#Bedrooms]* bedroom/*[#Baths]* bath *[Style of Home]* home and the polished wooden floors. Why just read about it when you can see it in person? Call *[Listing Agent]* at *[Phone Number]* to preview this listing today. *[Listing Code Number]*
**(Ad #25)**

### You'll Need Cowboy Boots

to appreciate and enjoy all *[Acres]* acres of this new farm we listed. Wall-length bookshelves provide the perfect backdrop to the family room with its wooden beamed ceilings and brick fireplace. Expanded kitchen and breakfast room make way for great conversations viewing the backyard and patio area. *[#Bedrooms]* bedrooms and *[#Baths]* baths, along with *[Feature 1]*, *[Feature 2]*, and *[Feature 3]*. This home is our "Special of the Week" on our Web site. See all the photos online at *[Web Site Address]* or call *[Listing Agent]* at *[Phone Number]*. *[Listing Code Number]*
**(Ad #26)**

### Ask Your Feet if It's Okay to Buy Cowboy Boots

You'll need them with this *[#Bedrooms]* bedroom/*[#Baths]* bath *[Style of Home]* home on *[Acres]* acres. Extra features included are *[Feature 1]*, *[Feature 2]*, and *[Feature 3]*. *[List Price]*! Call quickly on this one; it's sure to go quick at this price! Call *[Phone Number]* and ask for *[Listing Agent]*. *[Listing Code Number]*
**(Ad #27)**

### Get Rid of the Tie

This is a farm you're buying! Beautiful *[Acres]*-acre ranch with a large barn, new fencing, pond, *[Feature 1]*, and *[Feature 2]*.
A good balance of cleared and wooded acreage make this the perfect setup for most any operation. Call *[Listing Agent]* at *[Phone Number]* for all of the details. *[Listing Code Number]*
**(Ad #28)**

### No More Sport Coat and Tie

when you buy this lovely *[Acres]* acre ranch. Several outbuildings are included with this property as well as two ponds. Nice and cozy *[#Bedrooms]* bedroom/*[#Baths]* bath *[Style of Home]* home, complete with *[Feature 1]*, *[Feature 2]*, and *[Feature 3]*. See for yourself! Call *[Listing Agent]* at *[Phone Number]* for a private showing today. *[Listing Code Number]*
**(Ad #29)**

### Well Water Never Tasted So Good

until you've tasted the water from this *[#Bedrooms]* bedroom/*[#Baths]* bath *[Style of Home]* home sitting on *[Acres]* acres just minutes from town. Lots of extras and great views with this new listing. View virtual tours and photos online at *[Web Site Address]* or call *[Listing Agent]* at *[Phone Number]* for more information. *[Listing Code Number]*
**(Ad #30)**

### Requires a Pony

or two, or three, especially if you have children or grandchildren. This farm consists of over *[Acres]* acres on lush pasture land. Excellent outbuildings for equipment and livestock. *[#Bedrooms]* bedroom/*[#Baths]* bath *[Style of Home]* home with *[Feature 1]*, *[Feature 2]*, and *[Feature 3]*. See for yourself! Call *[Listing Agent]* at *[Phone Number]* for a private showing today. *[Listing Code Number]*
*(Ad #31)*

### A Real Country Kitchen

in a real country home! Striking *[#Bedrooms]* bedroom/*[#Baths]* bath *[Style of Home]* home with lots of extras, including a gourmet kitchen with a center island and pantry area. Large breakfast nook with bay window provides great natural light and view of back acreage. Features over *[Acres]* acres that are ideal for horses or cattle. Call *[Listing Agent]* at *[Phone Number]* for all of the details. *[Listing Code Number]*
*(Ad #32)*

### The Kids Will Love It

when you purchase this *[Acres]*-acre ranch featuring a nice *[Style of Home]* home with *[#Bedrooms]* bedroom and *[#Baths]* baths. Over *[# of Square Feet]* sq. ft. to enjoy with this spacious new listing, along with *[Feature 1]*, *[Feature 2]*, and *[Feature 3]*. A great buy at only *[List Price]*! For more information, contact *[Listing Agent]* at *[Phone Number]* or visit us on the Web at *[Web Site Address]*. *[Listing Code Number]*
*(Ad #33)*

### You'll Need a Flannel Shirt to Enjoy the Crisp Fall Mornings

with this *[#Bedrooms]* bedroom/*[#Baths]* bath *[Style of Home]* home. This farm includes just over *[Acres]* acres of prime pasture land at the foot of a gorgeous set of mountains. Great workshop included with additional outbuildings for farm equipment. Pond, good fencing, and more. For a private tour, call *[Listing Agent]* at *[Phone Number]* or e-mail *[Listing Agent]* at *[Listing Agent E-mail]*. *[Listing Code Number]*
*(Ad #34)*

### A Stone Home to Call Home!

That's right, this home is made out of stone and will be there for many years to come. Large fireplace adorns the family room with floor-to-ceiling bookcases on both sides. Wood beams provide a nice touch to the open airy room that also adjoins kitchen. Screened-in back porch to keep watch over your *[Acres]* acres. See for yourself! Contact *[Phone Number]* and ask for *[Listing Agent]*. *[Listing Code Number]*
*(Ad #35)*

### Mini-Farm in the Woods with High-Speed Internet Access!

This *[Acres]*-acre farm features a satellite dish for high-speed Internet so you can enjoy the comfort of city amenities with country living benefits. Lovely *[#Bedrooms]* bedroom/*[#Baths]* bath *[Style of Home]* home, with *[Feature 1]* and *[Feature 2]*. See for yourself! Contact *[Phone Number]* and ask for *[Listing Agent]*. *[Listing Code Number]*
*(Ad #36)*

### Overlooking the River

Log home with wrap-around front porch providing superb views of the countryside and nearby river. This home offers *[Feature 1]*, *[Feature 2]*, and *[Feature 3]*, along with *[#Bedrooms]* bedrooms and *[#Baths]* baths. Call *[Listing Agent]* at *[Phone Number]* for all of the details. *[Listing Code Number]* *(Ad #37)*

### Plenty of Firewood

with this *[#Bedrooms]* bedroom/*[#Baths]* bath *[Style of Home]* home sitting on *[Acres]* acres. Excellent fencing and outbuildings offered with this new listing. Spacious country kitchen with nook and adjoining family room with fireplace. Extra features included are *[Feature 1]*, *[Feature 2]*, and *[Feature 3]*. A great buy at only *[List Price]*! For more information, contact *[Listing Agent]* at *[Phone Number]* or visit us on the Web at *[Web Site Address]*. *[Listing Code Number]* *(Ad #38)*

### Burn a Fire Every Night

in this magnificent stone fireplace featured in this *[#Bedrooms]* bedroom/*[#Baths]* bath *[Style of Home]* home with over *[Acres]* wooded acres. You'll appreciate nature at its very best with this new listing and most of all you'll appreciate the price! *[List Price]*! Call *[Phone Number]* and ask for *[Listing Agent]*. *[Listing Code Number]* *(Ad #39)*

### Old McDonald Would Have Loved This Farm

especially the barn and the *[Acres]* acres of cleared pasture. All fencing has recently been updated, spring-fed pond, and more. Mrs. McDonald would have loved the *[# of Square Feet]* sq. ft. *[Style of Home]* home with the newly remodeled kitchen and breakfast nook. *[#Bedrooms]* bedrooms and *[#Baths]* baths, and so much more! *[List Price]*! Call quickly on this one; it's sure to go quick at this price! Call *[Phone Number]* and ask for *[Listing Agent]*. *[Listing Code Number]* *(Ad #40)*

### Living a Dream!

Driving up the extended paved road, a precious *[Style of Home]* home greets you. *[Acres]* acres surround this *[#Bedrooms]* bedroom/*[#Baths]* bath delight along with a open and airy floor plan. Lots of windows fill the room with natural light throughout the day. Screened-in porch off back of the home provides a great view of the countryside. This is a winner and waiting just for you! See for yourself! Contact *[Phone Number]* and ask for *[Listing Agent]*. *[Listing Code Number]* *(Ad #41)*

### Close to the City—But Nestled in the Woods

you'll discover a lovely *[#Bedrooms]* bedroom/*[#Baths]* bath *[Style of Home]* home on *[Acres]* acres of cleared pasture. Fine wood moldings are featured throughout this home, along with large windows and six panel doors. Newly updated kitchen and range chimney will make any cook proud! Why just read about it when you can see it in person? Call *[Listing Agent]* at *[Phone Number]* to preview this listing today. *[Listing Code Number]* *(Ad #42)*

# Land and Acreage  10

It is sometimes difficult to write advertisements for unimproved land. Most people looking for land just want the facts—the number of acres included, whether or not there is water, road status, the balance of cleared land versus wooded land, etc. Still, creating an interest in your product is important if you want the marketing efforts to be effective. When creating the ads, you must keep in mind that some buyers in this real estate market are looking for hunting purposes while others may plan to farm or use the land for investment purposes.

Whatever category or purpose your potential buyer falls into, make sure you have the details about your land listing! If available, list property dimensions and use topography maps, plats, surveys, and lots of photographs. Try to incorporate as much of this information as possible on your Web site or in your marketing materials. Consider using a feature, such as Google Maps to locate your property and link this to your Web site or local Multiple Listing Service if available.

# Sample Headings

It's Okay to Feed the Fish *(Ad #1)*

You Might Hear a Coyote at Night *(Ad #2)*

Deer Crossing *(Ad #3)*

Horse Trails and Hiking Trials *(Ad #4)*

Carefully Crafted Farmhouse Will Go Perfect with This Land *(Ad #5)*

Enjoy the Good Life *(Ad #6)*

Land Opportunity *(Ad #7)*

No More Hustle and Bustle *(Ad #8)*

Cowboy Boots Not Included *(Ad #9)*

Get Rid of the Tie *(Ad #10)*

Country Living with High-Speed Internet Access *(Ad #11)*

Requires a Pony *(Ad #12)*

Well Water Never Tasted So Good *(Ad #13)*

Requires an Occasional Visit to the Feed Store *(Ad #14)*

Luxurious Farm Living *(Ad #15)*

On Top of a Hill *(Ad #16)*

Country Paradise *(Ad #17)*

Black and White Cows Scattered Throughout *(Ad #18)*

You'll Appreciate the Countryside *(Ad #19)*

You + This Land = A Great Investment *(Ad #20)*

The Cows May Look at You Funny *(Ad #21)*

Three Red Barns *(Ad #22)*

Newly Painted Barn *(Ad #23)*

Wireless Internet to the Barn *(Ad #24)*

Your Dog Will Love to Visit *(Ad #25)*

Your Own Private Waterfalls *(Ad #26)*

Hang Out Here on Your Day Off! *(Ad #27)*

Own Your Own Vineyard *(Ad #28)*

Close to the City, but Nestled in the Woods *(Ad #29)*

That Is Called a Cow Chip *(Ad #30)*

It's Better Than Gold *(Ad #31)*

A Good Balance *(Ad #32)*

Nature at It's Very Best *(Ad #33)*

Attention Hunters! *(Ad #34)*

Fresh Air Never Smelled So Good *(Ad #35)*

A Section of Land Equals 40 Acres *(Ad #36)*

In the Country with Paved Roads *(Ad #37)*

Wide Open Country *(Ad #38)*

A Place to Get Away *(Ad #39)*

A Dream Come True *(Ad #40)*

Watch the Squirrels inside Your Great Room *(Ad #41)*

No Need to Buy Firewood *(Ad #42)*

Requires Lemonade When You Spend the Day *(Ad #43)*

Hard to Find *(Ad #44)*

Build Your Own Golf Driving Range *(Ad #45)*

Horseback Riding, Gardening, Golf, or Hunting. . . You Make the Decision *(Ad #46)*

It's Okay to Name the Trees *(Ad #47)*

You'll Need a Tractor *(Ad #48)*

Yes, You Still Get Wireless Cell Service with This Country Setting *(Ad #49)*

Needs a Log Cabin *(Ad #50)*

NOTE TO THE READER: The ad copy in this chapter has been repeated with the various ads to help show examples of how your ad copy can read with the various ad headings. Please feel free to use the copy that fits your listed property or change the wording to match your needs.

### It's Okay to Feed the Fish

*[# of Acres]* cleared acres with a gently rolling terrain. This parcel of land also includes *[Feature 1]* and *[Feature 2]* plus much more. Call *[Listing Agent]* at *[Phone Number]* for more information. *[Listing Code Number]* *(Ad #1)*

### You Might Hear a Coyote at Night

*[# of Acres]* wooded acres. You'll appreciate the *[Feature 1]* and *[Feature 2]*. Call *[Listing Agent]* at *[Phone Number]* for more information. *[Listing Code Number]* *(Ad #2)*

### Deer Crossing

Lots of road frontage with these *[# of Acres]* wooded acres. Features *[Feature 1]* and *[Feature 2]*, and is close to town. *[List Price]*! Call *[Phone Number]* and ask for *[Listing Agent]*. *[Listing Code Number]* *(Ad #3)*

### Horse Trails and Hiking Trials

Lots of road frontage with these *[# of Acres]* cleared acres. Features *[Feature 1]* and *[Feature 2]*. Ideal for developing or subdividing. See for yourself! Call *[Phone Number]* and ask for *[Listing Agent]*. *[Listing Code Number]* *(Ad #4)*

### Carefully Crafted Farmhouse Will Go Perfect with This Land

Gently rolling hills describe this *[# of Acres]*-acre parcel just minutes from town. Great amenities with this tract of ground including *[Feature 1]* and *[Feature 2]*. Call *[Listing Agent]* at *[Phone Number]* for all of the details. *[Listing Code Number]* *(Ad #5)*

### Enjoy the Good Life

Great views included with these *[# of Acres]* cleared acres along with *[Feature 1]* and *[Feature 2]*. *[List Price]*! Call quickly on this one; it's sure to go quick at this price! Call *[Phone Number]* and ask for *[Listing Agent]*. *[Listing Code Number]* *(Ad #6)*

### Land Opportunity

Attention subdividers—here's your chance! Great layout with this *[# of Acres]*-acre parcel of property. Includes *[Feature 1]*, *[Feature 2]*, and *[Feature 3]*. Don't let this once-in-a-lifetime business proposition pass you by. Call *[Listing Agent]* at *[Phone Number]* to find out more. *[Listing Code Number]*
**(Ad #7)**

### No More Hustle and Bustle

A good balance of cleared and wooded acreage with these *[# of Acres]* acres. Features *[Feature 1]* and *[Feature 2]*. A great buy at only *[List Price]*! For more information, contact *[Listing Agent]* at *[Phone Number]* or visit us on the Web at *[Web Site Address]*. *[Listing Code Number]*
**(Ad #8)**

### Cowboy Boots Not Included

Nature at its very best describes these *[# of Acres]* wooded acres. Lovely views and nice timber are found as you walk and explore your own special parcel of land. For a private tour, call *[Listing Agent]* at *[Phone Number]* or e-mail *[Listing Agent]* at *[Listing Agent E-mail]*. *[Listing Code Number]*
**(Ad #9)**

### Get Rid of the Tie

Trees and more trees can be found on these *[# of Acres]* wooded acres. The owners will miss the *[Feature 1]* and *[Feature 2]*. Here's your opportunity to own a lovely parcel of land! Call *[Listing Agent]* at *[Phone Number]* for all of the details. *[Listing Code Number]*
**(Ad #10)**

### Country Living with High-Speed Internet Access

Peace and tranquility make up the most of these *[# of Acres]* cleared acres. Lovely views and nice paved road to property. For more information, call *[Listing Agent]* at *[Phone Number]*. *[Listing Code Number]*
**(Ad #11)**

### Requires a Pony

You can see the stars great from these *[# of Acres]* cleared acres located minutes from town. Features *[Feature 1]*, *[Feature 2]*, *[Feature 3]*, and much more. Don't delay in calling about this new listing; it's sure to go quick! Call *[Listing Agent]* at *[Phone Number]* to preview this listing today. *[Listing Code Number]*
**(Ad #12)**

### Well Water Never Tasted so Good

Attention hunters—here are *[# of Acres]* wooded Acres that are complete with a deer stand and a private drilled well! Excellent parcel of land that will make you a great investment. See for yourself! Call *[Listing Agent]* at *[Phone Number]* for a private showing today. *[Listing Code Number]*
**(Ad #13)**

### Requires an Occasional Visit to the Feed Store

*[# of Acres]* cleared acres with a gently rolling terrain. This parcel of land also includes *[Feature 1]* and *[Feature 2]*, plus much more. Let *[Listing Agent]* show you this listing today. Call *[Phone Number]* to schedule your appointment. *[Listing Code Number]*
**(Ad #14)**

Land and Acreage

### Luxurious Farm Living

*[# of Acres]* cleared acres. You'll appreciate the *[Feature 1]*, *[Feature 2]*. Interactive CD-ROM available by contacting *[Listing Agent]* at *[Phone Number]*. *[Listing Code Number]*
**(Ad #15)**

### On Top of a Hill

Lots of road frontage with these *[# of Acres]* wooded acres. Features *[Feature 1]* and *[Feature 2]*, and is close to town. Call *[Listing Agent]* at *[Phone Number]* for more information. *[Listing Code Number]*
**(Ad #16)**

### Country Paradise

Lots of road frontage with these *[# of Acres]* cleared acres. Features *[Feature 1]* and *[Feature 2]*. Ideal for developing or subdividing. Call *[Listing Agent]* at *[Phone Number]* for more information. *[Listing Code Number]*
**(Ad #17)**

### Black and White Cows Scattered Throughout

gently rolling hills describes this *[# of Acres]*-acre parcel just minutes from town. Great amenities with this tract of ground including *[Feature 1]* and *[Feature 2]*. *[List Price]*! Call *[Phone Number]* and ask for *[Listing Agent]*. *[Listing Code Number]*
**(Ad #18)**

### You'll Appreciate the Countryside

Great views included with these *[# of Acres]* cleared acres along with *[Feature 1]* and *[Feature 2]*. See for yourself! Call *[Phone Number]* and ask for *[Listing Agent]*. *[Listing Code Number]*
**(Ad #19)**

### You + This Land = A Great Investment!

Attention subdividers—here's your opportunity! Great layout with this *[# of Acres]*-acre parcel of property. Includes *[Feature 1]*, *[Feature 2]*, and *[Feature 3]*. Don't let this once-in-a-lifetime business proposition pass you by. Call *[Listing Agent]* at *[Phone Number]* for all of the details. *[Listing Code Number]*
**(Ad #20)**

### The Cows May Look at You Funny

A good balance of cleared and wooded acreage with these *[# of Acres]* acres. Features *[Feature 1]* and *[Feature 2]*. *[List Price]*! Call quickly on this one; it's sure to go quick at this price! Call *[Phone Number]* and ask for *[Listing Agent]*. *[Listing Code Number]*
**(Ad #21)**

### Three Red Barns

Nature at its very best describes these *[# of Acres]* wooded acres. Lovely views and nice timber are found as you walk and explore your own special parcel of land. Call *[Listing Agent]* at *[Phone Number]* for more information. *[Listing Code Number]*
**(Ad #22)**

### Newly Painted Barn

Trees and more trees can be found on these *[# of Acres]* wooded acres. The owners will miss the *[Feature 1]* and *[Feature 2]*. Here's your opportunity to own a lovely parcel of land! A great buy at only *[List Price]*! For more information, contact *[Listing Agent]* at *[Phone Number]* or visit us on the Web at *[Web Site Address]*. *[Listing Code Number]*
**(Ad #23)**

### Wireless Internet to the Barn

Peace and tranquility make up the most of these *[# of Acres]* cleared acres. Lovely views and nice paved road to property. For a private tour, call *[Listing Agent]* at *[Phone Number]* or e-mail *[Listing Agent]* at *[Listing Agent E-mail]*. *[Listing Code Number]*
**(Ad #24)**

### Your Dog Will Love to Visit

these *[# of Acres]* cleared acres with a gently rolling terrain. This parcel of land also includes *[Feature 1]* and *[Feature 2]*, plus much more. Call *[Listing Agent]* at *[Phone Number]* for all of the details! *[Listing Code Number]*
**(Ad #25)**

### Your Own Private Waterfalls

*[# of Acres]* wooded acres with a rugged terrain and your own private waterfall. This parcel of land also includes *[Feature 1]* and *[Feature 2]*, plus much more. For more information, call *[Listing Agent]* at *[Phone Number]*. *[Listing Code Number]*
**(Ad #26)**

### Hang Out Here on Your Day Off!

Lots of road frontage with these *[# of Acres]* wooded acres. Features *[Feature 1]* and *[Feature 2]*, and is close to town. Why just read about it when you can see it in person? Call *[Listing Agent]* at *[Phone Number]* to preview this listing today. *[Listing Code Number]*
**(Ad #27)**

### Own Your Own Vineyard

Lots of road frontage with these *[# of Acres]* cleared acres. Features *[Feature 1]* and *[Feature 2]*. Ideal for fruit crops! See for yourself! Call *[Listing Agent]* at *[Phone Number]* for a private showing today. *[Listing Code Number]*
**(Ad #28)**

### Close to the City, but Nestled in the Woods

Gently rolling hills describe this *[# of Acres]* acre parcel just minutes from town. Great amenities with this tract of ground like *[Feature 1]* and *[Feature 2]*. Let *[Listing Agent]* show you this lovely listing today. Call *[Phone Number]* to schedule your appointment. *[Listing Code Number]*
**(Ad #29)**

### That Is Called a Cow Chip

Great views included with these *[# of Acres]* cleared acres along with *[Feature 1]* and *[Feature 2]*. Present owners run several head of cattle. More information is available by contacting *[Listing Agent]* at *[Phone Number]*. *[Listing Code Number]*
**(Ad #30)**

### It's Better Than Gold!

Attention subdividers—here's your opportunity! Great layout with this *[# of Acres]*-acre parcel of property. Includes *[Feature 1]*, *[Feature 2]*, and *[Feature 3]*. Don't let this once-in-a-lifetime business proposition pass you by. Call *[Listing Agent]* at *[Phone Number]* for more information. *[Listing Code Number]*
**(Ad #31)**

### A Good Balance

of cleared and wooded acreage with these *[# of Acres]* acres. Features *[Feature 1]* and *[Feature 2]*. For more information, contact *[Listing Agent]* at *[Phone Number]*. *[Listing Code Number]*
**(Ad #32)**

### Nature at It's Very Best

describes these *[# of Acres]* wooded acres. Lovely views and nice timber are found as you walk and explore your own special parcel of land. *[List Price]*! Call *[Phone Number]* and ask for *[Listing Agent]*. *[Listing Code Number]*
**(Ad #33)**

### Attention Hunters!

Trees and more trees can be found on these *[# of Acres]* wooded acres. The owners will miss the *[Feature 1]* and *[Feature 2]*. Here's your opportunity to own a lovely parcel of land! See for yourself! Call *[Phone Number]* and ask for *[Listing Agent]*. *[Listing Code Number]*
**(Ad #34)**

### Fresh Air Never Smelled So Good

Peace and tranquility make up the most of these *[# of Acres]* cleared acres. Lovely views and nice paved road to property. Call *[Listing Agent]* at *[Phone Number]* for all of the details. *[Listing Code Number]*
**(Ad #35)**

### A Section of Land Equals 40 Acres

You can see the stars well from these *[# of Acres]* cleared acres located minutes from town. Features *[Feature 1]*, *[Feature 2]*, *[Feature 3]*, and much more. Don't delay in calling about this new listing; it's sure to go quick! *[List Price]*! Call *[Phone Number]* and ask for *[Listing Agent]*. *[Listing Code Number]*
**(Ad #36)**

### In the Country with Paved Roads

Take note hunters—here are *[# of Acres]* wooded acres that are complete with a deer stand! Excellent parcel of land that will make you a great investment. Call *[Listing Agent]* at *[Phone Number]* for all the details. *[Listing Code Number]*
**(Ad #37)**

### Wide Open Country

*[# of Acres]* cleared acres with a gently rolling terrain. This parcel of land also includes *[Feature 1]* and *[Feature 2]*, plus much more. A great buy at only *[List Price]*! For more information, contact *[Listing Agent]* at *[Phone Number]* or visit us on the Web at *[Web Site Address]*. *[Listing Code Number]*
**(Ad #38)**

### A Place to Get Away

[# of Acres] wooded acres. You'll appreciate the [Feature 1] and [Feature 2]. For a private tour, call [Listing Agent] at [Phone Number] or e-mail [Listing Agent] at [Listing Agent E-mail]. [Listing Code Number]
*(Ad #39)*

### A Dream Come True

Lots of road frontage with these [# of Acres] wooded acres. Features [Feature 1] and [Feature 2], and is close to town. Call [Listing Agent] at [Phone Number] for all of the details! [Listing Code Number]
*(Ad #40)*

### Watch the Squirrels inside Your Great Room

Lots of road frontage with these [# of Acres] wooded acres. Features [Feature 1] and [Feature 2]. For more information, call [Listing Agent] at [Phone Number]. [Listing Code Number]
*(Ad #41)*

### No Need to Buy Firewood

Gently rolling hills describe these [# of Acres]-acre wooded parcel just minutes from town. Great amenities with this tract of ground including [Feature 1] and [Feature 2]. Why just read about it when you can see it in person? Call [Listing Agent] at [Phone Number] to preview this listing today. [Listing Code Number]
*(Ad #42)*

### Requires Lemonade When You Spend the Day

Great views included with these [# of Acres] cleared acres, along with [Feature 1] and [Feature 2]. See for yourself! Call [Listing Agent] at [Phone Number] for a private showing today. [Listing Code Number]
*(Ad #43)*

### Hard to Find

Attention subdividers—here's your opportunity! Great layout with this [# of Acres]-acre parcel of property. Includes [Feature 1], [Feature 2], and [Feature 3]. Don't let this once-in-a-lifetime business proposition pass you by. Let [Listing Agent] show you this lovely listing today. Call [Phone Number] to schedule your appointment. [Listing Code Number]
*(Ad #44)*

### Build Your Own Golf Driving Range

A good balance of cleared and wooded acreage with these [# of Acres] acres. Features [Feature 1] and [Feature 2]. Interactive CD-ROM available by contacting [Listing Agent] at [Phone Number]. [Listing Code Number]
*(Ad #45)*

### Horseback Riding, Gardening, Golf, or Hunting . . . You Make the Decision

Nature at its very best describes these [# of Acres] wooded acres. Lovely views and nice timber are found as you walk and explore your own special parcel of land. Call [Listing Agent] at [Phone Number] for more information. [Listing Code Number]
*(Ad #46)*

### It's Okay to Name the Trees

Trees and more trees can be found on these *[# of Acres]* wooded acres. The owners will miss the *[Feature 1]* and *[Feature 2]*. Here's your opportunity to own a lovely parcel of land! Call *[Listing Agent]* at *[Phone Number]* for all the details. *[Listing Code Number]*
**(Ad #47)**

### You'll Need a Tractor

Peace and tranquility make up the most of these *[# of Acres]* cleared acres. Lovely views and nice paved road to property. *[List Price]*! Call *[Phone Number]* and ask for *[Listing Agent]*. *[Listing Code Number]*
**(Ad #48)**

### Yes, You Still Get Wireless Cell Service with This Country Setting

You can see the stars well from these *[# of Acres]* cleared acres located minutes from town. Features *[Feature 1]*, *[Feature 2]*, *[Feature 3]*, and much more. Don't delay in calling about this new listing; it's sure to go quick! Call *[Phone Number]* and ask for *[Listing Agent]* for all the details. *[Listing Code Number]*
**(Ad #49)**

### Needs a Log Cabin

Attention hunters and fisherman! Here are *[# of Acres]* wooded acres that are complete with a deer stand and a small fishing lake hidden in the middle of nowhere! Excellent parcel of land just waiting for you to build a small cabin. Call *[Listing Agent]* at *[Phone Number]* for all of the details. *[Listing Code Number]*
**(Ad #50)**

# Historic and Older Homes  11

Older and historic homes have a place with many homebuyers' hearts in today's marketplace. Normally the buyers who are looking for an older home would like many details when they call in your office to inquire about more information. Make sure you have facts and figures about the age of the utility systems, costs for heating and cooling, year built (if available), and a list of updates and when the additions were completed. Photos are king to the historic and older home market. Showcasing this information on your Web site or having trifold brochures can be a plus when beginning your marketing endeavors. As with other types of properties (lake and resort and homes with acreage and farms) older and historic homes do well in my marketplace by advertising in the metropolitan area. Make sure you place your older home ads in the right publications to gain the maximum exposure for your clients.

Remember too that your sellers will be a "wealth" of information for you when you begin to write your advertisements for older and historic homes. Have them list features they feel should be included in the ad. Even though many real estate agents want to go this road alone, know the historic homeowner who is selling may have a, like mind to the historic homeowner wanting to buy. Incorporating the sellers' ideas and main points for the ad may be a good advantage that is often overlooked by many real estate professionals today.

# Sample Headings

Pre-Civil War Delight *(Ad #1)*

Abe Lincoln Never Slept Here *(Ad #2)*

Three-Story Victorian *(Ad #3)*

A Fireplace in Every Room (Almost) *(Ad #4)*

If These Walls Could Talk *(Ad #5)*

Plantation Setting *(Ad #6)*

Turn of the Century *(Ad #7)*

It Took Years to Build *(Ad #8)*

Relax—It's Been Restored *(Ad #9)*

Requesting Restoration *(Ad #10)*

Fabulous Victorian *(Ad #11)*

You'll Love the Staircase and Foyer *(Ad #12)*

Everyone's Favorite *(Ad #13)*

The Talk of the Town *(Ad #14)*

On the Historic Registry *(Ad #15)*

It Has Been There for Years *(Ad #16)*

Tree-Lined Street *(Ad #17)*

A Porch for the Entire Family *(Ad #18)*

Hold Your Family Reunion on the Porch *(Ad #19)*

A Little Bit of History *(Ad #20)*

Stop Your Looking *(Ad #21)*

You Won't Believe the Size of the Pantry *(Ad #22)*

Gothic Gem *(Ad #23)*

A Victorian Veranda *(Ad #24)*

Built to Last Forever *(Ad #25)*

Enormous Foyer and Staircase *(Ad #26)*

You Won't Believe the Woodwork *(Ad #27)*

Plenty of Pocket Doors *(Ad #28)*

Among the Shade Trees *(Ad #29)*

Among the Magnolias *(Ad #30)*

A Home That's Been Photographed *(Ad #31)*

Portrayed in Paintings *(Ad #32)*

Pretty in Pink *(Ad #33)*

A Painted Lady *(Ad #34)*

### Pre-Civil War Delight

Gracious and stately *[#Bedrooms]* bedrooms/*[#Baths]* bath *[Style of Home]* home on 16 acres, features a large parlor with fireplace, formal dining room with built-in china cabinet and hutch, along with an open staircase in foyer. For a private tour, call *[Listing Agent]* at *[Phone Number]*. Or you can e-mail *[Listing Agent]* at *[Listing Agent E-mail]*. *[Listing Code Number]*
**(Ad #1)**

### Abe Lincoln Never Slept Here

but he could have since this home was built prior to his presidency. A magnificent *[Style of Home]* home with spectacular stained glass windows adjoining the foyer. There's a screened back porch that's perfect for entertaining on summer evenings. Every room has a warm and cozy feeling. Call *[Listing Agent]* at *[Phone Number]* for all of the details! *[Listing Code Number]*
**(Ad #2)**

### Three-Story Victorian

with *[#Bedrooms]* bedrooms/*[#Baths]* baths would make the perfect bed and breakfast. Features a fireplace in every bedroom, large country kitchen recently updated with granite countertops, and wide pine flooring with walk-in pantry. All woodwork restored to its original condition. For more information, call *[Listing Agent]* at *[Phone Number]*. *[Listing Code Number]*
**(Ad #3)**

### A Fireplace in Every Room (Almost)

We couldn't believe how many fireplaces this *[#Bedrooms]* bedroom home had. There are seven fireplaces located throughout this new listing. Beautiful mantels and brickwork accompany each fireplace. State-of-the-art kitchen has been completely remodeled, central air-conditioning, new wiring, and so much more. You can't go wrong with this new home! See for yourself! Call *[Listing Agent]* at *[Phone Number]* for a private showing today. *[Listing Code Number]*
**(Ad #4)**

### If These Walls Could Talk

I'm sure we would hear stories since it's over 150 years old. Enormous formal dining room with a large chandelier will make every entertaining opportunity a joy. Spacious foyer, many updates added to home, and detached garage and workshop are just a few of the extras you'll find in this new listing. *[List Price]*! Call quickly on this one; it's sure to go quick at this price! Call *[Phone Number]* and ask for *[Listing Agent]*. *[Listing Code Number]*
**(Ad #5)**

## Plantation Setting

This *[Style of Home]* home has always been an eye catcher as people drive down *[Street Address]*. Features *[#Bedrooms]* bedrooms and *[#Baths]* baths, formal living and dining rooms, chef's kitchen with all new appliances, granite countertops, and more. You'll love this home! Why just read about it when you can see it in person? Call *[Listing Agent]* at *[Phone Number]* to preview this listing today. *[Listing Code Number]*
*(Ad #6)*

## Turn of the Century

This *[Style of Home]* home features a lovely wooded lot and wrap-around porch to enjoy the fresh air during spring, summer, and fall evenings. Beautiful open staircase with original woodwork greets your guests in the formal foyer. Italian marble floors wind throughout the biggest portion of the downstairs. Features *[#Bedrooms]* bedrooms and *[#Baths]* baths and is ready for immediate occupancy. A great buy at only *[List Price]*! For more information, contact *[Listing Agent]* at *[Agency Phone Number]* or visit us on the Web at *[Web Site Address]*. *[Listing Code Number]*
*(Ad #7)*

## It Took Years to Build

this *[# of Square Feet]* sq. ft. home took over four years for the owner to complete. The story is told that every detail had to be just right. Features *[#Bedrooms]* bedrooms and *[#Baths]* baths, den, sitting parlor, and special remodeled game room in the finished basement. Spectacular setting and a once-in-a-lifetime opportunity for you to own. Call *[Listing Agent]* at *[Phone Number]* for all of the details! *[Listing Code Number]*
*(Ad #8)*

## Relax—It's Been Restored

This *[#Bedrooms]* bedroom and *[#Baths]* bath *[Style of Home]* home has been totally renovated by the present owner. Some of the remodeling includes new plumbing, wiring, refinishing of hardwood floors, and more. You must see to appreciate all the details and work the owners have labored throughout this property. See for yourself! Call *[Listing Agent]* at *[Phone Number]* for a private showing today. *[Listing Code Number]*
*(Ad #9)*

## Requesting Restoration

This *[Style of Home]* home with a beautiful wrap-around porch is begging for someone to give it a little tender care. Features *[#Bedrooms]* bedrooms and *[#Baths]* baths and lots of potential. Why just read about it when you can see it in person? Call *[Listing Agent]* at *[Phone Number]* to preview this listing today. *[Listing Code Number]*
*(Ad #10)*

## Fabulous Victorian

*[#Bedrooms]* bedroom and *[#Baths]* bath *[Style of Home]* home with all the gingerbread you'd expect in your next home. A large foyer accompanied by breathtaking oak wood floors greets you as you enter this delightful piece of history. Kitchen cabinets with glass doors line the airy room with all new appliances including jet air range and stainless steal appliances. A home to be proud of, and priced at only *[List Price]*. See for yourself! Call *[Listing Agent]* at *[Phone Number]* for a private showing today. *[Listing Code Number]*
*(Ad #11)*

### You'll Love the Staircase and Foyer

in this 18<sup>th</sup>-century colonial home. This massive open foyer showcases a breathtaking staircase winding up to a private sitting area. Large windows overlook the professional manicured grounds you'll discover on the extra large lot. To find out more details and for a private e-mail containing a special Web site address with photos, virtual tours, and more, contact *[Listing Agent]* at *[Phone Number]*. *[Listing Code Number]*
**(Ad #12)**

### Everyone's Favorite

Go ahead and ask anyone in *[Local Area]* what their favorite home is and chances are they'll name this one. This *[#Bedrooms]* bedrooms/ *[#Baths]* bath *[Style of Home]* home has been totally renovated and remodeled for your pleasure. Row of sash windows in the kitchen and breakfast nook brings in plenty of morning sunlight to make every day begin with a great start. Too many upgrades to mention, you must see for yourself how adorable this home is. *[List Price]*! Call *[Phone Number]* and ask for *[Listing Agent]*. *[Listing Code Number]*
**(Ad #13)**

### The Talk of the Town

When the *[Owner's Last Name]* built this *[Style of Home]* home in 1876, I'm sure it was the talk of the town. *[#Bedrooms]* bedrooms and *[#Baths]* baths with a large wrap-around porch are just a few of the extras you'll appreciate in this new listing. Steeply gabled roof provides a look of character and sophistication. Living and dining rooms both provide built-in bookcases. It's such a neat home that it's still the talk of the town. See for yourself! Contact *[Phone Number]* and ask for *[Listing Agent]*. *[Listing Code Number]*
**(Ad #14)**

### On the Historic Registry

Vertical floor-to-ceiling wood paneling makes this home a special treat when you walk into the large open living room in this *[Style of Home]* home. Gorgeous picket fence surrounds the home along with elaborate landscaping. Features garden shed, workshop, and many more items too numerous to mention. Call *[Listing Agent]* at *[Phone Number]* for all of the details. *[Listing Code Number]*
**(Ad #15)**

### It Has Been There for Years

This *[Style of Home]* home features *[#Bedrooms]* bedrooms and *[#Baths]* baths with over *[# of Square Feet]* sq. ft. of living area. Will provide you with all of the room and comfort you desire. A real gem and priced to sale at only *[List Price]*. Call *[Listing Agent]* at *[Phone Number]* for all of the details. *[Listing Code Number]*
**(Ad #16)**

### Tree-Lined Street

begins the focal point of this new listing in *[Listing Area]*. *[#Bedrooms]* bedrooms/ *[#Baths]* bath *[Style of Home]* has been totally renovated by the current owners. Central air and heat, upgraded insulation, new wiring, and all new plumbing are just a few of the recent upgrades. See for yourself! Contact *[Phone Number]* and ask for *[Listing Agent]*. *[Listing Code Number]*
**(Ad #17)**

### A Porch for the Entire Family

This *[#Bedrooms]* bedroom/*[#Baths]* bath home features one of the prettiest porches we have ever seen. Two porch swings, lots of wicker furniture, and plants provide the perfect backdrop for a cool summer evening and nice long conversations with friends and family. Good garden spot in backyard along with garden shed for all your tools. *[List Price]*! Call quickly on this one; it's sure to go quick at this price! Call *[Phone Number]* and ask for *[Listing Agent]*. *[Listing Code Number]*
*(Ad #18)*

### Hold Your Family Reunion on the Porch

This *[#Bedrooms]* bedroom/*[#Baths]* bath *[Style of Home]* home has such a big porch you could all go outside and hold the after-dinner conversation from this area. Large country kitchen with walk-in pantry make up a small part of the newly renovated room. Master bath has also been totally remodeled with new whirlpool tub and black marble shower. *[List Price]*! Call *[Phone Number]* and ask for *[Listing Agent]*. *[Listing Code Number]*
*(Ad #19)*

### A Little Bit of History

is found in this *[Style of Home]* home off *[Street Address]*. Built prior to the turn of the century, this home has seen a lot of history. Features a formal living room, formal dining room, and setting room with built-in bookcases. Formal foyer is an attractive feature for all of your guests as they come to visit. A lovely home that's perfect for you and your family. To see this piece of history, contact *[Listing Agent]* at *[Phone Number]*. *[Listing Code Number]*
*(Ad #20)*

### Stop Your Looking

Because we've found the perfect *[Style of Home]* home. Exquisite *[#Bedrooms]* bedrooms/*[#Baths]* bath framed sided delight features all of the warmth and comfort you'd expect in a new home. New sheet rock throughout the interior, original woodwork restored, updated wiring, and new roof are just a few of the extras you'll find. For a private tour, call *[Listing Agent]* at *[Phone Number]* or e-mail *[Listing Agent]* at *[Listing Agent E-mail]*. *[Listing Code Number]*
*(Ad #21)*

### You Won't Believe the Size of the Pantry

The original owner wanted to have plenty of room for the canning she performed each year. Did she ever! Remodeled eat-in kitchen with formal dining room nearby makes this new listing a winner! Master bedroom located on main level, two staircases, and more. See for yourself! Call *[Listing Agent]* at *[Phone Number]* for a private showing today. *[Listing Code Number]*
*(Ad #22)*

### Gothic Gem

This *[#Bedrooms]* bedrooms/*[#Baths]* bath *[Style of Home]* home has been restored by the present owners with class and detail. Polished wooden floors make way throughout the formal dining room, living room, and study. Artist studio on second floor, eat-in kitchen, and large pantry. Let *[Listing Agent]* show you this lovely listing today. Call *[Phone Number]* to schedule your appointment. *[Listing Code Number]*
*(Ad #23)*

### A Victorian Veranda

Here's a lovely large wrap-around front porch you don't find with many homes for sale today. You'll also discover a flag stone patio with a rock walkway through the flower gardens. The inside has been restored and kept to the look of its original condition. You'll be amazed at how well this home shows. Newly listed and priced to move quick! Call *[Listing Agent]* at *[Phone Number]*. *[Listing Code Number]*
**(Ad #24)**

### Built to Last Forever

Cotswold moulded-stone fireplace is the center point to this *[#Bedrooms]* bedrooms/*[#Baths]* bath home constructed in the late 1800s when homes were built to last for many years. A cobbled courtyard awaits you as you exit the large country kitchen onto the backyard. This home also features a vintage cook stove, pantry, and more. A great buy at only *[List Price]*! For more information, contact *[Listing Agent]* at *[Phone Number]* or visit us on the Web at *[Web Site Address]*. *[Listing Code Number]*
**(Ad #25)**

### Enormous Foyer and Staircase

will greet your guests in a big way in this *[#Bedrooms]* bedroom/*[#Baths]* bath *[Style of Home]* home. Imported Italian marble floors help give a hearty welcome from the foyer, too. Screened-in patio off of breakfast room provides summer dining at its best. Call *[Listing Agent]* at *[Phone Number]* for all of the details. *[Listing Code Number]*
**(Ad #26)**

### You Won't Believe the Woodwork!

The owners have stripped and refinished all of the woodwork to give it a glorious shine and a look of yesteryear. *[#Bedrooms]* bedrooms and *[#Baths]* baths give way to a newly renovated kitchen with new cherry wood cabinets and granite countertops. See for yourself! Contact *[Phone Number]* and ask for *[Listing Agent]*. *[Listing Code Number]*
**(Ad #27)**

### Plenty of Pocket Doors

are found throughout the main floor of this newly listed *[Style of Home]* home. This diamond in the rough offers three fireplaces, breakfast room, study, and formal sitting room. Only two owners in the last 75 years have made claim to this home. Call *[Listing Agent]* at *[Phone Number]* for all of the details. *[Listing Code Number]*
**(Ad #28)**

### Among the Shade Trees

you'll find a *[Style of Home]* *[#Bedrooms]* bedroom/*[#Baths]* bath home that sparkles like a ray of sunshine. Refurbished hardwood floors is just the beginning in describing how cozy and comfortable this home will be for your family. Twelve-over-twelve sash windows provide much sunlight to brighten each and everyday. *[List Price]*! Call *[Phone Number]* and ask for *[Listing Agent]*. *[Listing Code Number]*
**(Ad #29)**

### Among the Magnolias

you'll discover a gorgeous *[Style of Home]* *[#Bedrooms]* bedroom/*[#Baths]* bath dwelling. Huge rooms will be a big hit for everyone in the family. Also included is a spectacular chef's kitchen with all newly upgraded appliances. See for yourself! Contact *[Phone Number]* and ask for *[Listing Agent]*. *[Listing Code Number]* *(Ad #30)*

### A Home That's Been Photographed

With its charm and delightful appearance, this home has been photographed by many people as they pass by. Many local residents have longed to own this *[Style of Home]* home. This residence offers *[#Bedrooms]* bedrooms and *[#Baths]* baths and more. Call *[Listing Agent]* at *[Phone Number]* for all of the details. *[Listing Code Number]* *(Ad #31)*

### Portrayed in Paintings

This home has been painted by several artists in the community because of its look, feel, and character. The neighboring shade trees provide a detailed backdrop for everyone who passes by. *[#Bedrooms]* bedrooms and *[#Baths]* baths, parlor off foyer, and sitting room on main floor. Lots of charm with this new listing! *[List Price]*! Call quickly on this one; it's sure to go quick at this price! Call *[Phone Number]* and ask for *[Listing Agent]*. *[Listing Code Number]* *(Ad #32)*

### Pretty in Pink

This *[Style of Home]* home is absolutely stunning in pink with white trim. Gorgeous wrap-around porch will almost certainly delight your guests. You'll discover a cozy alcove for a bed in the upper attic room. Great buy for the money. For a private tour, call *[Listing Agent]* at *[Phone Number]* or e-mail *[Listing Agent]* at *[Listing Agent E-mail]*. *[Listing Code Number]* *(Ad #33)*

### A Painted Lady

This *[Style of Home]* home was professionally sandblasted down to the original wood and then painted to give it the cheerful and homey feel that it now provides. A gorgeous kitchen with center island and glass front refrigerator door provides a sensational look and feel. It's not very often we can find a *[Style of Home]* in such good condition. Call *[Listing Agent]* at *[Phone Number]* for all of the details. *[Listing Code Number]* *(Ad #34)*

Historic and Older Homes

# Commercial Properties 12

Writing ads for commercial and investment properties can be a challenging area. Oftentimes, sellers want their information private so that the consuming public will not wonder why the business is for sale, thus hurting future profits. Before you begin writing commercial ads, it is recommended that you always visit with the clients and make sure they approve of your advertising copy before you put it in the paper. This could be a very sticky situation with most clients and sellers, so always get their input and approval prior to running ads.

# Sample Headings

Investor's Delight *(Ad #1)*

Live and Work *(Ad #2)*

Great Investment Opportunity *(Ad #3)*

How's Your Retirement Account? *(Ad #4)*

Looking for a Better Return on Your Investment? *(Ad #5)*

Looking for a Way to Increase Your Retirement Income? *(Ad #6)*

Better Than a 401K? *(Ad #7)*

Better Than an IRA? *(Ad #8)*

You Be the Landlord *(Ad #9)*

Think of the Equity *(Ad #10)*

Want to Be Your Own Boss? *(Ad #11)*

Landmark Business for Sale *(Ad #12)*

Do You Like to Cook? *(Ad #13)*

The Employees Are Looking for a New Boss *(Ad #14)*

Enjoy the Good Life and Work for Yourself *(Ad #15)*

Tell Your Boss to Take This Job and Shove It! *(Ad #16)*

Looking for a Better Way of Life? *(Ad #17)*

Tired of Taking Orders from Someone Else? *(Ad #18)*

Expand Your Potential *(Ad #19)*

Enjoy Going to Work in the Morning? *(Ad #20)*

Looking for Mr. Fix It? *(Ad #21)*

It's Almost Like Money Growing on Trees *(Ad #22)*

A Great Way to Retire *(Ad #23)*

Mom and Pop Business Can Now Be Yours *(Ad #24)*

There Is a Bright Future in Your Life When You Invest in This Business *(Ad #25)*

No Brainer *(Ad #26)*

Don't Pass Up This Opportunity *(Ad #27)*

Quick Fix for the Working Man Blues *(Ad #28)*

No More Rent *(Ad #29)*

Live on One Side and Rent the Other *(Ad #30)*

Caretaker's Quarters *(Ad #31)*

Did We Sell Rental Income? *(Ad #32)*

How Bright Is Your Future? *(Ad #33)*

Let the Good Times Roll *(Ad #34)*

Even Your Accountant Will Agree This Is a Great Deal *(Ad #35)*

Don't Tell Anyone—They May Buy This Out from Under You *(Ad #36)*

Even Your Banker Will Agree This Is a Great Deal *(Ad #37)*

Put the Kids to Work *(Ad #38)*

Closed on Sundays *(Ad #39)*

Investor's Dream *(Ad #40)*

A Great Way to Spend Your Workweek *(Ad #41)*

Go Ahead and Retire Early—We Have Another Job for You *(Ad #42)*

Retiring from Your Old Job Never Felt So Good *(Ad #43)*

Go Ahead—Give Your Two Weeks Notice *(Ad #44)*

The Perfect Investment *(Ad #45)*

Better Than a Money Machine *(Ad #46)*

Established Business Opportunity Awaiting *(Ad #47)*

Guess Who Is Selling Their Business? *(Ad #48)*

Living Quarters with This Business Opportunity *(Ad #49)*

A New Job and New Home *(Ad #50)*

Finally, Freedom Awaits You *(Ad #51)*

Turnkey Business Waits for You to Turn the Key *(Ad #52)*

Lonely Business Looking for Someone *(Ad #53)*

Lonely Business Looking for New Soul Mate *(Ad #54)*

All This Business Needs Is a Little TLC *(Ad #55)*

Owners Willing to Sell Their Business Secrets *(Ad #56)*

You're Not Only Buying the Restaurant, You're Buying Family Recipes, Too! *(Ad #57)*

Everything Is Great about This Business *(Ad #58)*

### Investor's Delight

Four-unit apartment building completely refurbished. Tenants pay all utilities and a great cash flow. See for yourself! Contact *[Phone Number]* and ask for *[Listing Agent]*. *[Listing Code Number]*
**(Ad #1)**

### Live and Work

Great opportunity with commercial building. Features *[Sq. Ft.]* square feet for retail or office with a live-in 2-bedroom apartment above. Save time and money by combining home and work in one payment. *[List Price]*! Call quickly on this one; it's sure to go quick at this price! Call *[Phone Number]* and ask for *[Listing Agent]*. *[Listing Code Number]*
**(Ad #2)**

### Great Investment Opportunity

Six-unit apartment complex with excellent cash flow. 2 bedroom/2 bath units, laundry facility provides extra income too! Call *[Listing Agent]* at *[Phone Number]* for all of the details. *[Listing Code Number]*
**(Ad #3)**

### How's Your Retirement Account?

This eight-unit apartment building can help provide excellent income for your future retirement. All units feature two bedrooms, two baths, living and dining rooms, and kitchen. Carport facilities for each unit. Detailed fact sheet with expenses and income available to qualified buyers. Call *[Listing Agent]* at *[Phone Number]* for all of the details! *[Listing Code Number]*
**(Ad #4)**

### Looking for a Better Return on Your Investment?

Here's an excellent moneymaker with this 50-unit apartment complex. Excellent income, plus living quarters for property manager. For more information, contact *[Listing Agent]* at *[Phone Number]* or visit us on the Web at *[Web Site Address]*. A great buy at only *[List Price]*. *[Listing Code Number]*
**(Ad #5)**

### Looking for a Way to Increase Your Retirement Income?

This 4-unit, 5-bedroom/2 bath townhouse apartment complex is ideal for any investor. For more information, call *[Listing Agent]* at *[Phone Number]* for all of the details! *[Listing Code Number]*
**(Ad #6)**

### Better Than a 401K?

Although there are risks involved with any investment, this 12-unit apartment building has provided the current owner with a good stream of income over the last few years. Features laundry facilities for added income. Tenants pay their own utilities. For more information, call *[Listing Agent]* at *[Phone Number]*. *[Listing Code Number]*
*(Ad #7)*

### Better Than an IRA?

This laundry mat and car wash combo provides a fantastic steady stream of income for the current owner. Tax records available for verified qualified buyers. Call *[Listing Agent]* at *[Phone Number]* for all of the details. *[Listing Code Number]*
*(Ad #8)*

### You Be the Landlord

Now's your chance with this 6-unit apartment complex. Each unit features two bedrooms and two baths with washer and dryer hook-ups. Tenants pay their own utilities! Excellent cash flow and low, low vacancy rate. *[List Price]*! Call quickly on this one; it's sure to go quick at this price! Call *[Phone Number]* and ask for *[Listing Agent]*. *[Listing Code Number]*
*(Ad #9)*

### Think of the Equity

This 16-unit apartment complex will pay for itself over a short length of time based on its current financial income. Excellent return on investment and priced for immediate sale. Call *[Listing Agent]* at *[Phone Number]* for all of the details! *[Listing Code Number]*
*(Ad #10)*

### Want to Be Your Own Boss?

Great business opportunity for sale with excellent financial statements. Owners willing to train new buyers the tricks of the trade of this business. For more information, call *[Listing Agent]* at *[Phone Number]*. *[Listing Code Number]*
*(Ad #11)*

### Landmark Business for Sale

We'd love to disclose the name and location of this excellent business opportunity but the owners have requested we not do so at this time. If you are seriously thinking about buying a new business and have the financial qualifications available to disclose, we would love to visit with you on this great investment. Call *[Listing Agent]* at *[Phone Number]* for all of the details! *[Listing Code Number]*
*(Ad #12)*

### Do You Like to Cook?

You'll love this business opportunity! Casual dining establishment for sale with good business clientele. Turnkey operation. Contact *[Listing Agent]* at *[Phone Number]* to find out more! *[Listing Code Number]*
*(Ad #13)*

### The Employees Are Looking for a New Boss

Here's an excellent business opportunity for you to invest in. You'll agree this is an astounding financial return on your investment after you study this proposal. Serious inquiries only please! Call *[Listing Agent]* at *[Phone Number]* for all of the details! *[Listing Code Number]*
*(Ad #14)*

### Enjoy the Good Life and Work for Yourself

This great business opportunity is available for sale, which includes real estate, personal property, and goodwill. Complete turnkey operation is waiting for your phone call. A great buy at only *[List Price]*! For more information, contact *[Listing Agent]* at *[Phone Number]* or visit us on the Web at *[Web Site Address]*. *[Listing Code Number]*
**(Ad #15)**

### Tell Your Boss to Take This Job and Shove It!

Well maybe don't go that far, but you can tell him you are going to be your own boss after you investigate this business opportunity for sale. Qualified financial inquiries only please! For more information, call *[Listing Agent]* at *[Phone Number]*. *[Listing Code Number]*
**(Ad #16)**

### Looking for a Better Way of Life?

Here's your chance with this business we just listed. Includes all real estate and inventory, plus you'll benefit from the 20 years of proud business history in *[Local Area]*. For complete details and information, contact *[Listing Agent]* at *[Phone Number]*. *[Listing Code Number]*
**(Ad #17)**

### Tired of Taking Orders from Someone Else?

Now's your opportunity to be your own boss. Small sporting goods store for sale with excellent relationship to local schools and a great repeat business for local community sporting associations. For more information, contact *[Listing Agent]* at *[Phone Number]*. *[Listing Code Number]*
**(Ad #18)**

### Expand Your Potential

Small factory and production plant for sale. Owner is willing to train and teach new buyers. This is an excellent business potential to technology savvy buyer who can use the Internet to grow the company. Contact *[Listing Agent]* at *[Phone Number]* for a full detailed informational packet on this opportunity. *[Listing Code Number]*
**(Ad #19)**

### Enjoy Going to Work in the Morning?

If not, then perhaps you should consider investing in your own business. Just listed, this profitable florist shop in *[Local Area]* has a good clientele and a successful long business history. Don't delay on this once-in-a-lifetime opportunity. Call *[Listing Agent]* at *[Phone Number]* for more information. *[Listing Code Number]*
**(Ad #20)**

### Looking for Mr. Fix It?

This eight-unit apartment complex needs some tender love and care but is in an excellent location that will provide security to your investment. Most units are currently not rented due to the extensive work needed. Have an open mind when you look. *[List Price]*! Call quickly on this one; it's sure to go quick at this price! Call *[Phone Number]* and ask for *[Listing Agent]*. *[Listing Code Number]*
**(Ad #21)**

### It's Almost Like Money Growing on Trees

This quality laundry mat is a real moneymaker. The present owners have completely remodeled this facility along with adding all new machines! Tax returns available to financially qualified buyers. Owner will consider exchange for other properties. Call *[Listing Agent]* at *[Phone Number]* for all of the details! *[Listing Code Number]*

**(Ad #22)**

### A Great Way to Retire

This recreational park in resort community provides excellent income during the summer months. Spend your winters relaxing off your profits! Present owner willing to assist training new owners. Call *[Listing Agent]* at *[Phone Number]* for all of the details. *[Listing Code Number]*

**(Ad #23)**

### Mom and Pop Business Can Now Be Yours!

Deli and grocery store has been in the family for years and has an excellent business clientele visiting the store weekly. The owners are willing to share famous recipes to new buyers. Call *[Listing Agent]* at *[Phone Number]* for all of the details. *[Listing Code Number]*

**(Ad #24)**

### There Is a Bright Future in Your Life When You Invest in This Business

Established beauty shop with 15 rental stations (all currently rented). Includes real estate and all personal property. Turnkey operation! Present owner willing to stay and rent station. See for yourself! Contact *[Phone Number]* and ask for *[Listing Agent]*. *[Listing Code Number]*

**(Ad #25)**

### No Brainer

This 24-unit apartment complex is just blocks from the university. Features two bedroom/one bath units, laundry facilities for extra income, and covered parking stalls for tenants. Fantastic cash flow! A great buy at only *[List Price]*! For more information, contact *[Listing Agent]* at *[Phone Number]* or visit us on the Web at *[Web Site Address]*. *[Listing Code Number]*

**(Ad #26)**

### Don't Pass Up This Opportunity

12-unit apartment complex with small rental home available in *[Local Area]*. Tenants pay all utilities. Good cash flow and very, very low tenant vacancy rate for past 24 months. *[List Price]*! Call quickly on this one; it's sure to go quick at this price! Call *[Phone Number]* and ask for *[Listing Agent]*. *[Listing Code Number]*

**(Ad #27)**

### Quick Fix for the Working Man Blues

15 single-family units for sale. All properties are located within *[Local Area]*. For a complete portfolio and detailed information on all properties for sale, contact *[Listing Agent]* at *[Phone Number]*. Please note all units to be sold in one package. *[Listing Code Number]*

**(Ad #28)**

### No More Rent

This 6-unit apartment complex features living quarters for owner. Your area includes three bedrooms, two-and-a-half baths, living room, dining room, and family room. Let someone else pay your mortgage payment each month while you live in one unit and rent the others. This is a great opportunity! For more information, call *[Listing Agent]* at *[Phone Number]*. *[Listing Code Number]*
*(Ad #29)*

### Live on One Side and Rent the Other

Newly renovated two-bedroom/two-bath duplex for sale. Also has a two-car garage. Perfect chance to cut your monthly mortgage payment in half! Call on this one before it is too late. For all the specifics, call *[Listing Agent]* at *[Phone Number]*. *[Listing Code Number]*
*(Ad #30)*

### Caretaker's Quarters

This 8-unit apartment building features an add-on for the property manager or caretaker to oversee the operation. All units recently renovated two years ago. Don't pass up this investment. Owner will consider exchange for other properties. Call *[Listing Agent]* at *[Phone Number]* for all of the details! *[Listing Code Number]*
*(Ad #31)*

### Did We Sell Rental Income?

Here is a 36-unit apartment complex with a good rental history. Tenants pay all utilities. Plus, you'll find very low monthly expense associated with this investment. Excellent return on investment! Call *[Listing Agent]* at *[Phone Number]* for all of the details. *[Listing Code Number]*
*(Ad #32)*

### How Bright Is Your Future?

This gas station/food convenience mart is located on a busy corner intersection in *[Local Area]*. The present owners are looking to retire and offering this business opportunity at a discount. For more information, call *[Listing Agent]* at *[Phone Number]*. *[Listing Code Number]*
*(Ad #33)*

### Let the Good Times Roll

This drive-in restaurant provides some of the best custard in the *[Local Area]* area. Turnkey operation! Business hours are spring, summer, and fall. For a complete package of information, contact *[Listing Agent]* at *[Agency Phone Number]*. *[Listing Code Number]*
*(Ad #34)*

### Even Your Accountant Will Agree This Is a Great Deal

Four-unit apartment building for sale. Each unit contains two bedrooms and two baths, along with washer and dryer hook-ups. All units recently refurbished! Owners have discounted price for a quick sale. Call *[Listing Agent]* at *[Phone Number]* for all of the details. *[Listing Code Number]*
*(Ad #35)*

Commercial Properties

### Don't Tell Anyone—They May Buy This out from Under You

Elegant 6-unit apartment building has class and appeal. Perhaps this is why the rental income is so good with this investment. It's the perfect introduction if you're new to the rental market. Excellent return on investment! Call *[Listing Agent]* at *[Phone Number]* for all of the details! *[Listing Code Number]*
*(Ad #36)*

### Even Your Banker Will Agree This Is a Great Deal

Newly listed duplex features three bedrooms and two baths in each unit. Two-car garage, fireplaces in each unit, and oversized patios. Great cash flow if used for rental property. Also works well if you want to live in one side and rent out the other. For more information, call *[Listing Agent]* at *[Phone Number]*. *[Listing Code Number]*
*(Ad #37)*

### Put the Kids to Work

This recreational park includes miniature golf and snack bar. Located on a busy street in resort area. You're sure to catch a good crowd almost every evening. A great buy at only *[List Price]*! For more information, contact *[Listing Agent]* at *[Phone Number]* or visit us on the Web at *[Web Site Address]*. *[Listing Code Number]*
*(Ad #38)*

### Closed on Sundays

Established florist shop for sale in *[Local Area]*. Turnkey operation includes real estate and all personal property with this business. Owner willing to train new buyers for up to six months. For more information, call *[Listing Agent]* at *[Phone Number]*. *[Listing Code Number]*
*(Ad #39)*

### Investor's Dream

400-unit storage building facility with a multitude of unit sizes available. Features fenced lot and security cameras for all units. Office facility on complex. Call quickly on this one; it's sure to move fast. Interactive CD-ROM available by contacting *[Listing Agent]* at *[Phone Number]*. *[Listing Code Number]*
*(Ad #40)*

### A Great Way to Spend Your Workweek

This 22-unit apartment complex is fully rented and provides excellent income for the current owners. Small office on property allows for good oversight of facilities. The monthly expenses are very minimal as shown on the current financial statements. Qualified buyers only! To find out more details and for a private e-mail containing a special Web site address with photos, virtual tours, and more, contact *[Listing Agent]* at *[Phone Number]*. *[Listing Code Number]*
*(Ad #41)*

### Go Ahead and Retire Early—We Have Another Job for You

This one-owner business has been in operation for over 15 years. Excellent clientele that should not vary when property changes hands. Turnkey operation that includes real estate and personal property. Serious and qualified financial buyers only. For more information, call *[Listing Agent]* at *[Phone Number]*. *[Listing Code Number]*
**(Ad #42)**

### Retiring from Your Old Job Never Felt So Good

will be your sentiments after you work at this business opportunity we have for you and your family. No special training needed! Excellent income and minimal hours for each workday. This business information is confidential and will only be available for financially qualified buyers. Please ask for *[Listing Agent]* at *[Phone Number]*. *[Listing Code Number]*
**(Ad #43)**

### Go Ahead—Give Your Two Weeks Notice

Once you look at this business opportunity we have for sale, you'll be sold on it. Good steady cash stream each month. No prior experience needed. Owners willing to train until you feel comfortable to take over on your own. Call *[Listing Agent]* at *[Phone Number]* for all of the details. *[Listing Code Number]*
**(Ad #44)**

### The Perfect Investment

4-unit apartment building in good condition includes all maintenance-free exterior, covered carports, and patio area for tenants. All you pay is water; tenants pay everything else. Good positive cash flow each month. See for yourself! Contact *[Phone Number]* and ask for *[Listing Agent]*. *[Listing Code Number]*
**(Ad #45)**

### Better Than a Money Machine

This six-bay car wash facility is a favorite by many of the locals. Excellent location, and owners always keep area clean. Newly refurbished equipment in car wash bays will provide low maintenance to the new owner. Financial statements are available to qualified buyers. A great buy at only *[List Price]*! For more information, contact *[Listing Agent]* at *[Agency Phone Number]* or visit us on the Web at *[Web Site Address]*. *[Listing Code Number]*
**(Ad #46)**

### Established Business Opportunity Awaiting

This excellent dining establishment *[Local Area]* has been in operation for over seven years. There is a private dining room for local groups and organizations who normally book in advance. *[List Price]*! Call quickly on this one; it's sure to go quick at this price! Call *[Phone Number]* and ask for *[Listing Agent]*. *[Listing Code Number]*
**(Ad #47)**

### Guess Who Is Selling Their Business?

Unfortunately, we cannot give the name in our advertisement but we can provide it to qualified buyers in our office. It's a once-in-a-lifetime opportunity if you're serious about buying your own business. For more information, call *[Listing Agent]* at *[Phone Number]*. *[Listing Code Number]*
*(Ad #48)*

### Turnkey Business Waits for You to Turn the Key

We just listed a bakery and coffee shop with an established customer base. Owners will train and help oversee the operation for as long as you need them too. For a complete portfolio of information, contact *[Listing Agent]* at *[Phone Number]*. *[Listing Code Number]*
*(Ad #52)*

### Living Quarters with This Business Opportunity

Small retail shop with downtown location features complete living quarters upstairs for the new owners. You can also rent out both units for a good positive cash flow. Willing to take less than the appraised price! Call *[Listing Agent]* at *[Phone Number]* to find out more. *[Listing Code Number]*
*(Ad #49)*

### Lonely Business Looking for Someone

This bookstore and coffee shop needs someone to help jump start it with some fresh ideas. Plenty of room for expansion and historic building offers lots of character to someone with an imagination. See for yourself! Contact *[Phone Number]* and ask for *[Listing Agent]*. *[Listing Code Number]*
*(Ad #53)*

### A New Job and New Home

Here's your opportunity to purchase a thriving antique store in the heart of *[Local Area]*. This property comes complete with living quarters upstairs. Located on highly traveled walking street between restaurants will aid in lots of consumer traffic. See for yourself! Contact *[Phone Number]* and ask for *[Listing Agent]*. *[Listing Code Number]*
*(Ad #50)*

### Lonely Business Looking for New Soul Mate

Established furniture store in an excellent location will offer you the satisfaction you've been looking for in a new business. Property includes a large showroom and retail facility plus a big storage facility included across town. In business for over 20 years, you can't go wrong with this investment opportunity. For more information, call *[Phone Number]* and ask for *[Listing Agent]*. *[Listing Code Number]*
*(Ad #54)*

### Finally, Freedom Awaits You

This convenience store provides the current owner with a great monthly income. Turnkey operation includes real estate and all personal property. Priced for immediate sale! Call *[Listing Agent]* at *[Phone Number]* for all of the details! *[Listing Code Number]*
*(Ad #51)*

### All This Business Needs Is a Little TLC

A nice convenience store with gas facilities in prime commercial location offered to a smart investor. Once a thriving commercial cornerstone, this property does need a facelift to attract more customers. *[List Price]*! Call quickly on this one; it's sure to go quick at this price! Call *[Phone Number]* and ask for *[Listing Agent]*. *[Listing Code Number]*
**(Ad #55)**

### Owners Willing to Sell Their Business Secrets

Posh and popular restaurant for sale with excellent clientele in downtown location. Turnkey operation plus owners willing to assist new buyers in anyway. Call *[Listing Agent]* at *[Phone Number]* for all of the details. *[Listing Code Number]*
**(Ad #56)**

### You're Not Only Buying the Restaurant, You're Buying Family Recipes, too!

Due to the confidentiality of this business we are only able to provide information to qualified buyers. Please stop by our office or call *[Listing Agent]* at *[Phone Number]*. *[Listing Code Number]*
**(Ad #57)**

### Everything Is Great about This Business

Great hours, great cash flow, and great opportunity! For more information, contact *[Listing Agent]* at *[Phone Number]*. *[Listing Code Number]*
**(Ad #58)**

### If You're Looking for the Perfect Business for Sale, then Look No Further

Corner convenience mart with gas pumps. Good business clientele and good monthly profits. This is a business to be proud of! To find out more details and for a private e-mail containing a special Web site address with photos, virtual tours, and more, contact *[Listing Agent]* at *[Phone Number]*. *[Listing Code Number]*
**(Ad #59)**

### Go Ahead and Put the Extra Hours in—It's Your Business!

40-unit hotel with all the amenities to bring your guests back time and time again. Great clientele and very profitable. All rooms recently refurbished. Interactive CD-ROM available by contacting *[Listing Agent]* at *[Phone Number]*. *[List Price]*. *[Listing Code Number]*
**(Ad #60)**

### Work Hard Now, Enjoy Life Later!

This rare business opportunity will require a little extra work and a few more hours, but the end result will be well worth the investment. For more information, call *[Listing Agent]* at *[Phone Number]*. *[Listing Code Number]*
**(Ad #61)**

### A Sign of Success Awaits You

Here's an opportunity you don't find very often with an established business and a good reputation for sale. Confidential and qualified financial buyers inquire only. Call *[Listing Agent]* at *[Phone Number]* for all of the details. *[Listing Code Number]*
**(Ad #62)**

### Your Future Success Begins Here

Established men's and ladies' downtown retail clothing store available. Very upscale clientele who demand the best. If this is an opportunity you feel challenged by and would like to invest in, then call *[Listing Agent]* at *[Phone Number]* for all of the details! *[Listing Code Number]*
**(Ad #63)**

### A New Day, a New Opportunity, a New Start!

Here's your chance at a fresh new start with this business. Excellent net income each month will provide the stable and secure environment you desire. Information will only be provided to qualified buyers. Call *[Listing Agent]* at *[Phone Number]* for all of the details! *[Listing Code Number]*
**(Ad #64)**

### Make the Turn Down This Road to Happiness

Established business that incorporates many friends who patronize week after week. Serious inquires only. Excellent return on investment! Call *[Listing Agent]* at *[Phone Number]* for all of the details! *[Listing Code Number]*
**(Ad #65)**

### Collecting Rent Never Felt So Good

16-unit apartment complex is fully occupied; in fact, there has not been an empty unit for over two years! All tenants pay their own utilities, new roof, and most units have had the carpeting replaced in the last few years. Don't pass up this once-in-a-lifetime opportunity. To find out more details and for a private e-mail containing a special Web site address with photos, virtual tours, and more, contact *[Listing Agent]* at *[Phone Number]*. *[Listing Code Number]*
**(Ad #66)**

# Holiday Ads 13

Sometimes it is good to develop theme ads for your real estate listings to create attention. Theme advertisements work well with current events such as holidays, sporting events, movies, and songs. *5 Minutes to a Great Real Estate Ad* has included several categories for theme advertisements. This particular section on holiday advertisements might work well to create attention for your real estate listing. However, one word of caution to the real estate professional is to not go overboard with theme advertisements. Although they may seem funny and cute, it may not be as effective to the consumer. Therefore, I would encourage you to use the theme ads provided in this book on a limited basis.

Hopefully, after reading some of the heading titles for these holiday ads, you will think of a few more you can use throughout your real estate career.

**Valentine's Day Headings**

Sweetheart of a Deal *(Ad #1)*

Tell Your Sweetheart How Much You Love Her *(Ad #2)*

Better than a Box of Chocolates *(Ad #3)*

Better than a Dozen Roses *(Ad #4)*

Better than a Diamond Ring *(Ad #5)*

Tell Her You Love Her *(Ad #6)*

The Perfect Valentine's Gift *(Ad #7)*

A Home to Fall in Love All Over Again *(Ad #8)*

A Pretty Home for Your Pretty Valentine *(Ad #9)*

Cupid's Special *(Ad #10)*

Be My Valentine *(Ad #11)*

With All My Love *(Ad #12)*

Lonely Valentine Needs Perfect Family *(Ad #13)*

**St. Patrick's Day Headings**

It's Your Lucky Day *(Ad #14)*

The Luck of the Irish *(Ad #15)*

Irish Green Already Included *(Ad #16)*

Better than a Pot of Gold *(Ad #17)*

St. Patrick Would Love It *(Ad #18)*

A Lucky Home for a Lucky Couple *(Ad #19)*

We Can't Promise You Irish Luck, but We Can Promise You an Irish Home! *(Ad #20)*

Irish All My Homes Were This Nice *(Ad #21)*

You May Not Find a Pot of Gold, but You Will Find a Great Home *(Ad #22)*

**Fourth of July Headings**

A Popping Good Deal *(Ad #23)*

4th of July Special *(Ad #24)*

Ooh! Ahh! Look at That House *(Ad #25)*

You'll Sparkle with This Home *(Ad #26)*

Sit on the Nice Big Yard and Watch the Fireworks **(Ad #27)**

**Halloween Headings**

Priced So Low, It's Spooky *(Ad #28)*

Put Your Pumpkin on the Porch *(Ad #29)*

This Is No Trick, but It Sure Is a Treat *(Ad #30)*

You'll Be Haunted if You Pass This One By *(Ad #31)*

It's Not the Addams Family Home, but It's Just as Big! *(Ad #32)*

**Thanksgiving Headings**

You'll Be Thankful if You Buy This Home *(Ad #33)*

A Dining Room Even the Pilgrims Would Love *(Ad #34)*

Your Thanksgiving Dinner Will Be So Easy to Host *(Ad #35)*

Thanksgiving Gatherings Will Go Great *(Ad #36)*

**Christmas Headings**

Great Place to Hang Your Stockings *(Ad #37)*

All This Home Needs for Christmas Is You! *(Ad #38)*

We'll Help You Put the Ribbon and Bow on This Home for Your Family *(Ad #39)*

A Great Way to Start the New Year *(Ad #40)*

Just in Time for Christmas! *(Ad #41)*

A Christmas to Always Remember *(Ad #42)*

You Will Need Plenty of Exterior Christmas Lights *(Ad #43)*

Rumor Has It This Is Santa's Favorite Christmas Stop *(Ad #44)*

Joy to the World *(Ad #45)*

Rockin' around the Christmas Tree *(Ad #46)*

There's a Chimney for Santa *(Ad #47)*

Merry Christmas! It's Your Lucky Day *(Ad #48)*

Santa May Stop and Look Around at This BIG Home *(Ad #49)*

**April Fool's Day Headings**

Don't Be Fooled by This Price *(Ad #50)*

This Is No April Fool's Joke *(Ad #51)*

We'll Tell the Appraiser This Is Not an April Fool's Joke *(Ad #52)*

We'll Tell Your Lender This Is Not an April Fool's Prank *(Ad #53)*

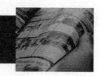

### Sweetheart of a Deal

Gracious and stately *[#Bedrooms]* bedroom/ *[#Baths]* bath *[Style of Home]* home on 16 acres. Features a large parlor with fireplace, and a formal dining room with built-in china cabinet and hutch, along with an open staircase in foyer. For a private tour, call *[Listing Agent]* at *[Phone Number]* or e-mail *[Listing Agent]* at *[Listing Agent E-mail]*. *[Listing Code Number]*
***(Ad #1)***

### Tell Your Sweetheart How Much You Love Her

by investing in this exquisite *[#Bedrooms]* bedroom/*[#Baths]* bath condominium. Many upgrades are found throughout this home, including walls framed by wood moldings. A great buy at only *[List Price]*! For more information, contact *[Listing Agent]* at *[Phone Number]* or visit us on the Web at *[Web Site Address]*. *[Listing Code Number]*
***(Ad #2)***

### Better than a Box of Chocolates

This Mediterranean style *[#Bedrooms]* bedroom/*[#Baths]* bath home has a cobbled courtyard with lovely wild flowers as a backdrop. It has all the flare you've been looking for, including a large eat-in kitchen with newly installed cabinets, granite countertops, and fireplace in the living room. A real charmer! For a private tour, call *[Listing Agent]* at *[Phone Number]* or you can e-mail *[Listing Agent]* at *[Listing Agent E-mail]*. *[Listing Code Number]*
***(Ad #3)***

### Better than a Dozen Roses

*[#Bedrooms]* bedroom/*[#Baths]* bath *[Style of Home]* home. Floor-to-ceiling casement windows provide a dramatic backdrop in this open and spacious living room. *[Feature 1]*, *[Feature 2]*, and *[Feature 3]* also adorn this gorgeous home. Priced to sell! Let *[Listing Agent]* show you this lovely listing today. Call *[Phone Number]* to schedule your appointment. *[Listing Code Number]*
***(Ad #4)***

### Better than a Diamond Ring

You'll ooh and aah as you approach this stately home from its lengthy paved tree-lined driveway. Every attention to detail has been included in this *[# of Square Feet]* sq. ft. showplace. The circular drive in front of the home greets you with fountains, flowers, and scrubs. The rear of the home features several patios, more flowers, and an Olympic size in-ground swimming pool. Full finished basement, culinary kitchen to die for, and so much more! CD-ROM is available with photos, floor plan, and virtual tours. For more information, call *[Listing Agent]* at *[Phone Number]*. *[Listing Code Number]*
***(Ad #5)***

### Tell Her You Love Her

There's plenty of room on this 10-acre parcel, complete with a small barn and two stalls. Lovely [#Bedrooms] bedroom/[#Baths] bath [Style of Home] home with family room, finished basement, and more. A great opportunity at [List Price]. Call [Listing Agent] at [Phone Number] for more information. [Listing Code Number]
*(Ad #6)*

### The Perfect Valentine's Gift

This home has everything you could imagine! Two bowling lanes in the basement, large billiard room with other recreational activities, plus a private movie theater! Passionate cooks will love this kitchen with all the extra amenities. A great buy at only [List Price]! For more information contact [Listing Agent] at [Agency Phone Number] or visit us on the Web at [Web Site Address]. [Listing Code Number]
*(Ad #7)*

### A Home to Fall in Love All Over Again

Believe it or not, this [# of Square Feet] sq. ft. estate was patterned after a castle seen in Europe. Features [#Bedrooms] bedrooms and [#Baths] baths, and large open veranda with stone walls and arches for breathtaking views of the countryside. Would make ideal bed and breakfast facility. Enormous living room with massive stone fireplace and beamed ceilings. This is truly a one-of-a-kind estate. Interactive CD-ROM available by contacting [Listing Agent] at [Phone Number]. [Listing Code Number]
*(Ad #8)*

### A Pretty Home for Your Pretty Valentine

A magnificent [Style of Home] home with spectacular stained glass windows adjoining the foyer. There's a screened-in back porch that's perfect for entertaining on summer evenings. Every room has a warm and cozy feeling. Call [Listing Agent] at [Phone Number] for all of the details. [Listing Code Number]
*(Ad #9)*

### Cupid's Special

With a large in-ground swimming pool, tennis courts, and a walking track, you'll enjoy living at [Name of Condo Development]. This condo offers [#Bedrooms] bedrooms and [#Baths] baths with a 2-car attached garage. Call today before it is too late! Ask for [Listing Agent] at [Phone Number]. [Listing Code Number]
*(Ad #10)*

### Be My Valentine

It's not often we find a home to sell that's nestled among the trees with a cobblestone brook nearby! You'll appreciate the attention to detail the original builder put into the woodwork and trim. An absolute gorgeous setting! Sure to go quick at this low price! Extra features included are [Feature 1], [Feature 2], and [Feature 3]. For more information, call [Listing Agent] at [Phone Number]. [Listing Code Number]
*(Ad #11)*

### With All My Love

This *[Style of Home]* has over *[# of Square Feet]* square feet of living area, complete with full finished basement. Master bath includes his and her walk-in closets, and Mediterranean tile in the kitchen with granite countertops make this a real "one of a kind!" Call *[Listing Agent]* at *[Phone Number]* for all of the details. *[Listing Code Number]*

**(Ad #12)**

### Lonely Valentine Needs Perfect Family

This *[# of Square Feet]* sq. ft. two-story French provincial home includes everything you would demand for upscale living. Wall-length bookshelves provide a dramatic backdrop to the family room. Gorgeous enclosed sunroom off back overlooks wooded backyard and pool and patio area. Also features *[Feature 1]*, *[Feature 2]*, and *[Feature 3]*. Let *[Listing Agent]* show you this lovely listing today. Call *[Phone Number]* to schedule your appointment. *[Listing Code Number]*

**(Ad #13)**

### It's Your Lucky Day

with this *[#Bedrooms]* bedroom/*[#Baths]* bath *[Style of Home]* home on six acres. You'll find plenty of large shade trees for rest and relaxation. Don't delay on this one! It's priced to move at *[List Price]*. Call *[Listing Agent]* to arrange a showing at *[Phone Number]*. *[Listing Code Number]*

**(Ad #14)**

### The Luck of the Irish

Great opportunity with this commercial building. Features *[# of Square Feet]* square feet for retail or office with a live-in *[#Bedrooms]* bedroom apartment above. Save time and money by combining home and work in one payment. *[List Price]*! Call quickly on this one; it's sure to go quick at this price! Call *[Phone Number]* and ask for *[Listing Agent]*. *[Listing Code Number]*

**(Ad #15)**

### Irish Green Already Included

This two-story English tudor home has been completely refurbished and updated to every modern convenience. Kitchen has large walk-in pantry that is accented by a large breakfast nook overlooking the back patio and grounds. Full finished basement with big screen television and surround sound stereo provide the perfect backdrop for the kids and their friends. Extra features included are *[Feature 1]*, *[Feature 2]*, and *[Feature 3]*. Why just read about it when you can see it in person? Call *[Listing Agent]* at *[Phone Number]* to preview this listing today. *[Listing Code Number]*

**(Ad #16)**

### Better than a Pot of Gold

This *[#Bedrooms]* bedroom/*[#Baths]* bath home would make the perfect bed and breakfast. Features a fireplace in every bedroom, large country kitchen recently updated with granite countertops, and wide pine flooring with walk-in pantry. All woodwork restored to its original condition. For more information, call *[Listing Agent]* at *[Phone Number]*. *[Listing Code Number]*

**(Ad #17)**

### St. Patrick Would Love It

and so will you, with all the great amenities this condo has to offer. Features whirlpool tub, walk-in closets, gourmet kitchen, and more! A great buy for the money! Call *[Listing Agent]* today to schedule a showing. Call *[Phone Number]*. *[Listing Code Number]*
*(Ad #18)*

### A Lucky Home for a Lucky Couple

This charming *[#Bedrooms]* bedroom/*[#Baths]* bath bungalow is a dollhouse! Fresh herbs await your picking off the rock patio. Large kitchen with nook area, pantry, and more. Just listed! Call quickly on this one! Call *[Phone Number]* and ask for *[Listing Agent]*. *[Listing Code Number]*
*(Ad #19)*

### We Can't Promise You Irish Luck, but We Can Promise You an Irish Home

This *[#Bedrooms]* bedroom/*[#Baths]* bath home sits on an oversized lot in town. Large eat-in kitchen leads out to a screened-in porch area that's ideal for summer dining. Arched windows in family room give a dramatic look both inside and outside this home. For more information, call *[Listing Agent]* at *[Phone Number]*. *[Listing Code Number]*
*(Ad #20)*

### Irish All My Homes Were This Nice

English tudor is nestled on a three-acre parcel of land in *[Subdivision Name]*. Features large kitchen with nook, sitting room, and stone fireplace in master suite. Powder room, walk-in closets, and a full finished basement with home theater. For more information, call *[Listing Agent]* at *[Phone Number]*. *[Listing Code Number]*
*(Ad #21)*

### You May Not Find a Pot of Gold, but You Will Find a Great Home

This 15-acre listing includes a *[#Bedrooms]* bedroom/*[#Baths]* bath *[Style of Home]* farmhouse. Constructed at the turn of the century, you'll find one-of-a-kind craftsmanship with built-in bookcases, china cabinets, and French doors. A real showplace and priced at *[List Price]*. Call *[Listing Agent]* at *[Phone Number]* to arrange a showing or visit this property online at *[Web Site Address]*. *[Listing Code Number]*
*(Ad #22)*

### A Popping Good Deal

Pamper yourself with all the extras this *[Style of Home]* home has to offer! *[#Bedrooms]* bedrooms/*[#Baths]* baths are only the beginning that you'll find when you visit this charming retreat. Extra features included are *[Feature 1]*, *[Feature 2]*, and *[Feature 3]*. Why just read about it when you can see it in person? Call *[Listing Agent]* at *[Phone Number]* to preview this listing today. *[Listing Code Number]*
*(Ad #23)*

### 4th of July Special

We couldn't believe how many fireplaces this *[#Bedrooms]* bedroom/*[#Baths]* bath home had. There are seven fireplaces located throughout this new listing. Beautiful mantels and brickwork accompany each fireplace. State-of-the-art kitchen has been completely remodeled, central air-conditioning, new wiring, and so much more. You can't go wrong with this new home! See for yourself! Call *[Listing Agent]* at *[Phone Number]* for a private showing today. *[Listing Code Number]*
***(Ad #24)***

### Ooh! Ahh! Look at That House

This *[#Bedrooms]* bedroom/*[#Baths]* bath bungalow has been the home to only one owner and has offered many enjoyable holidays for this family. Large dining room adjoins formal living room with fireplace and floor-to-ceiling built-in bookcases. *[Feature 1]* and *[Feature 2]*. See for yourself! Call *[Phone Number]* and ask for *[Listing Agent]*. *[Listing Code Number]*
***(Ad #25)***

### You'll Sparkle with This Home

No grass to mow, no snow to shovel, no windows to wash. With this home located at *[Name of Condo Development]*, you'll have easy access to golf. For a private tour, call *[Listing Agent]* at *[Phone Number]* or e-mail *[Listing Agent]* at *[Listing Agent E-mail]*. *[Listing Code Number]*
***(Ad #26)***

### Sit on the Nice Big Yard and Watch the Fireworks

*[#Bedrooms]* bedroom/*[#Baths]* bath home with all of the extras you would expect in a grand estate. Features open foyer with winding staircase, private study area with fireplace, three-car garage, and full finished basement. A great buy at only *[List Price]*! For more information, contact *[Listing Agent]* at *[Phone Number]* or visit us on the Web at *[Web Site Address]*. *[Listing Code Number]*
***(Ad #27)***

### Priced So Low, It's Spooky!

This two-story home is only three years old and features many upgrades and extras you won't find available in other homes on the market. Large open great room views upstairs loft, beamed ceilings, and culinary kitchen with soap stone countertops and oak cabinets. You'll be sorry if you let this opportunity pass you by! For a private tour, call *[Listing Agent]* at *[Phone Number]* or e-mail *[Listing Agent]* at *[Listing Agent E-mail]*. *[Listing Code Number]*
***(Ad #28)***

### Put Your Pumpkin on the Porch

Here's a lovely large wrap-around front porch you don't find with many homes for sale today. You'll also discover a flag stone patio with a rock walkway through the flower gardens. The inside has been restored and kept to the look of its original condition. You'll be amazed at how well this home shows. Newly listed and priced to move quick! Call *[Listing Agent]* at *[Phone Number]*. *[Listing Code Number]*
***(Ad #29)***

### This Is No Trick, but It Sure Is a Treat

This 8-unit apartment building can help provide excellent income for your future retirement. All units feature two bedrooms, two baths, living and dining rooms, and kitchen. Carport facilities for each unit. Detailed fact sheet with expenses and income available to qualified buyers. Call *[Listing Agent]* at *[Phone Number]* for all of the details. *[Listing Code Number]*
*(Ad #30)*

### You'll Be Haunted if You Pass This One By

This *[# of Square Feet]* sq. ft. home includes a little bit of everything you would want in your next home. Dazzling enclosed sunroom off back overlooks wooded backyard and pool and patio area. Also features *[Feature 1]*, *[Feature 2]*, and *[Feature 3]*. Let *[Listing Agent]* show you this lovely listing today. Call *[Phone Number]* to schedule your appointment. *[Listing Code Number]*
*(Ad #31)*

### It's Not the Addams Family Home, but It's Just as Big!

I'm sure we would hear stories since it's over 150 years old. Enormous formal dining room with a large chandelier will make every entertaining opportunity a joy. Spacious foyer, many updates added to home, and detached garage and workshop are just a few of the extras you'll find in this new listing. *[List Price]*! Call quickly on this one; it's sure to go quick at this price! Call *[Phone Number]* and ask for *[Listing Agent]*. *[Listing Code Number]*
*(Ad #32)*

### You'll Be Thankful if You Buy This Home

This *[#Bedrooms]* bedroom/*[#Baths]* bath home contains many special extras like a formal dining room, master bath and suite, screened-in porch, and more. It's a great place to call home and it is affordably priced. Call *[Listing Agent]* at *[Phone Number]* for all of the details. *[Listing Code Number]*
*(Ad #33)*

### A Dining Room Even the Pilgrims Would Love

Only one proud owner has enjoyed the comfort and warmth they're now offering to you. *[Feature 1]*, *[Feature 2]*, and *[Feature]*. Features a large open dining room with ten-foot ceilings along with a large fireplace and pocket doors that lead to a separate sitting area. Let *[Listing Agent]* show you this lovely listing and all of the charm and character it has to offer. Call *[Phone Number]* to schedule your appointment. *[Listing Code Number]*
*(Ad #34)*

### Your Thanksgiving Dinner Will Be So Easy to Host

in this *[#Bedrooms]* bedroom/*[#Baths]* bath home with over *[# of Square Feet]* square feet of lush living space. Exotic finished basement with private screening room, wet bar, rec. room, sleeping quarters, and in-ground swimming pool with hot tub nearby. For a private tour, call *[Listing Agent]* at *[Phone Number]* or e-mail *[Listing Agent]* at *[Listing Agent E-mail]*. *[Listing Code Number]*
*(Ad #35)*

### Thanksgiving Gatherings Will Go Great

in this *[#Bedrooms]* bedroom/*[#Baths]* bath *[Style of Home]* farmhouse on a 40-acre parcel of real estate. Features a large country kitchen, walk-in pantry, and screened-in porch off the side. It's hard to find anything as nice as this and it's only been on the market for a short time. Call *[Listing Agent]* at *[Phone Number]* for a private showing today. *[Listing Code Number]*
*(Ad #36)*

### Great Place to Hang Your Stockings

This *[Style of Home]* home has always been an eye catcher as people drive down *[Street Address]*. Features *[#Bedrooms]* bedrooms and *[#Baths]* baths, formal living and dining rooms, chef's kitchen with all new appliances, granite countertops, and more. You'll love this home! Why just read about it when you can see it in person? Call *[Listing Agent]* at *[Phone Number]* to preview this listing today. *[Listing Code Number]*
*(Ad #37)*

### All This Home Needs for Christmas Is You

Lots of extras are included with this *[Style of Home]* home we just listed including over *[# of Square Feet]*. Open foyer includes a winding staircase that leads to an upper sitting room. Features *[#Bedrooms]* bedrooms/*[#Baths]* baths and so much more. The vaulted ceiling in the great room will be perfect for your Christmas tree! Call *[Listing Agent]* at *[Phone Number]* for more information. *[Listing Code Number]*
*(Ad #38)*

### We'll Help You Put the Ribbon and Bow on This Home for Your Family

This *[#Bedrooms]* bedroom/*[#Baths]* bath bungalow features a large kitchen with breakfast nook, overlooking patio, and flower gardens in the backyard. There's a small den that could be used as an additional bedroom or computer room. See for yourself how tidy this home is. Call *[Phone Number]* and ask for *[Listing Agent]*. *[Listing Code Number]*
*(Ad #39)*

### A Great Way to Start the New Year

This *[# of Square Feet]* sq. ft. *[Style of Home]* home features all of the fine qualities you demand for upscale living. Top-of-the-line appliances, along with large walk-in pantry. Keeping room nearby with river stone fireplace for cozy winter evenings. You'll also find a large screened-in porch for summer dining and a finished basement with billiard room. This home is a must see! Interactive CD-ROM available by contacting *[Listing Agent]* at *[Phone Number]*. *[Listing Code Number]*
*(Ad #40)*

### Just in Time for Christmas!

This *[#Bedrooms]* bedroom/*[#Baths]* bath home on 20 acres with plenty of cedar and pine trees for your Christmas decor. Private walking trail, workshop, full finished basement, and covered patio make up small portion of the many additions this mini-farm has to offer. Listed for sale at only *[List Price]*! *[Listing Agent]* is ready to show you this property at your convenience. Call *[Phone Number]*. *[Listing Code Number]*
*(Ad #41)*

### A Christmas to Always Remember

*[# of Square Feet]* sq. ft., along with *[#Bedrooms]* bedrooms and *[#Baths]* baths provides an array of natural light almost any time of the day in this *[Style of Home]* home. Enter the stunning oversized kitchen and you'll immediately be drawn to the mile-high hood vent over the commercial grade gas range. For a private tour, call *[Listing Agent]* at *[Phone Number]* or e-mail *[Listing Agent]* at *[Listing Agent E-mail]*. *[Listing Code Number]*
**(Ad #42)**

### You Will Need Plenty of Exterior Christmas Lights

with this *[Style of Home]* home featuring a lovely wooded lot and wrap-around porch to enjoy the fresh air during spring, summer, and fall evenings. Beautiful open staircase with original woodwork greets your guests in the formal foyer. Italian marble floors wind throughout the biggest portion of the downstairs. Features *[#Bedrooms]* bedrooms and *[#Baths]* baths, and is ready for immediate occupancy. A great buy at only *[List Price]*! For more information, contact *[Listing Agent]* at *[Agency Phone Number]* or visit us on the Web at *[Web Site Address]*. *[Listing Code Number]*
**(Ad #43)**

### Rumor Has It This Is Santa's Favorite Christmas Stop

Immaculate *[# of Square Feet]* sq. ft. *[Style of Home]* home. Features a unique open floor plan with vaulted ceilings and vintage style windows. Gorgeous patio area with swimming pool and hot tub area. Oversized laundry facility with built-in desk and cabinets that doubles for a computer room. Full finished basement, wine cellar, and much more. Call *[Listing Agent]* at *[Phone Number]* for all of the details. *[Listing Code Number]*
**(Ad #44)**

### Joy to the World

Angled door frames and open beams provide a look and feel that is unmatched with this new listing. This *[#Bedrooms]* bedroom/*[#Baths]* bath also features a lovely stone entry foyer, *[Feature 1]*, *[Feature 2]*, and *[Feature 3]*. A real dollhouse and priced for a quick sale. Call *[Phone Number]* and ask for *[Listing Agent]*. *[Listing Code Number]*
**(Ad #45)**

### Rockin' around the Christmas Tree

Here's a *[# of Square Feet]* square foot home with dozens of amenities too numerous to mention. Keeping room with cooking hearth provides the perfect backdrop for the large kitchen with center island rectangular field tiles and cherry wood cabinets. Full finished basement, too! There's even a separate workshop area off the back of the garage. Call *[Listing Agent]* at *[Phone Number]* for all of the details. *[Listing Code Number]*
**(Ad #46)**

### There's a Chimney for Santa

Dormer windows peak out from a steeply tiled roof with this *[#Bedrooms]* bedroom/ *[#Baths]* bath *[Style of Home]* home. A romantic and exciting entrance welcomes you as you drive up the lengthy stove paved roadway. You'll appreciate the detail to every minute part of this home. Spectacular kitchen cabinetry appliqués, and mosaic tile and woodwork throughout home. Nothing has been missed! You must see this one for yourself to fully appreciate. Contact *[Phone Number]* and ask for *[Listing Agent]* for more information. *[Listing Code Number]*
**(Ad #47)**

### Merry Christmas! It's Your Lucky Day

This *[# of Square Feet]* sq. ft. *[Style of Home]* home features *[#Bedrooms]* bedrooms and *[#Baths]* baths. Boxed hedges line the front of this grand estate with vast windows that provide lots of afternoon sunlight. There's a covered pavilion with grill and wet bar and an outdoor fireplace to entertain guests and family. A home to be proud of! A great buy at only *[List Price]*! For more information, contact *[Listing Agent]* at *[Phone Number]* or visit us on the Web at *[Web Site Address]*. *[Listing Code Number]*
**(Ad #48)**

### Santa May Stop and Look Around at This BIG Home

*[#Bedrooms]* bedroom/ *[#Baths]* bath *[Style of Home]* with over *[# of Square Feet]* sq. ft.? You heard right! Listen to some of these extra amenities included with this home: *[Feature 1]*, *[Feature 2]*, and *[Feature 3]*. You can read and see all about it by clicking on "Home of the Week" on our Web site at *[Web Site Address]*. You can also call *[Listing Agent]* at *[Phone Number]* for more information. *[Listing Code Number]*
**(Ad #49)**

### Don't Be Fooled by This Price

First time offered for sale! This two-story Georgian farmhouse has been completely renovated with posh and elegance. Features spacious rooms and large eat-in kitchen with nook. For your enjoyment, there's also an in-ground pool with hot tub area flanked by a gorgeous rock patio. Priced at only *[List Price]*! Why just read about it when you can see it in person? Call *[Listing Agent]* at *[Phone Number]* to preview this listing today. *[Listing Code Number]*
**(Ad #50)**

### This Is No April Fool's Joke

There's 60 wooded acres to explore with this *[#Bedrooms]* bedroom/*[#Baths]* bath *[Style of Home]* home. Two fireplaces, finished family room in basement, and screened-in porch in the back for summer dining and visits with friends. An absolute treat and priced at only *[List Price]*! You can view this property online at *[Web Site Address]* or call *[Listing Agent]* at *[Phone Number]* for more information. *[Listing Code Number]*
**(Ad #51)**

### We'll Tell the Appraiser This Is Not an April Fool's Joke

We just listed a *[#Bedrooms]* bedroom/*[#Baths]* bath *[Style of Home]* with over *[# of Square Feet]* sq. ft. Lovely kitchen with center island and sink. Features a large master suite with double closets, full finished basement and *[Feature 1]*, *[Feature 2]*, and *[Feature 3]*. For more information, call *[Listing Agent]* at *[Phone Number]*. *[Listing Code Number]*
**(Ad #52)**

**We'll Tell Your Lender This Is Not an April Fool's Prank**

This *[#Bedrooms]* bedroom/*[#Baths]* bath bungalow with stenciled box-beamed ceilings sits on a quiet corner lot with large shade trees. Also boast *[Feature 1]*, *[Feature 2]*, and a huge country kitchen with pantry. A great buy at only *[List Price]*! For more information, contact *[Listing Agent]* at *[Phone Number]* or visit us on the Web at *[Web Site Address]*. *[Listing Code Number]*
**(Ad #53)**

# Sports-Related Ads 14

Sometimes it is good to take a different approach for advertising. One way to do that is through "theme advertising." Sporting events and sporting activities are a good way to accomplish this type of advertising. Normally, you might want to use these types of headings or slogans around a major sporting event such as the Super Bowl, World Series, Final Four, or some event that is creating a lot of national media attention throughout the week. I have included several examples of sporting-type headings in this chapter you might consider to use in your advertising. Again, these are only optional-type ads and more than anything they are included in the text for you to think about, consider, and hopefully get your creative juices moving so you may consider other types of alternative advertising ideas to create a buzz and recognition in your marketplace.

# Sample Headings

Shoot, Score, and You're a Winner *(Ad #1)*

Buy This Home and You Will Score the Perfect Game *(Ad #2)*

Three Strikes and You're Out! *(Ad #3)*

If You Don't Call on This Home Today, You're Out! *(Ad #4)*

Catch a Winner When You Buy This Home *(Ad #5)*

Trophy Catch *(Ad #6)*

A Grand Slam Any Way You Look at It *(Ad #7)*

It's a Touchdown for the Home Team When You Buy This Property *(Ad #8)*

Don't Strike Out—Buy This One Today *(Ad #9)*

Match Point with This Home *(Ad #10)*

Kick Off the Football Season in a New Family Room *(Ad # 11)*

Better than a Hole-in-One *(Ad #12)*

It's Like Scoring a Hole-in-One *(Ad #13)*

There's No Throwing This Fish Out *(Ad #14)*

Checkmate—You Have Found the Perfect Home *(Ad #15)*

Fore! A Great Deal Is Coming Your Way *(Ad #16)*

The Perfect Place for Your Next Super Bowl Party *(Ad #17)*

A Checkered Flag Is Waiting for You *(Ad #18)*

It's a Yellow Caution Flag but Only if You Pass This Deal By *(Ad #19)*

This Is Not a Foul Ball—It's a HOMERUN! *(Ad #20)*

### Shoot, Score, and You're a Winner

Gracious and stately *[#Bedrooms]* bedroom/ *[#Baths]* bath *[Style of Home]* home on 16 acres. Features a large parlor with fireplace, formal dining room with built-in china cabinet and hutch, along with an open staircase in foyer. For a private tour, call *[Listing Agent]* at *[Phone Number]* or e-mail *[Listing Agent]* at *[Listing Agent E-mail]*. *[Listing Code Number]* **(Ad #1)**

### Buy This Home and You Will Score the Perfect Game

by investing in this exquisite *[#Bedrooms]* bedroom/*[#Baths]* bath condominium. Many upgrades are found throughout this home including walls framed by wood moldings. A great buy at only *[List Price]*. For more information, contact *[Listing Agent]* at *[Phone Number]* or visit us on the Web at *[Web Site Address]*. *[Listing Code Number]* **(Ad #2)**

### Three Strikes and You're Out!

This Mediterranean style *[#Bedrooms]* bedroom/*[#Baths]* bath home has a cobbled courtyard with lovely wild flowers as a backdrop. It has all the flare you've been looking for, including a large eat-in kitchen with newly installed cabinets, granite countertops, and a fireplace in the living room. A real charmer! For a private tour, call *[Listing Agent]* at *[Phone Number]* or e-mail *[Listing Agent]* at *[Listing Agent E-mail]*. *[Listing Code Number]* **(Ad #3)**

### If You Don't Call on This Home Today, You're Out!

If so, we've got the perfect home for your family. Floor-to-ceiling casement windows provide a dramatic backdrop in this open and spacious living room. *[#Bedrooms]* bedroom/ *[#Baths]* bath home. *[Style of Home]* *[Feature 1]*, *[Feature 2]*, and *[Feature 3]* also adorn this gorgeous home. Priced to sell! Let *[Listing Agent]* show you this lovely listing today. Call *[Phone Number]* to schedule your appointment. *[Listing Code Number]* **(Ad #4)**

### Catch a Winner When You Buy This Home

You'll ooh and aah as you approach this stately home from its lengthy paved tree-lined driveway. Every attention to detail has been included in this *[# of Square Feet]* sq. ft. showplace. The circular drive in front of the home greets you with fountains, flowers, and scrubs. The rear of the home features several patios, more flowers, and an Olympic size in-ground swimming pool. Full finished basement, culinary kitchen to die for, and so much more! CD-ROM is available with photos, floor plan, and virtual tours. For more information, call *[Listing Agent]* at *[Phone Number]*. *[Listing Code Number]* **(Ad #5)**

### Trophy Catch

There's plenty of room on this 10-acre parcel, complete with a small barn and two stalls. Lovely *[#Bedrooms]* bedroom/*[#Baths]* bath *[Style of Home]* home with family room, finished basement, and more. A great opportunity at *[List Price]*. Call *[Listing Agent]* at *[Phone Number]* for more information. *[Listing Code Number]*
*(Ad #6)*

### A Grand Slam Any Way You Look at It

Four-unit apartment building completely refurbished. Tenants pay all utilities and a great cash flow. See for yourself! Contact *[Phone Number]* and ask for *[Listing Agent]*. *[Listing Code Number]*
*(Ad #7)*

### It's a Touchdown for the Home Team When You Buy This Property

A magnificent *[#Bedrooms]* bedroom/*[#Baths]* bath *[Style of Home]* home with spectacular stained glass windows adjoining the foyer. There's a screened back porch that's perfect for entertaining on summer evenings. Every room has a warm and cozy feeling. Call *[Listing Agent]* at *[Phone Number]* for all of the details. *[Listing Code Number]*
*(Ad #8)*

### Don't Strike Out—Buy This One Today

With a large in-ground swimming pool, tennis courts, and a walking track, you'll enjoy living at *[Name of Condo Development]*. This condo offers *[#Bedrooms]* bedrooms and *[#Baths]* baths with a 2-car attached garage. Call today before it is too late. Ask for *[Listing Agent]* at *[Phone Number]*. *[Listing Code Number]*
*(Ad #9)*

### Match Point with This Home

It's not often we find a home to sell that's nestled among the tress with a cobblestone brook nearby! You'll appreciate the attention to detail the original builder put into the woodwork and trim. An absolute gorgeous setting! Sure to go quick at this low price! Extra features included are *[Feature 1]*, *[Feature 2]*, and *[Feature 3]*. For more information, call *[Listing Agent]* at *[Phone Number]*. *[Listing Code Number]*
*(Ad #10)*

### Kick Off the Football Season in a New Family Room

We don't know if that's a good thing or not but this home is so big you can live in separate areas if you choose! Over *[# of Square Feet]* sq. ft. of living area, complete with full finished basement. Master bath includes his and her walk-in closets, and Mediterranean tile in the kitchen with granite countertops make this a real "one of a kind!" Call *[Listing Agent]* at *[Phone Number]* for all of the details. *[Listing Code Number]*
*(Ad #11)*

### Better than a Hole-in-One

This *[# of Square Feet]* sq. ft., two-story French provincial home includes everything you would demand for upscale living. Wall-length bookshelves provide a dramatic backdrop to the family room. Gorgeous enclosed sunroom off back overlooks wooded backyard and pool and patio area. Also features *[Feature 1]*, *[Feature 2]*, and *[Feature 3]*. Let *[Listing Agent]* show you this lovely listing today. Call *[Phone Number]* to schedule your appointment. *[Listing Code Number]*
*(Ad #12)*

### It's Like Scoring a Hole-in-One

and then some, with this *[#Bedrooms]* bedroom/*[#Baths]* bath *[Style of Home]* home on six acres. You'll find plenty of large shade trees for rest and relaxation. Don't delay on this one! It's priced to move at *[List Price]*. Call *[Listing Agent]* to arrange a showing at *[Phone Number]*. *[Listing Code Number]*
*(Ad #13)*

### There's No Throwing This Fish Out

Great opportunity with commercial building. Features *[# of Square Feet]* sq. ft. for retail or office with a live-in *[#Bedrooms]* bedroom apartment above. Save time and money by combining home and work in one payment. *[List Price]*! Call quickly on this one; it's sure to go quick at this price! Call *[Phone Number]* and ask for *[Listing Agent]*. *[Listing Code Number]*
*(Ad #14)*

### Checkmate—You Have Found the Perfect Home

This *[#Bedrooms]* bedroom/*[#Baths]* bath home would make the perfect bed and breakfast. Features a fireplace in every bedroom, large country kitchen recently updated with granite countertops, and wide pine flooring with walk-in pantry. All woodwork restored to its original condition. For more information, call *[Listing Agent]* at *[Phone Number]*. *[Listing Code Number]*
*(Ad #15)*

### Fore! A Great Deal Is Coming Your Way

with all the great amenities this condo has to offer. Features whirlpool tub, walk-in closets, gourmet kitchen, and more! A great buy for the money! Call *[Listing Agent]* today to schedule a showing. Call *[Phone Number]*. *[Listing Code Number]*
*(Ad #16)*

### The Perfect Place for Your Next Super Bowl Party

This charming *[#Bedrooms]* bedroom/ *[#Baths]* bath bungalow is a dollhouse! Fresh herbs await your picking off the rock patio. Large kitchen with nook area, pantry, and more. Just listed! Call quickly on this one! Call *[Phone Number]* and ask for *[Listing Agent]*. *[Listing Code Number]*
*(Ad #17)*

### A Checkered Flag Is Waiting for You

This *[#Bedrooms]* bedroom/*[#Baths]* bath home sits on an oversized lot in town. Large eat-in kitchen leads out to a screened-in porch area that's ideal for summer dining. Arched windows in family room give a dramatic look both inside and outside this home. For more information, call *[Listing Agent]* at *[Phone Number]*. *[Listing Code Number]*
**(Ad #18)**

### It's a Yellow Caution Flag but Only If You Pass This Deal By

English tudor is nestled on a three-acre parcel of land in *[Subdivision Name]*. Features large kitchen with nook, sitting room, and stone fireplace in master suite. Powder room, walk-in closets, and a full finished basement with home theater. For more information, call *[Listing Agent]* at *[Phone Number]*. *[Listing Code Number]*
**(Ad #19)**

### This Is Not a Foul Ball—It's a HOMERUN!

This 15-acre listing includes a *[#Bedrooms]* bedroom/*[#Baths]* bath *[Style of Home]* farmhouse. Constructed at the turn of the century, you'll find one-of-a-kind craftsmanship with built-in bookcases, china cabinets, and French doors. A real showplace and priced at *[List Price]*. Call *[Listing Agent]* at *[Phone Number]* to arrange a showing or visit this property online at *[Web Site Address]*. *[Listing Code Number]*
**(Ad #20)**

# Price Reductions  15

Occasionally some real estate listings do not sell as quickly as planned. When this happens many real estate sellers are forced to lower (adjust) their sales price downward to meet the equilibrium price for supply and demand. Normally the advertisement you have written works well for the property but now using a new heading to attract the readers attention is focused to the new price adjustment. This section contains previously written ads found throughout the book with the new "price reduction" headings. Keep in mind that you can use "any" ad found in the book where fitting for homes and substitute the heading with a price reduced heading from this chapter if you have a home and a newly adjust price.

It's important as real estate agents to oversee our listing inventory and recommend to our clients the need for reducing their list price if the property is seeing little activity or interest. Once you receive the price reduction from your clients, you can incorporate one of the ads from this section and it will help result in a sale. Good luck!

Just Reduced! *(Ad #1)*

For Sale at a Discount! *(Ad #2)*

30% Off *(Ad #3)*

March Madness *(Ad #4)*

Reduced, Reduced, Reduced *(Ad #5)*

Better than Half Price *(Ad #6)*

It's a Steal! *(Ad #7)*

You're Right, This Is a Steal! *(Ad #8)*

Bargain Bungalow *(Ad #9)*

Owner Says Sale! *(Ad #10)*

We Told the Owners It's Worth More than This *(Ad #11)*

Midnight Madness Sale *(Ad #12)*

Owners Say It's Okay to Offer at a Discount *(Ad #13)*

Hurry Before This One Is Gone *(Ad #14)*

Price Slashed! *(Ad #15)*

Hurry! This Won't Last Long *(Ad #16)*

There Is Nothing Wrong with This Home—The Owners Just Said Sell It Quick! *(Ad #17)*

Priced Below Market Value *(Ad #18)*

Instant Equity When You Buy This Home *(Ad #19)*

A Price to Be Happy with *(Ad #20)*

Your Appraiser Will Flip Out *(Ad #21)*

Deal of a Lifetime *(Ad #22)*

Deal of the Century *(Ad #23)*

Better than Being on *Wheel of Fortune* *(Ad #24)*

Unbelievable Price Reduction! *(Ad #25)*

Two for the Price of One *(Ad #26)*

Two for One at a Great Price *(Ad #27)*

What a Deal! *(Ad #28)*

It's Your Lucky Day *(Ad #29)*

Better than Winning the Lottery *(Ad #30)*

Here's Your Christmas Gift—I Hope It's Okay We Left the Price Tag On, Because It's a Great Deal *(Ad #31)*

Red Tag Special *(Ad #32)*

Blue Light Special *(Ad #33)*

Falling Price *(Ad #34)*

Massive Price Reduction *(Ad #35)*

Rock Bottom Price *(Ad #36)*

New Price Offering *(Ad #37)*

Slashed to the Bone *(Ad #38)*

Major Price Reduction *(Ad #39)*

Price Adjustment *(Ad #40)*

New Look, New Price *(Ad #41)*

Price Overhaul *(Ad #42)*

Priced below Agent's Recommendation *(Ad #43)*

A Brand New Price You Are Sure to Love *(Ad #44)*

A New Price to Help Sell This Home *(Ad #45)*

Unbelievable Price Break *(Ad #46)*

The Owners Have Reduced the Price and All the Agents Can Say Is "WOW" *(Ad #47)*

If They Would Have Priced It This Low, They Would Have Sold It a Month Ago *(Ad #48)*

If They Would Have Priced It This Low, They Would Have Sold It Months Ago *(Ad #49)*

If They Would Have Priced It This Low, They Would Have Sold It in the First Week *(Ad #50)*

Better than a Toy at This New Price *(Ad #51)*

10% Off *(Ad #52)*

# Sample Ads

### Just Reduced

Entry portico adds a warm touch to this *[#Bedrooms]* bedroom/*[#Baths]* bath cottage. Knotty pine walls accent the enclosed porch off the side of the home. Features plenty of closet space, *[Feature 1]*, and *[Feature 2]*. See for yourself! Call *[Phone Number]* and ask for *[Listing Agent]*. *[Listing Code Number]*
**(Ad #1)**

### For Sale at a Discount!

This majestic home has everything you've wanted and more. Welcoming foyer with large stone tiles greet guests as they view the winding staircase and open loft area above. There's also a grand room with vaulted ceilings, covered air-cooled veranda adjoining the large patio area, and in-ground pool and hot tub. Extra features included are *[Feature 1]*, *[Feature 2]*, and *[Feature 3]*. Why just read about it when you can see it in person? Call *[Listing Agent]* at *[Phone Number]* to preview this listing today. *[Listing Code Number]*
**(Ad #2)**

### 30% Off

With its charm and delightful appearance, this home has probably been photographed by many people as they pass by. Many local residents have longed to own this *[Style of Home]* home. This residence offers *[#Bedrooms]* bedrooms and *[#Baths]* baths, and more. Call *[Listing Agent]* at *[Phone Number]* for all of the details. *[Listing Code Number]*
**(Ad #3)**

### March Madness

Log home with wrap-around front porch providing superb views of the countryside and nearby river. This home offers *[Feature 1]*, *[Feature 2]*, and *[Feature 3]*, along with *[#Bedrooms]* bedrooms and *[#Baths]* baths. Call *[Listing Agent]* at *[Phone Number]* for all of the details. *[Listing Code Number]*
**(Ad #4)**

### Reduced, Reduced, Reduced

Ten-acre mini-farm complete with chicken house, barn, workshop, and fruit cellar. Enjoy the days of yesteryear with this *[#Bedrooms]* bedroom/*[#Baths]* bath *[Style of Home]* delight. Call *[Listing Agent]* at *[Phone Number]* for a showing today. *[Listing Code Number]*
**(Ad #5)**

### Better than Half Price

Angled door frames and open beams provide a look and feel that is unmatched with this new listing. This *[#Bedrooms]* bedroom/*[#Baths]* bath home also features a lovely stone entry foyer, *[Feature 1]*, *[Feature 2]*, and *[Feature 3]*. A real dollhouse and priced for a quick sale. Call *[Phone Number]* and ask for *[Listing Agent]*. *[Listing Code Number]*
**(Ad #6)**

### It's a Steal!

[# of Square Feet] sq. ft. [Style of Home] home with [#Bedrooms] bedrooms and [#Baths] baths for only [List Price]! Kitchen with path through to great room and cathedral ceilings give this home an airy feel. Large family room and rec. room in finished basement for the kids. [Feature 1] and [Feature 2]. Call [Phone Number] and ask for [Listing Agent]. [Listing Code Number]
(Ad #7)

### You're Right, This Is a Steal!

This home has been painted by several artists in the community because of its look, feel, and character. The neighboring shade trees provide a detailed backdrop for everyone who passes by. [#Bedrooms] bedrooms and [#Baths] baths, parlor off foyer, and sitting room on main floor. Lot's of charm with this new listing! [List Price]! Call quickly on this one; it's sure to go quick at this price! Call [Phone Number] and ask for [Listing Agent]. [Listing Code Number]
(Ad #8)

### Bargain Bungalow

You'll need them with this [#Bedrooms] bedroom and [#Baths] bath [Style of Home] home on [Acres] acres. Extra features included are [Feature 1], [Feature 2], and [Feature 3]. [List Price]! Call quick on this one, it's sure to go quick at this price! Call [Phone Number] and ask for [Listing Agent]. [Listing Code Number]
(Ad #9)

### Owner Says Sale!

25 gently rolling acres with a good balance of pasture and woods accompanies this [#Bedrooms] bedroom and [#Baths] bath [Style of Home] home. Why just read about it when you can see it in person? Call [Listing Agent] at [Phone Number] to preview this listing today. [Listing Code Number]
(Ad #10)

### We Told the Owners It's Worth More than This

This [#Bedrooms] bedroom/[#Baths] bath bungalow features a large kitchen with breakfast nook, overlooking patio, and flower gardens in the backyard. There's a small den that could be used as an additional bedroom or computer room. See for yourself how tidy this home is. Call [Phone Number] and ask for [Listing Agent]. [Listing Code Number]
(Ad #11)

### Midnight Madness Sale

[#Bedrooms] bedrooms/[#Baths] bath [Style of Home] home with over [# of Square Feet] sq. ft.? You heard right! Listen to some of these extra amenities included with this home: [Feature 1], [Feature 2], and [Feature 3]. You can read and see all about it on our Web site at [Web Site Address]. Click on "Home of the Week." You can also call [Listing Agent] at [Phone Number] for more information. [Listing Code Number]
(Ad #12)

### Owners Say It's Okay to Offer at a Discount

Cotswold moulded-stone fireplace is the centerpoint to this *[#Bedrooms]* bedroom/*[#Baths]* bath home constructed in the late 1800s when homes were built to last for many years. A cobbled courtyard awaits you as you exit the large country kitchen onto the backyard. This home also features a vintage cook stove, pantry, and more. A great buy at only *[List Price]*! For more information, contact *[Listing Agent]* at *[Phone Number]* or visit us on the Web at *[Web Site Address]*. *[Listing Code Number]*
*(Ad #13)*

### Hurry Before This One Is Gone

Over *[# of Acres]* mostly cleared acres that are ideal for horses or cattle. Wet weather creek and spring-fed pond make owning and raising livestock a breeze. All fencing is in excellent condition. A great buy at only *[List Price]*! For a full-color flyer, contact *[Listing Agent]* at *[Phone Number]* or visit us on the Web at *[Web Site Address]*. *[Listing Code Number]*
*(Ad #14)*

### Price Slashed!

Ten acre mini-farm complete with chicken house, barn, workshop, and fruit cellar. Enjoy the days of yesteryear with this *[#Bedrooms]* bedroom and *[#Baths]* bath *[Style of Home]* delight. Call *[Listing Agent]* at *[Phone Number]* for a showing today. *[Listing Code Number]*
*(Ad #15)*

### Hurry! This Won't Last Long

Stunning terra-cotta tile floor in kitchen leads to an open living room with fireplace and built-in window seat. This new listing has all of the updates you would require in preowned home. Perfect home and a great buy for the money. Why just read about it when you can see it in person? Call *[Listing Agent]* at *[Phone Number]* to preview this listing today. *[Listing Code Number]*
*(Ad #16)*

### There Is Nothing Wrong with This Home—The Owners Just Said Sell It Quick!

This *[# of Square Feet]* sq. ft. *[Style of Home]* home features *[#Bedrooms]* bedrooms and *[#Baths]* baths. Boxed hedges line the front of this grand estate with vast windows that provide lots of afternoon sunlight. There's a covered pavilion with grill and wet bar and an outdoor fireplace to entertain guests and family. A home to be proud of! A great buy at only *[List Price]*! For more information, contact *[Listing Agent]* at *[Phone Number]* or visit us on the Web at *[Web Site Address]*. *[Listing Code Number]*
*(Ad #17)*

### Priced Below Market Value

The owners have stripped and refinished all of the woodwork to give it a glorious shine and a look of yesteryear. *[#Bedrooms]* bedrooms and *[#Baths]* baths give way to a newly renovated kitchen with new cherry wood cabinets and granite countertops. See for yourself! Call *[Phone Number]* and ask for *[Listing Agent]*. *[Listing Code Number]*
*(Ad #18)*

### Instant Equity When You Buy This Home

This *[Style of Home]* was built just prior to the Civil War. Large rooms with wide woodwork frame every area with perfection. Open foyer greets your guests with a heavy sigh. Many original details have been preserved to give this new listing a special touch. A great buy at only *[List Price]*! For more information, contact *[Listing Agent]* at *[Phone Number]* or visit us on the Web at *[Web Site Address]*. *[Listing Code Number]*
**(Ad #19)**

### A Price to Be Happy with

This 45-acre wooded track of ground is nestled at the foot of *[City Name]*. The owner has his own private deer stand that has led to great success over the last few seasons. Lovely *[#Bedrooms]* bedroom/*[#Baths]* bath *[Style of Home]* home with over *[# of Square Feet]* sq. ft. of living area. Full basement, three-car garage, and large master bedroom and suite with jacuzzi tub and shower. Best of all, it's priced at only *[List Price]*! Call *[Listing Agent]* at *[Phone Number]* to look at this home today. *[Listing Code Number]*
**(Ad #20)**

### Your Appraiser Will Flip Out

Front door with adjacent side window give a hearty and warm greeting to you and your guests. This *[#Bedrooms]* bedroom/*[#Baths]* bath home on an oversized city lot is sure to sell fast at this low price! *[List Price]*! Call *[Phone Number]* and ask for *[Listing Agent]*. *[Listing Code Number]*
**(Ad #21)**

### Deal of a Lifetime

with this lovely *[# of Square Feet]* sq. ft. *[Style of Home]* home. Features *[#Bedrooms]* bedrooms and *[#Baths]* baths, *[Feature 1]*, *[Feature 2]*, and *[Feature 3]*. Expandable area on second floor gives way to more space if you think you need it. Full finished basement with billiard and theater. A must see, and priced at only *[List Price]*! Call *[Phone Number]* and ask for *[Listing Agent]*. *[Listing Code Number]*
**(Ad #22)**

### Deal of the Century

This *[#Bedrooms]* bedroom/*[#Baths]* bath home has a lovely large wrap-around front porch you don't find with many homes for sale today. You'll also discover a flag stone patio with a rock walkway through the flower gardens. The inside has been restored and kept to the look of its original condition. You'll be amazed at how well this home shows. Newly listed and priced to move quick! Call *[Listing Agent]* at *[Phone Number]*. *[Listing Code Number]*
**(Ad #23)**

### Better Than Being on Wheel of Fortune

Stunning *[# of Acres]*-acre horse farm complete with horse barn, stalls, and storage/tack room. The white board fencing goes great with this traditional *[Style of Home]* home. This new listing provides *[# of Square Feet]* sq. ft., along with *[#Bedrooms]* bedrooms and *[#Baths]* baths. For more information, visit our Web site at *[Web Address]* or call *[Listing Agent]* at *[Phone Number]*. *[Listing Code Number]*
**(Ad #24)**

### Unbelievable Price Reduction!

on this 30-acre resort-like setting on the *[River Name]*. Large wooden deck is ideal for family gatherings and quiet evenings. *[#Bedrooms]* bedrooms and *[#Baths]* bath *[Style of Home]* home with workshop. Best of all, there's a gazebo down by the river you have to see for yourself. For more information, contact *[Listing Agent]* at *[Phone Number]*. *[Listing Code Number]*
***(Ad #25)***

### Two for the Price of One

Great opportunity with this commercial building. Features *[# of Square Feet]* square feet for retail or office with a live-in *[#Bedrooms]* bedroom apartment above. Save time and money by combining home and work in one payment. *[List Price]*! Call quickly on this one; it's sure to go quick at this price! Call *[Phone Number]* and ask for *[Listing Agent]*. *[Listing Code Number]*
***(Ad #26)***

### Two for One at a Great Price

Here's your opportunity to purchase a thriving antique store in the heart of *[Local Area]*. This property comes complete with living quarters upstairs. Located on a highly traveled walking street between restaurants that will aid in lots of consumer traffic. See for yourself! Call *[Phone Number]* and ask for *[Listing Agent]*. *[Listing Code Number]*
***(Ad #27)***

### What a Deal!

This six-bay car wash facility is a favorite by many of the locals. Excellent location, and the owners always keep the area clean. Newly refurbished equipment in car wash bays will provide low maintenance to the new owner. Financial statements are available to qualified buyers. A great buy at only *[List Price]*! For more information, contact *[Listing Agent]* at *[Phone Number]* or visit us on the Web at *[Web Site Address]*. *[Listing Code Number]*
***(Ad #28)***

### It's Your Lucky Day

This 22-unit apartment complex is fully rented and provides excellent income for the current owners. Small office on property allows for good oversight of facilities. The monthly expenses are very minimal as shown on the current financial statements. Qualified buyers only! To find out more details and for a private e-mail containing a special Web site address with photos, virtual tours, and more, contact *[Listing Agent]* at *[Phone Number]*. *[Listing Code Number]*
***(Ad #29)***

### Better than Winning the Lottery

Established florist shop for sale in *[Local Area]*. Turnkey operation includes real estate and all personal property with this business. Owner willing to train new buyers for up to six months. For more information, call *[Listing Agent]* at *[Phone Number]*. *[Listing Code Number]*
***(Ad #30)***

### Here's Your Christmas Gift—I Hope It's Okay We Left the Price Tag on, Because It's a Great Deal

This *[# of Square Feet]* sq. ft. *[Style of Home]* home features *[#Bedrooms]* bedrooms and *[#Baths]* bath*s*. Boxed Hedges line the front of this grand estate with vast windows that provide lot's of afternoon sunlight. There's a covered pavilion with grill and wet bar and an outdoor fireplace to entertain guests and family. A home to be proud of! For more information contact *[Listing Agent]* at *[Agency Phone Number]* or visit us on the Web at *[Web Site Address]*. A great buy at only *[List Price]*. *[Listing Code Number]*
**(Ad #31)**

### Red Tag Special

Large arched windows make up the majority of the rear of this home and provide a grand view of the lake and surrounding hill country. You'll find lots of extras in this beautiful *[# of Square Feet]* sq. ft. *[Style of Home]* home. Welcoming foyer provides a perfect introduction to guests and friends. Keeping room off kitchen with small beehive fireplace makes a great conversation piece. Why just read about it when you can see it in person? Call *[Listing Agent]* at *[Phone Number]* to preview this listing today. *[Listing Code Number]*
**(Ad #32)**

### Blue Light Special

Although it's compact in nature, this *[#Bedrooms]* bedroom/*[#Baths]* bath *[Style of Home]* home is determined to provide you with all of the satisfaction you desire in your next home. *[Feature 1]*, *[Feature 2]*, and *[Feature 3]* are just a few of the many extras you'll be treated with in this home. A great buy at only *[List Price]*! For more information, contact *[Listing Agent]* at *[Phone Number]* or visit us on the Web at *[Web Site Address]*. *[Listing Code Number]*
**(Ad #33)**

### Falling Price

There is plenty of room on this ten-acre parcel, complete with a small barn and two stalls. Lovely *[#Bedrooms]* bedroom/*[#Baths]* bath *[Style of Home]* with family room, finished basement, and more. A great opportunity at *[List Price]*! Call *[Listing Agent]* at *[Phone Number]* for more information. *[Listing Code Number]*
**(Ad #34)**

### Massive Price Reductions

A covered veranda is just a small part of this *[#Bedrooms]* bedroom/*[#Baths]* bath *[Style of Home]* home. Features *[Feature 1]*, *[Feature 2]*, and *[Feature 3]*, along with a full finished basement. Why just read about it when you can see it in person? Call *[Listing Agent]* at *[Phone Number]* to preview this listing today. *[Listing Code Number]*
**(Ad #35)**

### Rock Bottom Price

Simple yet functional, this *[#Bedrooms]* bedroom/*[#Baths]* bath *[Style of Home]* features *[Feature 1]* and *[Feature 2]*, along with low-voltage halogen lighting in the kitchen. A real charmer that's sure to please everyone in the family! Why just read about it when you can see it in person? Call *[Listing Agent]* at *[Phone Number]* to preview this listing today. *[Listing Code Number]*
***(Ad #36)***

### New Price Offering

Over *[Acres]* acres mostly cleared that's ideal for horses or cattle. Wet weather creek and spring fed pond make owning and raising livestock a breeze. All fencing is in excellent condition. For a full color flyer contact *[Listing Agent]* at *[Agency Phone Number]* or visit us on the Web at *[Web Site Address]*. A great buy at only *[List Price]*. *[Listing Code Number]*
***(Ad #37)***

### Slashed to the Bone

Twelve acres of gently rolling pasture surround this *[#Bedrooms]* bedroom/*[#Baths]* bath *[Style of Home]* home. Extra clean and ready to move into. Call *[Listing Agent]* at *[Phone Number]* for all the details or to schedule an appointment to preview. *[Listing Code Number]*
***(Ad #38)***

### Major Price Reduction

Here is a *[# of Square Feet]* sq. ft. *[Style of Home]* home with *[#Bedrooms]* bedrooms and *[#Baths]* baths that is located on *[Name of Lake]*. Passionate cooks will love this kitchen especially the Thermador® appliances. Too many extra features to mention in this home. Let *[Listing Agent]* show you this lovely listing today. Call *[Phone Number]* to schedule your appointment. *[Listing Code Number]*
***(Ad #39)***

### Price Adjustment

Are words to describe this *[#Bedrooms]* bedroom and *[#Baths]* bath cozy home on three acres. Great spot for a garden, horse shoes, and other family outdoor activities. Features a 30 × 40 workshop with work bench and shelves designed for the craftsman. It is a real treat and sure to move fast at only *[List Price]*. Call *[Listing Agent]* at *[Phone Number]* to see this home before it is too late.
***(Ad #40)***

### New Look, New Price

Enjoy the good life with two other families on a four-acre lake nestled among the woods. *[Style of Home]* home with *[#Bedrooms]* bedrooms and *[#Baths]* baths. Spacious master bedroom and private deck overlooking the lake is a great way to greet every morning. Master bath features whirlpool tub and separate shower unit. Two walk-in closets plus much more. For a private tour, call *[Listing Agent]* at *[Phone Number]* or e-mail *[Listing Agent]* at *[Listing Agent E-mail]*. *[Listing Code Number]*
***(Ad #41)***

### Price Overhaul

You will have more than enough room for your outdoor activities with this 15-acre parcel land. Includes a good combination of woods and pasture, and a wet weather creek. *[#Bedrooms]* bedrooms and *[#Baths]* baths complimented by a large brick fireplace in family room. Priced at *[List Price]*! Call *[Listing Agent]* at *[Phone Number]* to arrange a showing.
***(Ad #42)***

### Priced Below Agent's Recommendation

Excellent golfing accommodations for homeowners in the *[Lake Development]*. You'll appreciate this *[#Bedrooms]* bedroom/*[#Baths]* bath *[Style of Home]* home. Features *[Feature 1]* and *[Feature 2]*. Tastefully decorated with an open and spacious floor plan. Call *[Listing Agent]* at *[Phone Number]* or e-mail *[Listing Agent]* at *[Listing Agent E-mail]*. *[Listing Code Number]*
***(Ad #43)***

### A Brand New Price You Are Sure to Love

It is a ten acre mini-farm complete with chicken house, barn, workshop, and fruit cellar. Enjoy the days of yesteryear with this *[#Bedrooms]* bedroom and *[#Baths]* bath *[Style of Home]* delight. Call *[Listing Agent]* at *[Phone Number]* for a showing today.
***(Ad #44)***

### A New Price to Help Sale This Home

This forty-five acre wooded track of ground is nestled at the foot of *[Name of Condo Development]*. The owner has his own private deer stand that has led to great success over the last few seasons. Lovely *[#Bedrooms]* bedroom and *[#Baths]* bath *[Style of Home]* home with over *[# of Square Feet]* sq. ft. of living area. Full basement, three-car garage, large master bedroom and suite with jacuzzi tub and shower. Best of all it is priced at only *[List Price]* call *[Listing Agent]* at *[Phone Number]* to look at this home today.
***(Ad #45)***

### Unbelievable Price Break

The owners have said they will miss the upper-floor sitting room that views the lake from several angles when they sell this home. A great place to read a book or to take an afternoon nap. This home also features *[#Bedrooms]* bedroom and *[#Baths]* baths and over *[# of Square Feet]* sq. ft. Full basement, great kitchen setup, and much more. Let *[Listing Agent]* show you this lovely listing today. Call *[Phone Number]* to schedule your appointment. *[Listing Code Number]*
***(Ad #46)***

### The Owners Have Reduced the Price and All the Agents Can Say Is "WOW"

This *[#Bedrooms]* bedroom/*[#Baths]* bath home is made out of stone and will be there for many years to come. Large fireplace adorns the family room with floor-to-ceiling bookcases on both sides. Wood beams provide a nice touch to the open airy room that also adjoins kitchen. Screened-in back porch to keep watch over your *[# of Acres]* acres. See for yourself! Call *[Phone Number]* and ask for *[Listing Agent]*. *[Listing Code Number]*
***(Ad #47)***

### If They Would Have Priced It This Low, They Would Have Sold It a Month Ago

Lovely *[#Bedrooms]* bedroom/*[#Baths]* bath *[Style of Home]* home with a large chef's kitchen and center island. You will also discover a walk-in pantry, breakfast bar, and many upgraded appliances. For more information, contact *[Listing Agent]* at *[Phone Number]*. *[Listing Code Number]*

*(Ad #48)*

### If They Would Have Priced It This Low, They Would Have Sold It Months Ago

*[#Bedrooms]* bedroom/*[#Baths]* bath *[Style of Home]* home located in *[Lake Development]* will provide you with access to your own fishing lake just a few short steps from your back door. This home includes a private covered boat dock and large deck to enjoy all the views of the lake. Extra features included are *[Feature 1]*, *[Feature 2]*, and *[Feature 3]*. *[List Price]*! Call *[Phone Number]* and ask for *[Listing Agent]*. *[Listing Code Number]*

*(Ad #49)*

### If They Would Have Priced It This Low, They Would Have Sold It in the First Week

with this *[#Bedrooms]* bedroom/*[#Baths]* bath *[Style of Home]* farmhouse. Spacious rooms adore oversized hallways and foyer. Your guests will be amazed at all of the room you have. Priced at only *[List Price]*! Call *[Listing Agent]* at *[Phone Number]* for more information. *[Listing Code Number]*

*(Ad #50)*

### Better than a Toy at This New Price

Cute and cozy *[#Bedrooms]* bedroom/*[#Baths]* bath home located in *[Lake Development]*. Lots of closet space, large eat-in kitchen, *[Feature 1]*, and *[Feature 2]*. Why just read about it when you can see it in person? Call *[Listing Agent]* at *[Phone Number]* to preview this listing today. *[Listing Code Number]*

*(Ad #51)*

### 10% Off

Log home with wrap-around front porch providing superb views of the countryside and nearby river. This home offers *[Feature 1]*, *[Feature 2]*, and *[Feature 3]* along with *[#Bedrooms]* bedrooms and *[#Baths]* baths. Call *[Listing Agent]* at *[Phone Number]* for all of the details. *[Listing Code Number]*

*(Ad #52)*

# Agent Promotion 16

When you think about products you use on a daily basis what is the first thing that comes to your mind? If I asked you to think about soda, what would you answer? Pizza? Your local bank? How about real estate? Hopefully, you added your own name when you think of real estate. The goal of any product or company or real estate professional is to get the buying public to think about you when they think about real estate. Agent promotional ads are very effective in accomplishing that goal. Over my long tenure in real estate I know firsthand how important it is to promote and market yourself. Unfortunately, sellers want to see their house in the newspaper! Many sellers believe that if their property is not in the newspaper then it will not sell. You and I both know that newspaper ads normally do not sell their property directly. Newspaper ads and other types of marketing are designed to obtain buyer leads to where it is our responsibility to determine what those buyer needs are and using that knowledge to find the right property for the buyer. So it is a double-edged sword to advertise yourself and not advertise your listings. I believe it is a good idea to balance the two and always market your client's property (you have a fiduciary obligation to do this under your listing contract) but it is also important to advertise yourself as the real estate expert in your area. Keeping a good balance of agent promotion and client properties in the public eye is essential for any real estate agent to be successful.

Normally, good agent promotion includes a photograph or a theme; or some other idea, slogan, or logo to grab the reader's attention. Some marketplaces running a short classified ad can be very effective too. The following section contains some sample ads that could be used in your newspapers without spending a lot of money but yet accomplishing the same goal—getting people to think about you when they think about real estate.

# Sample Headings

Now Accepting New Clients *(Ad #1)*
Don't Hire a Real Estate Agent! *(Ad #2)*
Have You Heard? *(Ad #3)*
Are You Lonely? *(Ad #4)*
Strange Words? *(Ad #5)*
Rough Road? *(Ad #6)*
Have a Heart Problem? *(Ad #7)*
Don't Get Lost in the Shuffle *(Ad #8)*
Quick Change Artist *(Ad #9)*
Sign Here *(Ad #10)*
Attention Senior Adults *(Ad #11)*
Mission Impossible *(Ad #12)*
It's Too Late *(Ad #13)*
Thank You! *(Ad #14)*

One Million Dollars *(Ad #15)*
Your Rent Is Due *(Ad #16)*
Warning!! *(Ad #17)*
Avoid Paying Taxes *(Ad #18)*
For Rent *(Ad #19)*
Stay Home *(Ad #20)*
Media Man *(Ad #21)*
At the Bridge *(Ad #22)*
A Ray of Sunshine *(Ad #23)*
Home Run *(Ad #24)*
Magic *(Ad #25)*
No Instructions Required *(Ad #26)*
Need a Professor? *(Ad #27)*
A Bad Taste *(Ad #28)*

# Sample Ads

### Now Accepting New Clients

*[Agent Name]* is pleased to announce that she is accepting new buyer and seller clients due to her recent flurry of activity. If you're thinking about buying or selling real estate, call *[Agent Name]* at *[Phone Number]*. *[Listing Code Number]*
**(Ad #1)**

### Don't Hire a Real Estate Agent!

That is right! Don't just hire any real estate agent. Hire someone who has experience and knows the real estate business forward and backward. Call *[Agent Name]* at *[Phone Number]* because experience counts! *[Listing Code Number]*
**(Ad #2)**

### Have You Heard?

More buyers and sellers in *[Office Location/Area]* rely on *[Agent Name]* for all of their real estate needs. *[Agent Name]* consistently lists and sells more real estate than 80% of the real estate agents in *[Office Location/Area]*. If you need a real estate professional, then you need *[Agent Name]*! Call *[Agent Name]* at *[Agency Phone Number]* for more information. *[Listing Code Number]*
**(Ad #3)**

### Are You Lonely?

Many real estate sellers complain of never hearing from their real estate agent. There is no need to be a lonely seller. *[Agent Name]* has over fifteen years experience working with buyers and sellers and their real estate needs and you will always hear from *[Agent Name]*. You can count on him! Call *[Agent Name]* at *[Agency Phone Number]* for all your real estate needs. *[Listing Code Number]*
**(Ad #4)**

### Strange Words?

Many real estate buyers and sellers complain about the real estate jargon and terminology that seems completely strange to them. Thanks to *[Agent Name]*, there's no need to worry about your next real estate transaction. *[Agent Name]* specializes in working with buyers and sellers and explaining all the details of the real estate transaction in simple, plain, and understanding phrases. If you're thinking about buying or selling real estate, don't make a move without *[Agent Name]*. Call today at *[Phone Number]*!
**(Ad #5)**

### Rough Road?

It doesn't have to be a rough road when you buy or sell real estate. *[Agent Name]* knows that buying or selling a home can be a traumatic experience and that's why she makes it a point for every real estate transaction to run smoothly. Don't let your real estate transaction be a rough road to hoe. Call *[Agent Name]* at *[Phone Number]* to help. *[Listing Code Number]*
*(Ad #6)*

### Have a Heart Problem?

You need to call a heart specialist. When you have a real estate problem, you need to call *[Agent Name]*. *[Agent Name]* is an experienced real estate agent that can help you with all of your real estate needs. For a free private consultation, call *[Phone Number]*. *[Listing Code Number]*
*(Ad #7)*

### Don't Get Lost in the Shuffle

If you're worried about getting lost in the shuffle with overworked and busy real estate agents, perhaps it's time you choose someone who can devote more time to your needs. Hi, my name is *[Agent Name]* and I'm ready to serve your real estate needs. Providing you with full-time attention and 110% service guaranteed. Call me, *[Agent Name]*, at *[Phone Number]* for all your real estate needs. *[Listing Code Number]*
*(Ad #8)*

### Quick Change Artist

I specialize in helping buyers and sellers with their real estate needs. For buyers, I will put you in a home as quickly as possible. Sellers don't just get listed, but get sold. Now is a great time to buy or sell real estate. Call me, *[Agent Name]*, at *[Phone Number]* for more information. *[Listing Code Number]*
*(Ad #9)*

### Sign Here

Many real estate agents ask for the signature without explaining the details. Don't get lost in the shuffle. Call me, *[Agent Name]*, and I will put your real estate worries at ease by explaining all the details. Call *[Phone Number]* or visit my Web site at *[Agent Web Site]* for more information. *[Listing Code Number]*
*(Ad #10)*

### Attention Senior Adults

Hi, my name is *[Agent Name]* and I specialize by working with senior citizens and their real estate needs. I understand how frustrating it can be to buy or sell real estate. That's why I would love to make your next real estate transaction run as smooth as possible. Call me *[Agent Name]* at *[Agency Phone Number]* for more information. *[Listing Code Number]*
*(Ad #11)*

### Mission Impossible

With some real estate agents, that might be the case. But with *[Agent Name]*, buying or selling a home is mission possible. Let *[Agent Name]* put her proven real estate principles to work for you. Call *[Agent Name]* at *[Phone Number]* or visit online at *[Agent Web Site]*. *[Listing Code Number]*
*(Ad #12)*

### It's Too Late

That seems to be the response many buyers and sellers get, but with *[Agent Name]*'s proven buyer's technology search system new matches for the type home you're looking for will be sent to your e-mail the minute they become available. Call *[Agent Name]* at *[Phone Number]* and let him explain how his proven home match system can work for you. *[Listing Code Number]*
*(Ad #13)*

### Thank You!

Those are the words *[Agent Name]* hears all the time from buyers and sellers who have been so pleased with their real estate transaction. *[Agent Name]* is now accepting new clients and is eager to work with you for all your real estate desires. For a FREE, no obligation consultation, call *[Phone Number]*. *[Listing Code Number]*
*(Ad #14)*

### One Million Dollars

Thinking about selling your home? Even though it may not be worth a million dollars, *[Agent Name]* will put his six-step home selling solution into practice for your home. For more information, contact *[Agent Name]* at *[Phone Number]*. You'll tell yourself it is worth a million dollars after you view all the details! *[Listing Code Number]*
*(Ad #15)*

### Your Rent Is Due

Why keep paying rent to your landlord when you can own your own home? Call *[Agent Name]* at *[Phone Number]* and find out how easy it is to own your own home. *[Listing Code Number]*
*(Ad #16)*

### Warning!!

Buying or selling a home might be hazardous to your health if you don't consult with the right real estate professional. There are a lot of great real estate agents out there with knowledge and information that can help you, but there is one agent that is ready to work for you today. Call *[Agent Name]* at *[Phone Number]* and let *[Agent Name]* show you how buying or selling a home can be a fascinating, fun, and rewarding experience. *[Listing Code Number]*
*(Ad #17)*

### Avoid Paying Taxes

*[Agent Name]* can show you how easy it is to sell your investment property without paying any capital gains tax. If you would like to know more about how 1031 tax free exchanges work, call *[Agent Name]* at *[Phone Number]* for more information. *[Listing Code Number]*
**(Ad #18)**

### For Rent

Great real estate agent with lots of experience and available for buyers or sellers on a full-time basis. Excellent attitude, friendly smile, and no high-pressure tactics are included. Best of all, available for immediate or long-term needs. Would like to be your present and future real estate agent forever. For more information, contact *[Agent Name]* at *[Phone Number]*. *[Listing Code Number]*
**(Ad #19)**

### Stay Home

Why get out and run all over town trying to find the perfect house when you can stay home and view my Web site with full color photos, virtual tours, school reports, and other information? Best of all, you can narrow down your selection to the two or three homes you really want to see. Call me *[Agent Name]* at *[Agency Phone Number]* or visit my Web site online at *[Agent Web Site]*. *[Listing Code Number]*
**(Ad #20)**

### Media Man

Looking for a Web site with homes for sale and plenty of photographs? Visit *[Agent Web Site]*. I put an average of 40–50 photos on all of my listings I have for sale. Maybe that's why they nicknamed me *[Agent Nickname]*. Whether you're buying or selling, the right photograph can make all the difference. Call me for ALL your real estate needs. Call *[Phone Number]*. *[Listing Code Number]*
**(Ad #21)**

### At the Bridge

Let me bridge the gap between buying a home and financing your mortgage. I have several lenders I work with so I can help find you the right mortgage. Call *[Agent Name]* at *[Phone Number]* for more information. *[Listing Code Number]*
**(Ad #22)**

### A Ray of Sunshine

is always available when you buy or sale a home from *[Agent Name]*. Call *[Agent Name]* at *[Phone Number]* or visit her online at *[Agent Web Site]*. *[Listing Code Number]*
**(Ad #23)**

### Home Run

You'll hit a home run every time when you use the real estate services of *[Agent Name]*. Call *[Agent Name]* at *[Phone Number]* for all your real estate needs. *[Listing Code Number]*
**(Ad #24)**

### Magic

Some people might think *[Agent Name]* uses a little bit of magic to sell his homes so fast. But, *[Agent Name]* will tell you it's just good old-fashion hard work. If that is the type of real estate professional you're looking for, call *[Agent Name]* at *[Phone Number]* for more information. *[Listing Code Number]*
*(Ad #25)*

### No Instructions Required

If you're thinking about buying or selling a home, let *[Agent Name]* handle all the details and answer all the questions. Call *[Agent Name]* at *[Phone Number]* and let him take care of all the instructions for your next real estate transaction. *[Listing Code Number]*
*(Ad #26)*

### Need a Professor?

If so, you have come to the right place when dealing with real estate. Call Professor *[Agent Name]* at *[Phone Number]* for assistance with your next real estate transaction. *[Listing Code Number]*
*(Ad #27)*

### A Bad Taste

There is no need to have a bad taste in your mouth over a sour real estate transaction. Call *[Agent Name]* to help you with your buying and selling needs. You'll be glad you did. Call *[Agent Name]* at *[Phone Number]*. *[Listing Code Number]*
*(Ad #28)*

# Open House Ads 17

Holding an open house can often be a topic of debate among real estate professionals. Many agents feel holding open houses is a waste of time and produces little business. Normally you will hear real estate agents make note that open houses only make sellers happy. Others find this real estate marketing a good source of leads for future buyers and sellers. Regardless of which school of thought you agree with, one fact is certain: holding open houses must be from an "active" approach if you want your open house to be a success. Advertising (in advance) of the open house is essential! Inviting neighbors to attend, promoting your Web site and local multiple listing service are a must. Many real estate agents only place ads in newspapers and a few directional open house signs expecting a big turnout. Putting a little effort into marketing your open house can usually provide a better turnout on your open house day.

One final note on open house advertising. Make sure you allow enough time to market your listing and "good" directions to your open house in all of your ads. Use proper directional signs on the day of your open house. Have a method on how you plan to market your event. Use the Internet and your Web site to publicize your open house.

# Sample Headings

Closed House (to the Family but Open to the Public) *(Ad #1)*

Take a Drive and Stop on By *(Ad #2)*

Stop in This Saturday *(Ad #3)*

Open for You to View *(Ad #4)*

Want to Look Inside? *(Ad #5)*

Come on By—It's Open This Weekend *(Ad #6)*

See for Yourself *(Ad #7)*

Have a First-Hand Look *(Ad #8)*

Have a Look and Feel Free to Sit on the Porch Swing *(Ad #9)*

The Old Timers Always Wanted to Look Inside *(Ad #10)*

The First Time Open to the Public *(Ad #11)*

We Couldn't Believe the Owners Would Let Us Hold It Open (It Is Such a Showplace) *(Ad #12)*

A Rare Opportunity *(Ad #13)*

Opportunity of a Lifetime *(Ad #14)*

We Could Charge Admission *(Ad #15)*

Look What Is Open This Weekend! *(Ad #16)*

A Victorian Open House *(Ad #17)*

Open House on the Beach *(Ad #18)*

Open House on the Lake *(Ad #19)*

Open House Down on the Farm *(Ad #20)*

Free Hot Dogs and Soda at This Open House *(Ad #21)*

Get a Free Credit Report This Weekend *(Ad #22)*

Open House Weekend Includes Free Credit Report and Appraisal *(Ad #23)*

Open House Bonanza *(Ad #24)*

Three in One! *(Ad #25)*

Want to Know How Close This House Is to the Lake? *(Ad #26)*

Look and Touch This Sunday *(Ad #27)*

Soak Up the Surroundings This Weekend *(Ad #28)*

### Closed House
### (to the Family but Open to the Public)

You'll appreciate all the detail and oak woodwork and trim in this lovely *[Style of Home]* home. Open this *[Day(s) of Open House]*, *[Time of Open House]*. Come visit *[Listing Agent]* at *[Street Address]*. *[Directions to Property]*. *[Listing Code Number]*
**(Ad #1)**

### Take a Drive and Stop on By

Recently listed, immaculate *[#Bedrooms]* bedroom/*[#Baths]* bath *[Style of Home]* home. For a special opportunity to preview this home, visit our open house *[Day(s) of Open House]*, *[Time of Open House]*. *[Street Address]*. *[Directions to Property]*. *[Listing Code Number]*
**(Ad #2)**

### Stop In This Saturday

Free coffee, cookies, and other light refreshments at our open house this weekend from *[Time of Open House]*. Lovely *[Style of Home]* home featuring a stunning kitchen that would delight any cooks heart. *[Street Address]*. *[Directions to Property]*. *[Listing Code Number]*
**(Ad #3)**

### Open for You to View

Gorgeous *[#Bedrooms]* bedroom/*[#Baths]* bath *[Style of Home]* home nestled on a one-acre lot in town. Open this *[Day(s) of Open House]*, *[Time of Open House]*. Come visit *[Listing Agent]* at *[Street Address]*. *[Directions to Property]*. *[Listing Code Number]*
**(Ad #4)**

### Want to Look Inside?

*[Listing Agent]* of *[Agency Name]* is hosting an open house this *[Day(s) of Open House]*, *[Time of Open House]*. Classy *[#Bedrooms]* bedroom/*[#Baths]* bath *[Style of Home]* home with all the extras. A must see! Come visit *[Listing Agent]* at *[Street Address]*. *[Directions to Property]*. *[Listing Code Number]*
**(Ad #5)**

### Come on By—It's Open This Weekend

Lovely pool area with hot tub is perfect for any family! Stop by our open house this *[Day(s) of Open House]*, *[Time of Open House]*. Free refreshments served. Come visit *[Listing Agent]* at *[Street Address]*. *[Directions to Property]*. *[Listing Code Number]*
**(Ad #6)**

### See for Yourself

Over *[# of Square Feet]* sq. ft. of spacious living area featuring a beautiful flower garden. Large shade trees and much more. Come see for yourself! Open this *[Day(s) of Open House]*, *[Time of Open House]*. Come visit *[Listing Agent]* at *[Street Address]*. *[Directions to Property]*. *[Listing Code Number]*
*(Ad #7)*

### Have a First-Hand Look

This *[#Bedrooms]* bedroom/*[#Baths]* bath *[Style of Home]* home has all the extras you have been looking for. Newly refurbished kitchen, gorgeous patio area, and more. There will be lemonade by the pool this *[Day(s) of Open House]*, *[Time of Open House]*. Come visit *[Listing Agent]* at *[Street Address]*. *[Directions to Property]*. *[Listing Code Number]*
*(Ad #8)*

### Have a Look and Feel Free to Sit on the Porch Swing

Here's your chance to view this special new listing this *[Day(s) of Open House]*, *[Time of Open House]*. Extra features included in this home are *[Feature 1]*, *[Feature 2]*, and *[Feature 3]*. Come visit *[Listing Agent]* at *[Street Address]*. *[Directions to Property]*. *[Listing Code Number]*
*(Ad #9)*

### The Old Timers Always Wanted to Look Inside

You will ooh and aah over the entry foyer and staircase in this new listing. Special invitation for you to preview this *[Day(s) of Open House]*, *[Time of Open House]*. Come visit *[Listing Agent]* at *[Street Address]*. *[Directions to Property]*. *[Listing Code Number]*
*(Ad #10)*

### The First Time Open to the Public

Explore all the charm and beauty of this rare find this *[Day(s) of Open House]*, *[Time of Open House]*. Come visit *[Listing Agent]* at *[Street Address]*. *[Directions to Property]*. *[Listing Code Number]*
*(Ad #11)*

### We Couldn't Believe the Owners Would Let Us Hold It Open (It Is Such a Showplace)

Gorgeous *[#Bedrooms]* bedroom/*[#Baths]* bath *[Style of Home]* home surrounded by *[# of Square Feet]* sq. ft. of living area. Open this *[Day(s) of Open House]*, *[Time of Open House]*. Come visit *[Listing Agent]* at *[Street Address]*. *[Directions to Property]*. *[Listing Code Number]*
*(Ad #12)*

### A Rare Opportunity

You won't believe it so come and experience it first hand. *[Style of Home]* home with charming courtyard and patio area. Refreshments will be served. Open this *[Day(s) of Open House]*, *[Time of Open House]*. Come visit *[Listing Agent]* at *[Street Address]*. *[Directions to Property]*. *[Listing Code Number]*
*(Ad #13)*

### Opportunity of a Lifetime

to preview this home during a rare open house weekend. This *[# of Square Feet]* sq. ft. *[Style of Home]* home has every possible amenity you would ask for. *[Feature 1]* and *[Feature 2]* are worth the tour. Free popcorn and soda for all in attendance. For a special opportunity to preview this home, visit our open house *[Day(s) of Open House]*, *[Time of Open House]*. *[Street Address]*. *[Directions to Property]*. *[Listing Code Number]*
*(Ad #14)*

### We Could Charge Admission

for this open house it is so magnificent, but we won't. Outstanding *[# of Square Feet]* sq. ft. estate is open *[Day(s) of Open House]*, *[Time of Open House]*. Come view the breathtaking foyer, open staircase, and then be sure to have a glass of cool lemonade and some small refreshments by the pool. *[Street Address]*. *[Directions to Property]*. *[Listing Code Number]*
*(Ad #15)*

### Look What Is Open This Weekend!

You'll appreciate all the restoration the owners have done to this magnificent home. Stop by our open house this *[Day(s) of Open House]*, *[Time of Open House]*. Free refreshments served. Come visit *[Listing Agent]* at *[Street Address]*. *[Directions to Property]*. *[Listing Code Number]*
*(Ad #16)*

### A Victorian Open House

We're serving Victorian snacks along with this open house on *[Day(s) of Open House]*, *[Time of Open House]*. Grace and beauty abound throughout this three-story home. This is a rare opportunity you don't want to miss. *[Street Address]*. *[Directions to Property]*. *[Listing Code Number]*
*(Ad #17)*

### Open House on the Beach

Come soak up the gorgeous views of the ocean at this open house on *[Day(s) of Open House]*, *[Time of Open House]*. Explore the possibilities of owning this home and see for yourself all the charm and character it has to offer. *[Street Address]*. *[Directions to Property]*. *[Listing Code Number]*
*(Ad #18)*

### Open House on the Lake

Here is your chance to view this beautiful two-story log home with full-length wooded deck overlooking its own lake. A real treat and a home you will appreciate by seeing first hand. Open this *[Day(s) of Open House]*, *[Time of Open House]*. Come visit *[Listing Agent]* at *[Street Address]*. *[Directions to Property]*. *[Listing Code Number]*
*(Ad #19)*

### Open House Down on the Farm

Neat and clean *[#Bedrooms]* bedroom/*[#Baths]* bath *[Style of Home]* home on *[Acres]* acres will be open this *[Day(s) of Open House]*, *[Time of Open House]*. Come visit *[Listing Agent]* at *[Street Address]*. *[Directions to Property]*. *[Listing Code Number]*
*(Ad #20)*

### Free Hot Dogs and Soda at This Open House

*[Mortgage Lender Name]* will be serving free hot dogs and soda for anyone in attendance at this unique and comfortable *[#Bedrooms]* bedroom/*[#Baths]* bath *[Style of Home]* home. Come see a great home and get prequalified for your next home loan "FREE" of charge. Open this *[Day(s) of Open House]*, *[Time of Open House]*. Come visit *[Listing Agent]* at *[Street Address]*. *[Directions to Property]*. *[Listing Code Number]*
*(Ad #21)*

### Get a Free Credit Report This Weekend

*[Mortgage Lender Name]* will be on hand this weekend providing free credit reports for the first 10 guests who visit this gorgeous *[#Bedrooms]* bedroom/*[#Baths]* bath *[Style of Home]* home. Open this *[Day(s) of Open House]*, *[Time of Open House]*. Come visit *[Listing Agent]* at *[Street Address]*. *[Directions to Property]*. *[Listing Code Number]*
*(Ad #22)*

*(Please note: Make sure your state real estate commission will allow such offers prior to running any ads with "FREE" gifts).*

### Open House Weekend Includes Free Credit Report and Appraisal

The first two guests who visit *[Street Address]* this *[Day(s) of Open House]*, *[Time of Open House]* will receive a free credit report and appraisal complements of *[Mortgage Lender Name]* if they get their next home loan through *[Mortgage Lender Name]*. You'll also have the opportunity to see a great *[#Bedrooms]* bedroom/*[#Baths]* bath *[Style of Home]* home that has been completely refurbished. *[Street Address]*. *[Directions to Property]*. *[Listing Code Number]*
*(Ad #23)*

*(Please note: Make sure your state real estate commission will allow such offers prior to running any ads with "FREE" gifts).*

### Open House Bonanza

We're holding three open houses in *[Subdivision Name]* this *[Day(s) of Open House]*, *[Time of Open House]*. Free refreshments at each house with other useful information provided by *[Mortgage Lender Name]*. Come visit *[Listing Agent]* at *[Street Address]*. *[Directions to Property]*. *[Listing Code Number]*
*(Ad #24)*

### Three in One!

That's right! Three open houses in one subdivision this weekend. Great opportunity to shop and compare in *[Subdivision Name]*. You can view all three homes on our Web site at *[Web Address]* in advance or come by and see the houses in person. Open this *[Day(s) of Open House]*, *[Time of Open House]*. Come visit *[Listing Agent]* at *[Street Address]*. *[Directions to Property]*. *[Listing Code Number]*
*(Ad #25)*

### Want to Know How Close This House Is to the Lake?

Stop by the open house this weekend and find out. Spacious *[#Bedrooms]* bedroom/*[#Baths]* bath *[Style of Home]* home has all the amenities you would dream for in your next residence. For a special opportunity to preview this home, visit our open house *[Day(s) of Open House]*, *[Time of Open House]*. *[Street Address]*. *[Directions to Property]*. *[Listing Code Number]*
*(Ad #26)*

### Look and Touch This Sunday

*[#Bedrooms]* bedroom/*[#Baths]* bath *[Style of Home]* home has been restored with pride. Excellent detail to refinished hardwood trim and crown molding. Cozy fireplace with side bookcases built in. This is the home you must see to appreciate! Here's your chance to view this special new listing this *[Day(s) of Open House]*, *[Time of Open House]*. Come visit *[Listing Agent]* at *[Street Address]*. *[Directions to Property]*. *[Listing Code Number]*
*(Ad #27)*

### Soak Up the Surroundings This Weekend

Exquisite *[#Bedrooms]* bedroom/*[#Baths]* bath *[Style of Home]* home on a wooded lot will be open this *[Day(s) of Open House]*, *[Time of Open House]*. Come visit *[Listing Agent]* at *[Street Address]*. *[Directions to Property]*. Beautiful home and a great opportunity! Don't miss it! *[Listing Code Number]*
*(Ad #28)*

# Recruitment Ads  18

As a bonus section, we have included a special set of classified advertisements for recruiting. These ads can be used by brokers or agents who are building teams inside a broker's office. Any organization having a superb and adequate sales staff is essential. For the broker, recruitment is like prospecting for listings for the real estate agent.

Whether you are a broker or an agent building a team, consider using some of these recruitment ads for building a profitable organization. One final note to remember: Be sure to follow all equal employment advertising rules and guidelines when running recruitment advertisements. (For editing purposes, all equal employment disclosures have been left out of the text.)

Looking for a Change? *(Ad #1)*

Looking for Something to Jump Start Your Career? *(Ad #2)*

Stop for Commissions *(Ad #3)*

Career Sliding? *(Ad #4)*

Straddling the Fence? *(Ad #5)*

Crash and Burn? *(Ad #6)*

You Have Options *(Ad #7)*

What Are You Waiting for? *(Ad #8)*

Are You SOLD? *(Ad #9)*

It's Time for a New Day *(Ad #10)*

Don't Waste Your Career *(Ad #11)*

The Choice Is Yours *(Ad #12)*

Look toward the Future *(Ad #13)*

Need a Helping Hand? *(Ad #14)*

High Voltage *(Ad #15)*

Real Estate Career Maze *(Ad #16)*

Every Four Days *(Ad #17)*

Need Help? *(Ad #18)*

New Beginnings *(Ad #19)*

Better Days *(Ad #20)*

Solid Roots *(Ad #21)*

Not Everyone Can Work Here *(Ad #22)*

STOP! *(Ad #23)*

Hunting? *(Ad #24)*

Don't Call *(Ad #25)*

More than a Job *(Ad #26)*

Be Your Own Boss *(Ad #27)*

It's a Secret *(Ad #28)*

It's No Secret *(Ad #29)*

Finally *(Ad #30)*

We've Moved *(Ad #31)*

Why? *(Ad #32)*

Don't Say Yes *(Ad #33)*

Trust *(Ad #34)*

Caution: Speed Zone Ahead *(Ad #35)*

Welcome Home *(Ad #36)*

Too Many Weeds *(Ad #37)*

Afternoon Delight *(Ad #38)*

Come Grow with Us *(Ad #39)*

Only a Few Left *(Ad #40)*

It's Not Magic *(Ad #41)*

You'll Flip *(Ad #42)*

Wake Up to a New Day *(Ad #43)*

# Sample Ads

### Looking for a Change?

*[Company Name]* now has positions available to join their team. For a confidential private interview, contact *[Broker or Manager Name]* at *[Phone Number]*. *[Listing Code Number]*
*(Ad #1)*

### Looking for Something to Jump Start Your Career?

*[Company Name]* has limited space available for new and experienced real estate agents. Excellent training programs available! Contact *[Broker or Manager Name]* at *[Phone Number]*. *[Listing Code Number]*
*(Ad #2)*

### Stop for Commissions

Are you looking for more income to put in your pocket each month? If so, contact *[Company Name]* about a career in real estate. Have immediate openings available for real estate agents. Experience not required. For a private, no obligation interview, contact *[Broker or Manager Name]* at *[Phone Number]*. *[Listing Code Number]*
*(Ad #3)*

### Career Sliding?

Is your real estate career taking a slide downhill that is out of control? If so, perhaps you need to place your license with an aggressive company that takes real estate seriously. We offer an aggressive compensation package and extensive in-house training. For a private consultation, call *[Broker or Manager Name]* at *[Phone Number]*. *[Listing Code Number]*
*(Ad #4)*

### Straddling the Fence?

If you're questioning where you should be with your real estate career, then you need a name and a company that you and your clients can trust. *[Company Name]* is providing refreshments and a meet and greet with the staff on Friday from 10 A.M. to 12 P.M. Contact *[Broker or Manager Name]* at *[Phone Number]* for more information. *[Listing Code Number]*
*(Ad #5)*

### Crash and Burn?

Does your real estate career feel like it has crashed and is about ready to burn? If so, perhaps you need a new fresh start with a new company. *[Company Name]* is now accepting positions for full- or part-time real estate agents. Call *[Broker or Manager Name]* at *[Phone Number]* for more information. *[Listing Code Number]*
*(Ad #6)*

### You Have Options

By choosing *[Company Name]*, you'll have plenty of options to jump start your real estate career. Great training and technology offered for all agents. Aggressive commission splits. Private office or work in open area—it's your choice! Contact *[Broker or Manager Name]* at *[Phone Number]. [Listing Code Number]*
***(Ad #7)***

### What Are You Waiting for?

Here is your opportunity to affiliate with one of the premier real estate offices in *[Office Location/Area]*. Aggressive compensation plans, advanced training, and a pleasant work environment will make your life easier. Call *[Broker or Manager Name]* at *[Phone Number]* to find out more. *[Listing Code Number]*
***(Ad #8)***

### Are You SOLD?

Are you really sold on your real estate career? If not, then perhaps it's time to make the change. *[Company Name]* is looking for new associates for their *[Office Location/Area]* office. New facility offers the option for private offices. Aggressive marketing and training programs available. For a private and confidential interview, contact *[Broker or Manager Name]* at *[Phone Number]. [Listing Code Number]*
***(Ad #9)***

### It's Time for a New Day

If your real estate career is not where it needs to be, then it's time for you to consider a career with *[Company Name]* agency. For years they've been providing real estate needs for the community along with helping real estate professionals advance their careers to new levels. Contact *[Broker or Manager Name]* at *[Phone Number]* for more information. *[Listing Code Number]*
***(Ad #10)***

### Don't Waste Your Career!

Don't throw away good commissions that you could earn! Consider a career with *[Company Name]*. We offer a generous compensation package along with advanced marketing programs and technology training that can't be matched! For more information, contact *[Broker or Manager Name]* at *[Phone Number]. [Listing Code Number]*
***(Ad #11)***

### The Choice Is Yours

You can either watch your real estate career stay in neutral or move it into high gear. *[Company Name]* has a limited opportunity for new real estate agents to join their team. Good compensation plan, marketing, technology, and other training available. The choice is up to you. Call *[Broker or Manager Name]* at *[Phone Number]* today. *[Listing Code Number]*
***(Ad #12)***

### Look toward the Future

Affiliating with the right real estate company is not only important for today but tomorrow as well. To make sure your professional career is on track for many years to come, consider affiliating with *[Company Name]*. We have a proven track record of helping families with their real estate needs for many years. For a private, risk-free interview, call *[Broker or Manager Name]* at *[Phone Number]*. *[Listing Code Number]*
*(Ad #13)*

### Need a Helping Hand?

If you are a real estate agent and feel like you have no help with your career, *[Company Name]* can help you get back on the right track. To learn more about all of the services and opportunities we provide our real estate professionals, call *[Broker or Manager Name]* at *[Phone Number]*. *[Listing Code Number]*
*(Ad #14)*

### High Voltage

If your real estate career needs a little spark, *[Company Name]* can provide you with the jump start you have been looking for. We have a "FREE" CD-ROM available for real estate agents considering a change. All inquires held strictly in confidence. For more information, contact *[Broker or Manager Name]* at *[Phone Number]*. *[Listing Code Number]*
*(Ad #15)*

### Real Estate Career Maze

Sometimes finding the right real estate office can truly be a task. Don't get yourself lost going down the wrong road. Before you affiliate with anyone, talk to *[Company Name]* and ask for *[Broker or Manager Name]*. *[Phone Number]*. *[Listing Code Number]*
*(Ad #16)*

### Every Four Days

At *[Company Name]*, our agents earn a commission check on average every four days! If you're not earning the commission income you would like, consider making a switch to *[Company Name]*. Ask for *[Broker or Manager Name]* for a private confidential interview and learn how you can join a team where the average agent earns a commission every four days. Call *[Broker or Manager Name]* at *[Phone Number]*. *[Listing Code Number]*
*(Ad #17)*

*(Please Note: Be sure and verify what the average commission is per day before running this type of ad.)*

### Need Help?

If your real estate career is in need of an overhaul or you're looking for new options to enhance your real estate career, why not consider a move to *[Company Name]*? We offer a wide array of benefits for our real estate agents. Contact *[Broker or Manager Name]* at *[Phone Number]*. *[Listing Code Number]*
*(Ad #18)*

### New Beginnings

At *[Company Name]*, we're unveiling a new name and a new way of doing real estate business in the *[Office Location/Area]*. To learn more about how you can be a part of this new real estate concept, call *[Broker or Manager Name]* at *[Phone Number]*. *[Listing Code Number]*
***(Ad #19)***

### Better Days

Does your real estate career seem stuck and you don't enjoy going to work everyday? Good news, better days are ahead at *[Company Name]*! We can provide you with excellent compensation splits, a comfortable and professional work environment, and the right tools to help your business grow. To find out more information, contact *[Broker or Manager Name]* at *[Phone Number]*. *[Listing Code Number]*
***(Ad #20)***

### Solid Roots

For many real estate professionals, one of the main elements for a successful career is to have a good longevity with a real estate firm. To accomplish this task you need to be with a company that has an aggressive marketing plan, good compensation splits, recognition, and award programs, along with good technology. *[Company Name]* can provide you with these real estate benefits and much more. To find out more about all of our services and features, contact *[Broker or Manager Name]* at *[Phone Number]* for a private confidential interview. *[Listing Code Number]*
***(Ad #21)***

### Not Everyone Can Work Here

At *[Company Name]*, we pride ourselves on only hiring the highest quality professional real estate agents in the market. If you would like to affiliate with a team that takes such pride in their hiring process, call *[Broker or Manager Name]* at *[Phone Number]* for a private confidential interview. *[Listing Code Number]*
***(Ad #22)***

### STOP!

Don't let your real estate career go down the wrong road and lead you to nowhere. Start your career in the right direction with the right company. Find out all the positive benefits of affiliating with *[Company Name]*. Call *[Broker or Manager Name]* at *[Phone Number]* for more information. *[Listing Code Number]*
***(Ad #23)***

### Hunting?

Hunting for a new real estate team to affiliate with? The search is over! *[Company Name]* has the tools and services to help you win more business in the marketplace. Call *[Broker or Manager Name]* at *[Phone Number]* to find out all of the positive benefits about affiliating with *[Company Name]*. *[Listing Code Number]*
***(Ad #24)***

### Don't Call

Thinking about switching real estate companies? If you hate to call to find out all of the benefits that *[Company Name]* has to offer, then go to our Web site and read about the success stories from some of our agents and all of the benefits and services we provide new team members. Go to *[Company Web Site]*. *[Listing Code Number]*
**(Ad #25)**

*(Please Note: This is a good ad to direct agents to your Web site to read about the benefits and agent testimonies on why to affiliate with your company.)*

### More than a Job

A career in real estate is more than just a job; it's a life changing opportunity for most people. Be your own boss, work your own hours, and allow yourself the opportunity to make as much money you desire. The choice is yours. To find out all of the great benefits there are to beginning a career in real estate, call *[Broker or Manager Name]* at *[Phone Number]*. *[Listing Code Number]*
**(Ad #26)**

### Be Your Own Boss

Find out how a career in real estate can allow you to work your own hours and determine your own income. Literally, you be your own boss! To find out more, call *[Broker or Manager Name]* at *[Phone Number]*. *[Listing Code Number]*
**(Ad #27)**

### It's a Secret

but we're willing to spill the beans at our real estate career workshop on why our agents are so productive and do so well. To find out the secrets, you'll have to attend. Call for a reservation at *[Phone Number]* and ask for *[Broker or Manager Name]*. *[Listing Code Number]*
**(Ad #28)**

### It's No Secret

why *[Company Name]* agents earn so much more income than the average real estate agent in *[Office Location/Area]*. From our aggressive marketing campaigns to our generous compensation packages, and of course our advanced training, it's no secret why we're number 1! For more information, contact *[Broker or Manager Name]* at *[Phone Number]*. *[Listing Code Number]*
**(Ad #29)**

*(Please Note: Only use this type of ad if you can document and verify that the agents from your office are earning more money than the other agents in the area.)*

### Finally

a real estate company that offers a full-time real estate trainer in the *[Office Location/Area]*. *[Company Name]* is pleased to announce the hiring of *[Agent Name]* as a part of their company staff. For more information about how you can take advantage of these new educational opportunities, contact *[Broker or Manager Name]* at *[Phone Number]*. *[Listing Code Number]*
**(Ad #30)**

## We've Moved

That's right! We've moved our real estate professionals to a whole new level in their selling careers by incorporating some of the latest technology advances and marketing skills available. You can move, too! Call *[Broker or Manager Name]* at *[Phone Number]* for more information on this exciting new program. *[Listing Code Number]*
*(Ad #31)*

## Why?

Why do so many real estate agents affiliate with *[Company Name]*? Could it be the marketing plans they offer their agents? The technology tools they provide their real estate professionals? The aggressive compensation splits each team member receives? Or perhaps it's just a great friendly professional environment. Whatever the case, you, too, can experience the same great benefits. For more information to find out how you can become part of the *[Company Name]* team, call *[Broker or Manager Name]* at *[Phone Number]*. *[Listing Code Number]*
*(Ad #32)*

## Don't Say Yes

in affiliating with a real estate company until you've spoken to *[Company Name]*. We offer the tools, technology, and education you'll require to be a success in the real estate industry. There is no cost or obligation to find out and to ask a few questions. Call *[Broker or Manager Name]* at *[Phone Number]*. *[Listing Code Number]*
*(Ad #33)*

## Trust

Affiliating with the right real estate company needs to have an element of trust. You'll need the support and education from your broker to help you learn the business. You'll need the ability to increase your compensation level as your sales increase. You'll need a company that is adapting to technology as the market place changes. You can trust *[Company Name]* to help you in all of these areas. For more information, contact *[Broker or Manager Name]* at *[Phone Number]*. [Listing Code Number]*
*(Ad #34)*

## Caution: Speed Zone Ahead

By affiliating your real estate career with *[Company Name]*, you'll be moving into the fast lane. Our company provides the latest marketing and technology advancements to our real estate professionals. Great educational opportunities along with many other benefits await you. For all of the information about how you can put your sales in the fast lane, contact *[Broker or Manager Name]* at *[Phone Number]*. [Listing Code Number]*
*(Ad #35)*

## Welcome Home

You'll never feel so good about your real estate career and the direction you're moving in until you affiliate with *[Company Name]*. We offer a professional and friendly work environment with colleagues committed to a teamwork environment. Come find out what a great opportunity awaits you at *[Company Name]*. Call *[Phone Number]* and ask for *[Broker or Manager Name]*. [Listing Code Number]*
*(Ad #36)*

### Too Many Weeds?

If your real estate career is being choked by too many unnecessary issues, let *[Company Name]* help with getting you weed free. We can provide the educational training you'll need to put your career back on track. To find out more, contact *[Broker or Manager Name]* at *[Phone Number]*. *[Listing Code Number]*
**(Ad #37)**

### Afternoon Delight

No more frustration from your present work environment when you affiliate with *[Company Name]*. Our team environment provides a great place to grow your real estate career. To learn all of the information about our company and why you'll enjoy each and every day working in our office, call *[Broker or Manager Name]* at *[Agency Phone Number]*. *[Listing Code Number]*
**(Ad #38)**

### Come Grow with Us

*[Company Name]* is one of the leading real estate companies in *[Office Location/Area]*. We're currently interviewing experienced and new real estate agents to help fill our demanding real estate needs. If you're interested in joining one of the fasting growing real estate firms, contact *[Broker or Manager Name]* at *[Phone Number]*. *[Listing Code Number]*
**(Ad #39)**

### Only a Few Left

That's right! *[Company Name]* only has a few spots left on their real estate roster. Call *[Broker or Manager Name]* at *[Phone Number]* today and find out how you can be a part of their fast growing and aggressive real estate team. Limited time only—so don't delay! Pick up the phone and call *[Broker or Manager Name]* today. *[Listing Code Number]*
**(Ad #40)**

### It's Not Magic

There's no secret or magic why real estate agents at *[Company Name]* do so well. We offer marketing, educational training, reputation, and other services for our agents. We also provide our real estate professionals with the latest technology tools. To find out more, call *[Broker or Manager Name]* at *[Phone Number]*. *[Listing Code Number]*
**(Ad #41)**

### You'll Flip

when you hear all of the great services and benefits we provide our real estate agents on a daily basis. Call *[Broker or Manager Name]* at *[Phone Number]* to schedule a private confidential interview and to receive your free portfolio of all of our special details. Now hiring new and experienced agents for a limited time only. Call before it's too late. Call *[Phone Number]*. *[Listing Code Number]*
**(Ad #42)**

### Wake Up to a New Day

Begin tomorrow with a new career at *[Company Name]*. We offer all of the tools and benefits that a real estate professional demands. Before you affiliate or change offices, make sure you go with a company that has experience and the backing you need to prosper your real estate career. Call *[Broker or Manager Name]* at *[Phone Number]* for more information. *[Listing Code Number]*

**(Ad #43)**

# Fair Housing Issues

One of the primary responsibilities of a real estate professional is to make sure all of your advertising copy conforms to the Fair Housing Advertising Guidelines. Since laws do change and with the wide vast of information available on the World Wide Web, you can visit the HUD Web site at http://www.hud.gov/ for the latest on Fair Housing advertising guidelines and laws.

When drafting your advertising copy, you should keep in mind the Golden Rule: "Do unto others as you would have them do unto you." Being discriminatory in any advertising is not fair to the recipient on the other end. Make a conscious effort to always examine your advertising copy and avoid any discriminatory advertising words, phrases, or other insulations that could remotely offend the reader. According to the 2004 National Association of REALTORS® Profile of Home Buyers and Sellers, the number one feature that buyers look for in choosing a real estate agent is their reputation.[1] It may only take one negatively worded advertisement to tarnish and ruin a person's reputation. If you destroy your character image, you can create long-term negative effects for your business.

---

[1] P. Bishop, T. M. Beers III, and S. D. Hightower from The National Association of REALTORS® Research Division, "2004 National Association of REALTORS® Profiles of Buyers' Home Feature Preferences," http://www.realtor.org/ Research.nsf/files/HFShilite2004.pdf/$FILE/HFShilite2004.pdf.

## PART 109—FAIR HOUSING ADVERTISING

Sec.

APPENDIX I TO PART 109—FAIR HOUSING ADVERTISING

AUTHORITY: Title VIII, Civil Rights Act of 1968, 42 U.S.C. 3600-3620; section 7(d), Department of HUD Act, 42 U.S.C. 3535(d).

SOURCE: 54 FR 3308, Jan. 23, 1989, unless otherwise noted.

### § 109.5　　Policy.

It is the policy of the United States to provide, within constitutional limitations, for fair housing throughout the United States. The provisions of the Fair Housing Act (42 U.S.C. 3600, *et seq.*) make it unlawful to discriminate in the sale, rental, and financing of housing, and in the provision of brokerage and appraisal services, because of race, color, religion, sex, handicap, familial status, or national origin. Section 804(c) of the Fair Housing Act, 42 U.S.C. 3604(c), as amended, makes it unlawful to make, print, or publish, or cause to be made, printed, or published, any notice, statement, or advertisement, with respect to the sale or rental of a dwelling, that indicates any preference, limitation, or discrimination because of race, color, religion, sex, handicap, familial status, or national origin, or an intention to make any such preference, limitation, or discrimination. However, the prohibitions of the act regarding familial status do not apply with respect to *housing for older persons*, as defined in section 807(b) of the act.

### § 109.10　　Purpose.

The purpose of this part is to assist all advertising media, advertising agencies and all other persons who use advertising to make, print, or publish, or cause to be made, printed, or published, advertisements with respect to the sale, rental, or financing of dwellings which are in compliance with the requirements of the

Fair Housing Act. These regulations also describe the matters this Department will review in evaluating compliance with the Fair Housing Act in connection with investigations of complaints alleging discriminatory housing practices involving advertising.

### § 109.15   Definitions.

As used in this part:

(a) *Assistant Secretary* means the Assistant Secretary for Fair Housing and Equal Opportunity.

(b) *General Counsel* means the General Counsel of the Department of Housing and Urban Development.

(c) *Dwelling* means any building, structure, or portion thereof which is occupied as, or designed or intended for occupancy as, a residence by one or more families, and any vacant land which is offered for sale or lease for the construction or location thereon of any such building, structure, or portion thereof.

(d) *Family* includes a single individual.

(e) *Person* includes one or more individuals, corporations, partnerships, associations, labor organizations, legal representatives, mutual companies, joint-stock companies, trusts, unincorporated organizations, trustees, trustees in cases under Title 11 of the United States Code, receivers, and fiduciaries.

(f) *To rent* includes to lease, to sublease, to let and otherwise to grant for a consideration the right to occupy premises not owned by the occupant.

(g) *Discriminatory housing practice* means an act that is unlawful under section 804, 805, 806, or 818 of the Fair Housing Act.

(h) *Handicap* means, with respect to a person—

(1) A physical or mental impairment which substantially limits one or more of such person's major life activities,

(2) A record of having such an impairment, or

(3) Being regarded as having such an impairment.

This term does not include current, illegal use of or addiction to a controlled substance (as defined in section 102 of the Controlled Substances Act (21 U.S.C. 802)). For purposes of this part, an individual shall not be considered to have a handicap solely because that individual is a transvestite.

(i) *Familial status* means one or more individuals (who have not attained the age of 18 years) being domiciled with—

(1) A parent or another person having legal custody of such individual or individuals; or

(2) The designee of such parent or other person having such custody, with the written permission of such parent or other person. The protections afforded against discrimination on the basis of familial status shall apply to any person who is pregnant or is in the process of securing legal custody of any individual who has not attained the age of 18 years.

### § 109.16      Scope.

(a) *General.* This part describes the matters the Department will review in evaluating compliance with the Fair Housing Act in connection with investigations of complaints alleging discriminatory housing practices involving advertising. Use of these criteria will be considered by the General Counsel in making determinations as to whether there is reasonable cause, and by the Assistant Secretary in making determinations that there is no reasonable cause, to believe that a discriminatory housing practice has occurred or is about to occur.

(1) *Advertising media.* This part provides criteria for use by advertising media in determining whether to accept and publish advertising regarding sales or rental transactions. Use of these criteria will be considered by the General Counsel in making determinations as to whether there is reasonable cause, and by the Assistant Secretary in making determinations that there is no reasonable cause, to believe that a discriminatory housing practice has occurred or is about to occur.

(2) *Persons placing advertisements.* A failure by persons placing advertisements to use the criteria contained in this part, when found in connection with the investigation of a complaint alleging the making or use of discriminatory advertisements, will be considered by the General Counsel in making a determination of reasonable cause, and by the Assistant Secretary in making determinations that there is no reasonable cause, to believe that a discriminatory housing practice has occurred or is about to occur.

(b) *Affirmative advertising efforts.* Nothing in this part shall be construed to restrict advertising efforts designed to attract persons to dwellings who would not ordinarily be expected to apply, when such efforts are pursuant to an affirmative marketing program or undertaken to remedy the effects of prior discrimination in connection with the advertising or marketing of dwellings.

[54 FR 308, Jan. 23 1989, as amended at 55 FR 53294, Dec. 28, 1990.]

## § 109.20 Use of words, phrases, symbols, and visual aids.

The following words, phrases, symbols, and forms typify those most often used in residential real estate advertising to convey either overt or tacit discriminatory preferences or limitations. In considering a complaint under the Fair Housing Act, the Department will normally consider the use of these and comparable words, phrases, symbols, and forms to indicate a possible violation of the act and to establish a need for further proceedings on the complaint, if it is apparent from the context of the usage that discrimination within the meaning of the act is likely to result.

(a) *Words descriptive of dwelling, landlord, and tenants*. White private home, Colored home, Jewish home, Hispanic residence, adult building.

(b) *Words indicative of race, color, religion, sex, handicap, familial status, or national origin*—

(1) *Race*—Negro, Black, Caucasian, Oriental, American Indian.

(2) *Color*—White, Black, Colored.

(3) *Religion*—Protestant, Christian, Catholic, Jew.

(4) *National origin*—Mexican American, Puerto Rican, Philippine, Polish, Hungarian, Irish, Italian, Chicano, African, Hispanic, Chinese, Indian, Latino.

(5) *Sex*—the exclusive use of words in advertisements, including those involving the rental of separate units in a single or multi-family dwelling, stating or tending to imply that the housing being advertised is available to persons of only one sex and not the other, except where the sharing of living areas is involved. Nothing in this part restricts advertisements of dwellings used exclusively for dormitory facilities by educational institutions.

(6) *Handicap*—crippled, blind, deaf, mentally ill, retarded, impaired, handicapped, physically fit. Nothing in this part restricts the inclusion of information about the availability of accessible housing in advertising of dwellings.

(7) *Familial status*—adults, children, singles, mature persons. Nothing in this part restricts advertisements of dwellings which are intended and operated for occupancy by older persons and which constitute *housing for older persons* as defined in Part 100 of this title.

(8) *Catch words*—Words and phrases used in a discriminatory context should be avoided, e.g., *restricted, exclusive, private, integrated, traditional, board approval or membership approval*.

(c) *Symbols or logotypes.* Symbols or logotypes which imply or suggest race, color, religion, sex, handicap, familial status, or national origin.

(d) *Colloquialisms.* Words or phrases used regionally or locally which imply or suggest race, color, religion, sex, handicap, familial status, or national origin.

(e) *Directions to real estate for sale or rent (use of maps or written instructions).* Directions can imply a discriminatory preference, limitation, or exclusion. For example, references to real estate location made in terms of racial or national origin significant landmarks, such as an existing black development (signal to blacks) or an existing development known for its exclusion of minorities (signal to whites). Specific directions which make reference to a racial or national origin significant area may indicate a preference. References to a synagogue, congregation or parish may also indicate a religious preference.

(f) *Area (location) description.* Names of facilities which cater to a particular racial, national origin or religious group, such as country club or private school designations, or names of facilities which are used exclusively by one sex may indicate a preference.

## § 109.25 Selective use of advertising media or content.

The selective use of advertising media or content when particular combinations thereof are used exclusively with respect to various housing developments or sites can lead to discriminatory results and may indicate a violation of the Fair Housing Act. For example, the use of English language media alone or the exclusive use of media catering to the majority population in an area, when, in such area, there are also available non-English language or other minority media, may have discriminatory impact. Similarly, the selective use of human models in advertisements may have discriminatory impact. The following are examples of the selective use of advertisements which may be discriminatory:

(a) *Selective geographic advertisements.* Such selective use may involve the strategic placement of billboards; brochure advertisements distributed within a limited geographic area by hand or in the mail; advertising in particular geographic coverage editions of major metropolitan newspapers or in newspapers of limited circulation which are mainly advertising vehicles for reaching a particular segment of the community; or displays or announcements available only in selected sales offices.

(b) *Selective use of equal opportunity slogan or logo.* When placing advertisements, such selective use may involve placing the equal housing opportunity slogan or logo in advertising reaching some geographic areas, but not others, or with respect to some properties but not others.

(c) *Selective use of human models when conducting an advertising campaign.* Selective advertising may involve an advertising campaign using human models primarily in media that cater to one racial or national origin segment of the population without a complementary advertising campaign that is directed at other groups. Another example may involve use of racially mixed models by a developer to advertise one development and not others. Similar care must be exercised in advertising in publications or other media directed at one particular sex, or at persons without children. Such selective advertising may involve the use of human models of members of only one sex, or of adults only, in displays, photographs or drawings to indicate preferences for one sex or the other, or for adults to the exclusion of children.

## § 109.30    Fair housing policy and practices.

In the investigation of complaints, the Assistant Secretary will consider the implementation of fair housing policies and practices provided in this section as evidence of compliance with the prohibitions against discrimination in advertising under the Fair Housing Act.

(a) *Use of Equal Housing Opportunity logotype, statement, or slogan.* All advertising of residential real estate for sale, rent, or financing should contain an equal housing opportunity logotype, statement, or slogan as a means of educating the homeseeking public that the property is available to all persons regardless of race, color, religion, sex, handicap, familial status, or national origin. The choice of logotype, statement or slogan will depend on the type of media used (visual or auditory) and, in space advertising, on the size of the advertisement. Table I (see Appendix I) indicates suggested use of the logotype, statement, or slogan and size of logotype. Table II (see Appendix I) contains copies of the suggested Equal Housing Opportunity logotype, statement and slogan.

(b) *Use of human models.* Human models in photographs, drawings, or other graphic techniques may not be used to indicate exclusiveness because of race, color, religion, sex, handicap, familial status, or national origin. If models are used in display advertising campaigns, the models should be clearly definable as reasonably representing majority and minority groups in the metropolitan area, both sexes, and, when appropriate, families with children. Models, if used, should portray persons in an equal social setting and indicate to the general public that the housing is open to all without regard to race, color, religion, sex, handicap, familial status, or national origin, and is not for the exclusive use of one such group.

(c) *Coverage of local laws.* Where the Equal Housing Opportunity statement is used, the advertisement may also include a statement regarding the coverage of any local fair housing or human rights ordinance prohibiting discrimination in the sale, rental or financing of dwellings.

(d) *Notification of fair housing policy—*

(1) *Employees.* All publishers of advertisements, advertising agencies, and firms engaged in the sale, rental or financing of real estate should provide a printed copy of their nondiscrimination policy to each employee and officer.

(2) *Clients.* All publishers or advertisements and advertising agencies should post a copy of their nondiscrimination policy in a conspicuous location wherever persons place advertising and should have copies available for all firms and persons using their advertising services.

(3) *Publishers' notice.* All publishers should publish at the beginning of the real estate advertising section a notice such as that appearing in Table III (see Appendix I). The notice may include a statement regarding the coverage of any local fair housing or human rights ordinance prohibiting discrimination in the sale, rental or financing of dwellings.

APPENDIX I TO PART 109—FAIR HOUSING ADVERTISING

The following three tables may serve as a guide for the use of the Equal Housing Opportunity logotype, statement, slogan, and publisher's notice for advertising:

Table I

A simple formula can guide the real estate advertiser in using the Equal Housing Opportunity logotype, statement, or slogan.

In all space advertising (advertising in regularly printed media such as newspapers or magazines) the following standards should be used:

| Size of advertisement | *Size of logotype in inches* |
|---|---|
| 1/2 page or larger ......................... | $2 \times 2$ |
| 1/8 page up to 1/2 page ................. | $1 \times 1$ |
| 4 column inches to 1/8 page ............ | $\frac{1}{2} \times \frac{1}{2}$ |
| Less than 4 column inches | ($^1$) |

$^1$Do not use.

In any other advertisements, if other logotypes are used in the advertisement, then the Equal Housing Opportunity logo should be of a size at least equal to the largest of the other logotypes; if no other logotypes are used, then the type should be bold display face which is clearly visible. Alternatively, when no other logotypes are used, 3 to 5 percent of an advertisement may be devoted to a statement of the equal housing opportunity policy.

In space advertising which is less than 4 column inches (one column 4 inches long or two columns 2 inches long) of a page in size, the Equal Housing Opportunity slogan should be used. Such advertisements may be grouped with other advertisements under a caption which states that the housing is available to all without regard to race, color, religion, sex, handicap, familial status, or national origin.

Table II

Illustrations of Logotype, Statement, and Slogan. Equal Housing Opportunity Logotype:

Equal Housing Opportunity Statement: We are pledged to the letter and spirit of U.S. policy for the achievement of equal housing opportunity throughout the Nation. We encourage and support an affirmative advertising and marketing program in which there are no barriers to obtaining housing because of race, color, religion, sex, handicap, familial status, or national origin.

Equal Housing Opportunity Slogan: "Equal Housing Opportunity."

Table III

Illustration of Media Notice—Publisher's notice: All real estate advertised herein is subject to the Federal Fair Housing Act, which makes it illegal to advertise "any preference, limitation, or discrimination because of race, color, religion, sex, handicap, familial status, or national origin, or intention to make any such preference, limitation, or discrimination."

We will not knowingly accept any advertising for real estate which is in violation of the law. All persons are hereby informed that all dwellings advertised are available on an equal opportunity basis.

# Conclusion

One final thought on advertising. Many times people will run advertisements or marketing campaigns for a short duration (sometimes only once) and not get the feedback or calls they were hoping for and in their mind the advertising or publication didn't work. Please don't use that rationale for your advertising plan. Some ads just won't produce calls, but that doesn't mean it's a bad ad. Some publications may feature your advertisements and the phone won't ring, but that doesn't make that publication a bad commodity. Advertising may not work all the time the way you and I expect it to. We need to continue to run advertisements for our clients and for us. We can't give up on a campaign or an ad just because the phone doesn't ring 20 times during its shelf life. We do, however, need to monitor our ads and the calls and where they're coming from. We also have to give the plan and the campaign some time to work. Don't give up easily, refuse to be discouraged, and keep tweaking and adjusting until you find the right combination that works.

Stewart Henderson Britt, from the *New York Herald Tribune*, once said, *"Doing business without advertising is like winking at a girl in the dark. You know what you are doing, but nobody else does"* (quoted in the *New York Herald Tribune*, October 1956). Like it or not, advertising is an essential part to our business economy. The adage supply and demand still exists for real estate professionals, too. In many parts of the country there's a large supply of real estate agents, thus spreading the demand over many licensees. As a real estate agent, it is important that we create a demand in our products (listings that we take) and our services (working with buyers and sellers). I hope that *5 Minutes to a Great Real Estate Ad* is valuable to your career. My goal is to help you become more creative with your ad writing. I'm sure that not everyone will read through this book and be excited about every ad heading that I've developed, but if I can get you to start thinking about headings and copy and making your creative juices flow, then my goal is fulfilled! I hope you will be able to write ads that will entice consumers to finish reading and, most of all, pick up the phone and call you for more information.

I wish you the best of luck with your ad writing and I hope more than anything that with the help of this book you are only "five minutes away from a great real estate ad!"

Good luck!

John D. Mayfield

**G**rab their attention! Develop a heading for your ad.

_____

_____

**E**ntice the reader's interest.

_____

_____

_____

**T**ruthful in all advertising!

❏ Check this box to remind you not to "over exaggerate" the benefits of the home!

**C**lose the sale! *This will go at the end of your ad!*

_____

_____

_____

**A**sk the sellers what they'll miss about their home. List one to three features about the property below:

1. _____

2. _____

3. _____

**L**ist key features about the home. Normally you would insert bedrooms and baths here. Other choices could include style, garage, and other amenities you would like to list in your ad.

1. _____

2. _____

3. _____

4. _____

5. _____

6. _____

**L**ook at other ads and pay attention to what other successful real estate agents are doing.

❏ Check this box to remind you of this task!

**S**pend time preparing and writing your ads, and write several ads for each listing you have!

❏ Check this box to remind you of this task!

*Insert the appropriate information from the book on the following lines.*

## Ad Copy #1

**Date Used** _____ **Publication Used** _____

G_____
E_____
L_____
L_____
C_____

## Ad Copy #2

**Date Used** _____ **Publication Used** _____

G_____
E_____
L_____
L_____
C_____

## Ad Copy #3

**Date Used** _____ **Publication Used** _____

G_____
E_____
L_____
L_____
C_____

# Book References

*English Country Interiors: Inside Cotswold Homes*, Sarah North, Mitchell Beazley, Octopus Publishing Group, Ltd., Heron Quays, London, 2004

*Inside the Bungalow: America's Arts & Crafts Interior*, Paul Duchscherer and Douglas Keister, Penguin Studio, Published by the Penguin Group, Penguin Putnam Inc., New York, NY, 1997

*Victorian Kitchen and Baths,* Franklin and Esther Schmidt, Gibbs Smith, Publisher, Salt Lake City UT 2005

*Colonial Style: Creating Classic Interiors In Your Cape, Colonial or Saltbox Home*, Treena Crochet, The Taunton Press, 2005

*French Country At Home,* Kathy Passero, Sterling Publishing Co., Inc., New York, NY, 2005

*Backyard Idea Book,* Lee Anne White, Taunton Press, Newton, CT, 2004

*The Kitchen Idea Book,* Joanne Kellar Bourknight, The Taunton Press, Newton, CT, 2004

**NOTES**

# NOTES

NOTES

# NOTES

# NOTES

# NOTES

**NOTES**

# NOTES

**NOTES**

# NOTES

**NOTES**

# NOTES

**NOTES**